Like a Mighty Army?

Like a Mighty Army?

The Salvation Army, the Church, and the Churches

DAVID TAYLOR

With a Foreword by John H. Y. Briggs

PICKWICK *Publications* · Eugene, Oregon

LIKE A MIGHTY ARMY?
The Salvation Army, the Church, and the Churches

Pickwick Publications
An Imprint of Wipf and Stock Publishers
199 W. 8th Av.e, Suite 3
Eugene, OR 97401

www.wipfandstock.com

ISBN 13: 978-1-62564-436-7

Cataloging-in-Publication data:

Taylor, David.

    Like a mighty army? : the Salvation Army, the church, and the churches / David Taylor ; foreword by John H. Y. Briggs

    xviii + 288 p. ; 23 cm. Includes bibliographical references and index.

    ISBN 13: 978-1-62564-436-7

    1. Salvation Army—Doctrines. 2. Church. 3. Barth, Karl, 1886–1968. I. Briggs, John H. Y. II. Title.

BX9721 T195 2014

Manufactured in the U.S.A.

To Kathy, Anna, Jenni, Sam and Samuel,
and the Church in Wood Green

Contents

Foreword

David Taylor's *Like a Mighty Army?* is a fine example of a study of the interplay of historical research, theological interrogation, and the analysis of emerging ecclesiastical practice, well illustrating the impact of the mental exercise of historical and theological enquiry on the practical issue presently confronting The Salvation Army in exploring the nature of its identity and mission in the modern world. Thus, the roots of the movement are traced back, religiously, to North American Holiness movements, derived as they were from John Wesley's own convictions about Christian perfectionism, and, organisationally, to English Methodism, particularly as expressed in its non-Wesleyan Methodist connexions. At the same time, the origins of the movement were also quite literally earthed in the desperate social situation confronting the new urban masses, and therefore the Churches, so robustly portrayed in *In Darkest England and the Way Out* first published in 1890. It was just here that William Booth sought to contextualise the mission of the Church

By that date the East London Mission had already morphed into The Salvation Army, thereby supplying two key words in the life of this ecclesiastical community—Mission and Army, spelling out both the urgency of the task, and the discipline needed to be effective in undertaking such a critical endeavour. The military metaphor, with its focus on an aggressive determination to secure well-defined goals, in the last decades of the nineteenth century spoke to and from a culture much influenced by the jingoism of empire, laying much emphasis on the subjective self, implicitly downplaying the significance of the corporate. This is not to deny that its life and work, as conceived by William Booth, had to do as much with the immediate deprivations of the urban working classes and with practical programmes to meet that need, as with the eternal salvation of the individual soul, so the dynamics of Mission and

ix

Army, evangelism and social welfare, the personal and the corporate, were early brought creatively together within the life of the movement.

Notwithstanding some criticism from the established Churches—as for example the jibe of an aged Earl of Shaftesbury who said of the Army that it was "in action as extravagant and in expression as offensive as any that ever disgraced the wildest fanaticism"—it was often seen as doing a job, namely effectively evangelising the lower orders in society, for which other branches of Christendom were ill-equipped, so that in some senses the Army was viewed as undertaking a particularly difficult task on behalf of all the churches. However, as a divided Christendom became more conscious of the need to establish relationships between its several parts, so the question as to the status of The Salvation Army became ever more pressing: was it or was it not a Church, and if a Church where were the classic marks of the life of the Church to be found within a body both non-sacerdotal and non-sacramental, and indeed in many respects non-ecclesial? Taylor tackles these critical questions both historically and theologically, the latter by submitting the Army's life to interrogation from the main contours of the doctrine of the Church as expounded in an ecumenical context by the reformed theologian, Karl Barth, an academic exercise prescient with potential suggestions for practical changes within the contemporary ordering of the Army.

Confusion on this issue existed at the highest level. For example, when the World Council of Churches was founded in 1948, the Army was admitted without question as a member Church. This, and other developing ecumenical relationships, increasingly placed upon the Army some examination of its own self-understanding of its ecclesial position, explorations of which are here properly and helpfully analysed. Living within an ecumenical context necessarily raised questions. One example of the pressure placed upon the Army by its ecumenical engagement can be seen in the debate at the Nairobi Assembly of the World Council in 1975 in which it was proposed to change the clause on "Functions and Purposes" within its constitution to read that the Council exists, amongst other purposes, "to call the Churches to the goal of visible unity in one faith and in one eucharistic fellowship." For Churches with an exclusivist view of the Church this was acceptable as a long-term aim though they were unable to contemplate any form of more intermediate inter-communion. The problem for The Salvation Army was of a different order: in the debate Commissioner Williams pointed out that the inclusion of the phrase "eucharistic fellowship" "acted against such denominations as The Salvation Army and the Society of Friends." This intervention called forth the clarification from the General Secretary that "the functions are not binding upon the member Churches but are what the WCC is expected to promote." In this interchange The Salvation Army clearly identifies itself as a "denomination," even though the WCC was in process of adopting language which was problematic for the Army.

In the event, three years later, the Army suspended its membership of the Council, in part because of the grant made by the WCC's programme to Combat Racism to the Patriotic Front in Zimbabwe in 1978. It also provided an opportunity for the Army to clarify the appropriate way in which it might relate to the Council, for the body which had joined in 1948 was not a national Church, as the WCC rules require, but the International Headquarters of the Army in the UK. The appropriate relationship after 1981was perceived to be that of a Christian World Communion, a status which provides for a presence in the counsels of the WCC but without voting rights. The latest Handbook of the WCC opens the section on the Army with the words "The Salvation Army is an integral part of the Christian Church, although distinctive in government and practice." It notes that whilst "no Army Churches are member Churches of the WCC," most of its national bodies are members of National Councils which are themselves associated with the WCC.

In streamlining its activities in the interests of its mission, the Army had deprived itself of what other Christians regarded as essential marks of the Church—particularly an ordained ministry and the sacraments of baptism and holy communion. Whilst there were emphases within the life of the Army which could be recognised as serving a similar purpose—the commissioning of officers as creating something akin to an ordained ministry, [and certainly at law Salvation Army officers are recognised as ministers of religion], a dedication service fulfilling some of the functions of infant baptism, the tendency was to stress the subjective experience of the believer, rather more than rejoicing in the objective nature of a grace already secured through the death and resurrection of Jesus Christ. There were accordingly weaknesses in the structure of the Army, for example the establishment of a hierarchical ruling class of officers, convenient for the effective implementation of policy but without theological rationale. Whilst lay participation was maintained in the guise of the positive service of the Christian soldier, it was highly regulated, disciplined and exclusive of individuals unwilling to take the necessary vows of "practical holiness."

Of course, Mission and Church belong closely together, in the sense that a Church indifferent to its mission to the world is grievously heretical, whilst mission cannot be isolated from the ongoing witness of the body of the Risen Christ. Whilst the current study carefully documents the development of Salvationist thinking on this relationship and on the Army as a Church, it convincingly argues that the thought in earlier times was essentially pragmatic, and only in the most recent decades has a more rigorously theological approach been adopted, a development which the present study will certainly advance.

Thus the present work is essential reading for all Salvationists seeking to deepen their understanding of their churchmanship and for all the Army's ecumenical partners, intent on understanding its ecclesial self-understanding, and deepening ecumenical partnership.

John H. Y. Briggs
sometime Director of the Baptist History and Heritage Centre, Regent's Park College, University of Oxford;
Honorary Research Professor the International Baptist Theological Seminary, Prague;
Emeritus Professor, the University of Birmingham, UK.

Preface

THIS BOOK CAME TO be written for three very specific reasons. Firstly, I happen to possess a possibly unique claim to two parents, four grandparents and eight great-grandparents, who were Salvation Army Officers stretching back to the very beginnings of the movement, with William and Catherine Booth. That heritage has understandably instilled in me a deep sense of loyalty and commitment to what has proved to be a quite remarkable phenomenon. Secondly, with my wife, I have been a Salvation Army Officer, offering leadership and service within a number of Salvation Army congregations for nearly thirty years, most recently in Wood Green, London, where we grew together, with other Christian partners, in a deepening understanding of *koinonia*, for nineteen years. Thirdly, I hold a deep longing to see the Church of God, in ecumenical unity and partnership, find a more robust theological foundation upon which it might visibly live and express the gospel of God's grace in a fractured world.

It is from those three perspectives that this study has sought to investigate and interrogate, what it might mean for The Salvation Army to live and demonstrate the reality of God's Church in the world, offering a gospel of grace in word , deed, and generous community. Whilst some might find the interrogation in places to be uncomfortable, I hope that ultimately it will be discerned to have stemmed from a genuine sense of loyalty for the honour and glory of God, and therefore faithfulness to the cause of The Salvation Army. Certainly, I cannot rest content to withstand Karl Barth's perceptive and striking challenge against all acquiescent and complacent denominationalism, in the face of the "one Church." Truly, the Church—*ecclesia semper reformanda*—is in need of constant reformation as it seeks to enter into God's mission.

David Taylor
August 8, 2014

Introduction

ECCLESIOLOGY MUST SURELY HAVE at its heart an earnest and passionate interest in the true nature, form and mission of the Church, including a clear understanding of its unity and diversity, at a time when there has been an explosion of Christian endeavor, particularly in many of the developing nations of the world. There are more Christian denominations and expressions of Christian community than ever. Reporting to the Ninth Assembly of the World Council of Churches at Porto Alegre, Brazil, in 2006, the Moderator of the WCC Central Committee, Aram I, Catholicos of Cilicia, admits that "for many, unity is no longer an ecumenical priority but, rather, an academic topic or, at best, an eschatological goal."[1] Recognizing that "a divided church cannot have a credible witness in a broken world" he calls for a renewed recognition that "being church" is "an ecumenical issue; it means challenging and helping the church to become an efficient and credible instrument of God's transformation in a changing world."[2] The Ninth Assembly, in its statement, *Called To Be The One Church,* urges churches to recognize their "*mutual responsibility* to one another" to "continue to facilitate *deep conversations* among various churches" and "to engage in the hard task of giving a candid account of the relation of their own faith and order to the faith and order of other churches."[3]

This study is principally an examination of The Salvation Army and its emerging ecclesiological conviction and practise within an ecumenical context. Founded in London, England, in 1865 by William and Catherine Booth, it has emerged as an international Christian denomination, with a presence in 121 nations of the world.[4] The last fifty years

---

1. Aram I, Catholicos of Cilicia, "Report of the Moderator," 125.
2. Ibid., 118f.
3. The World Council of Churches, "Called To Be The One Church," 259.
4. The Salvation Army, *The Salvation Army Year Book, 2011,* 27–28.

in particular have witnessed a significant shift in the denomination's self-understanding. In 1954 its sixth General, Albert Orsborn, informed Salvationists that whilst they were "part of the body of Christ called 'the Church militant," they were "not a Church," but "a permanent mission to the unconverted."[5] The most recent ecclesiological statement, issued in 2008, informs Salvationists that they are "an international Christian church in permanent mission to the unconverted . . . an integral part of the Body of Christ like other Christian churches, and that the Army's local corps are local congregations like the local congregations of other Christian churches."[6] Acknowledging this shift of emphasis John Larsson suggested in 2001 to the delegates of The Salvation Army's first International Theological Symposium, that "we are in a period of transition towards a fuller understanding of ourselves as a church—and theological concerns lie at the very heart of this process,"[7] in which "a great deal of thinking has yet to be done."[8]

This study is in two parts. The first part is an examination of the historical development of The Salvation Army's ecclesiological understanding in three phases: its origins as a Christian Mission in the East End of London, its establishment as The Salvation Army and its contemporary ecclesiological conviction as an international denomination of the Church. Under particular examination is the military metaphor of an army. Chosen pragmatically within the context of holiness revivalism as an aggressive means of Christian mission, it became established as a kind of spiritual emergency service or quasi-missionary religious order within and alongside the Church and ultimately has evolved as the dominant metaphor that informs Salvationists of what it means to be the Church. This study aims to assess the extent to which Larsson's comments have been heeded, in terms of firstly, the depth of internal theological reflection that has been given to the metaphor of the Church as an army, and secondly, the extent to which The Salvation Army has engaged in dialogue with the convictions of other churches. It concludes that in both cases the reflection and dialogue have been limited. Inasmuch as the metaphor of an army was the sociological and pragmatic outcome of a largely individualistic and subjective approach to salvation, it does not

5. Orsborn, "The World Council of Churches," 74.

6. The Salvation Army, *The Salvation Army in the Body of Christ*, 10.

7. Larsson, "Salvationist Theology," 12.

8. Ibid., 11.

adequately characterize the theological nature and form of the Christian community, and continues to afflict the Army's ecclesiology. In particular, this dominant metaphor presents a tangled cord of three separately identifiable ecclesial strands of mission, army and church.

In view of these findings, the second part of the study represents a dialogue with the ecclesiology of Karl Barth. Barth is chosen as a helpful discussion partner principally for the way in which, in the articulation of his ecclesiology and from his overall understanding of theological anthropology, he rejects both individualism and subjectivism, whilst strongly affirming The Salvation Army's own conviction about the priority of mission. Furthermore, his coherent Christological ecclesiology is able to assist The Salvation Army in addressing the tangled ecclesial cords of mission, army and church. His ecclesiology encourages Salvationists to examine their visible form from a deeper and more objective theological perspective.

Barth was himself intensely interested in Christian unity to which his recently re-published 1936 text, *The Church and the Churches*, delivered to the 1937 global Second World Conference on Faith and Order, in Edinburgh, clearly testifies. He believed that "the union of the churches is a thing which cannot be manufactured, but must be found and confessed, in subordination to that already accomplished oneness of the Church which is in Jesus Christ."[9] For Barth, the union of the churches was nothing short of "one unanimous confession"[10] without "taint of compromise, or of an assent to forms and formulae of union which would camouflage division without transcending it."[11] Barth encourages the churches, The Salvation Army included, to both deepen their internal theological reflection and engage in ecumenical discussion. He concludes that "only in our own church can we listen to Christ"[12] and "with humble but complete sincerity endorse the confession of our own church"[13] in such a way that confessions come "into the open, over

---

9. Barth, *The Church and the Churches*, 39.

10. Ibid. 41.

11. Ibid., 43.

12. Ibid., 49.

13. Ibid., 51.

against each other, in sharp and surprising contrast"[14] and we allow "thesis and antithesis well thought out to meet each other face to face."[15]

The highly pragmatic and activist nature of Salvation Army mission and service, has, from its founder William Booth's example, generally undervalued theological reflection. Barth offers a challenge to the Army's emerging ecclesiological conviction and practise, when he says that, "it is vital that once more in every church, in its own special atmosphere and thus with an ear attentive to Christ, real sober strict genuine theology should become active."[16] Ultimately therefore the aim of this study is, with the help of Barth, to demonstrate what it means for The Salvation Army to deepen theological reflection upon its identity and to engage wholeheartedly in an ecumenical journey with the churches, towards the goal of the visible unity of the one, holy, catholic and apostolic Church.

14. Ibid., 57.

15. Ibid., 58.

16. Ibid., 59.

PART ONE

Emerging Salvationist Ecclesiology

Introduction

This book proposes that there have been three defining phases in the emerging ecclesiological conviction and practise of The Salvation Army. The first phase began when William Booth and his wife Catherine, fresh from their independent itinerant holiness revivalism in England and Wales, took leadership of a group of "lay missioners" working from a tent in Whitechapel, London, and set about adapting holiness revivalism to the particular challenge of London's East End, with its stark poverty and low church attendance. During this phase, 1865–1878, the Booths, after a quick succession of several named organizations, ultimately founded "The Christian Mission." Characterized by William Booth's naïve declaration that he was not creating another sect or church, this phase was deeply influenced by the Booths' understanding of the current trans-Atlantic holiness revivalism that they so eagerly exploited. They could not foresee the eventual size, impact and influence of the organization that they had initiated.

The second phase emerged in the rapid growth and organization of a movement that quickly established the quasi-military identity and structure of an Army. In an ecclesial sense this phase dates from the failed negotiations for co-operation with the Church of England which fizzled out in the early 1880s, galvanizing Booth's perception of his Army as a kind of spiritual emergency service within the Church. The phase began with the Christian Mission's change of name to The Salvation Army in 1878, and characterizes the incipient and institutionalizing period of its first two Generals, William, and his son, Bramwell Booth, to the year 1929, though may for the purposes of this study be extended to the inception of the World Council of Churches (WCC) in 1948. It was a phase in which The Salvation Army, whilst still not claiming to be "a church," was nevertheless in its own opinion, and within its own militaristic and missional terms of reference, to be reckoned as an equal

3

partner, alongside other major denominations, as "part" of the universal Christian Church. It was a position which enabled The Salvation Army enigmatically to be a founding member of the WCC, whilst still officially disavowing that it was a church.

The third phase represents the development of this emerging conviction and practise, to The Salvation Army's contemporary ecclesiological understanding. It charts briefly the influence of twentieth-century ecumenism upon The Salvation Army, and in particular the WCC invitation to respond to the Faith and Order paper *Baptism, Eucharist and Ministry* (*BEM*), in which it found itself having to reflect more fully upon its own idiosyncratic ecclesiological convictions. The ecumenical movement, including *BEM* and the Army's response to it, has proved to be the catalyst towards the recent publication of a brief official clarification that seeks to outline The Salvation Army's current ecclesiological convictions. In this publication The Salvation Army, which continued for a large part of its history to strenuously deny that it was a church, asserts that in its own understanding it is to be understood in these terms.

The first part of this study represents the charting and analysis of emerging convictions and practise through these three phases, in order to assess their theological character and coherency. It is argued that these three phases also loosely describe three identifiable ecclesial strands that have in the historical development of The Salvation Army become tangled. In the first phase, the dominant influence of holiness revivalism and its espousal of what became popularly known as "aggressive Christianity" inspired the ecclesial strand of a Christian mission, in London's East End. In the second phase, this aggressive evangelical mission logically led to the establishing of the ecclesial strand of a Christian army; The Salvation Army. This quasi-military denomination, with its emphasis upon what it termed "practical holiness" rapidly developed the character of a quasi-missionary religious order within the wider church. Booth likened it to a spiritual emergency service, with a disciplined regime of order, regulation and lifestyle requirements. Finally in the third phase, partly through the familiar sociological development of a denomination, and partly the tentative theological enquiry of a movement exposed to an emerging ecumenical consensus, there has been an attempt to retrieve an understanding of The Salvation Army as a church. These three tangled strands are, for ease of identification in this study, simply termed "mission," "army" and "church." What follows in this first part of the study is the characterization of these three defining phases, together with the three identifiable ecclesial strands that loosely emerge within them.

part of the study is the manner in which one can show the underlying
together with the way in which each wist should, and that
over them.

1

The Origins of a "Christian Mission"

Introduction

The Methodist roots of William[1] and Catherine[2] Booth and The Salvation Army[3] which they founded, come as no surprise to Salvationists, bred on an understanding of William's teenage conversion in a Methodist chapel in Nottingham. The Salvation Army is viewed as the last of a series of schisms in the history of nineteenth-century Methodism.[4] On the other hand, The Salvation Army's origins in what is termed in this study the "holiness revivalism" of the nineteenth-century "holiness movement," are surprisingly poorly understood in Salvation Army literature, and much is still to be learned about these formative influences.[5] This book argues that William Booth's Methodism was mediated more through these influences, than directly from John Wesley. Paul Rader was right to recognise this in a brief article that just pre-

1. See in particular: Begbie, *Life of William Booth*; Ervine, *God's Soldier*; Stead, *General Booth*; Nicol, *General Booth*; Railton, *The Authoritative Life of General William Booth*; Bennett, *The General*; Green, *The Life and Ministry of William Booth*.

2. See in particular: Booth-Tucker, *The Life of Catherine Booth*; Stead, *Mrs. Booth of The Salvation Army*; Bramwell-Booth, *Catherine Booth*; Green, *Catherine Booth*; Kew, *Catherine Booth*.

3. The official history is recorded as *The History of the Salvation Army*, in 7 volumes. See in addition: Coutts, *No Discharge In This War*; Rhemick, *A New People of God*; Murdoch, *Origins of The Salvation Army*.

4. See Hattersley, *Blood and Fire*, 31.

5. See Kent, *Holding The Fort*; Carwardine, *Trans-Atlantic Revivalism*; Dieter, *The Holiness Revival*; Scotland, *Apostles of the Spirit and Fire*.

dated the research of John Kent and Richard Carwardine, who both linked William and Catherine Booth to holiness revivalism's predominant personalities:

> One can understand William Booth and The Salvation Army's heritage of holiness only in terms of the dynamic spiritual movement within which they were cradled. That movement may have had more to do with what the founders were and The Army became, than with their debt to Wesley and Methodism.[6]

In a letter of 1876 to his eldest son, Bramwell, whom he had been developing as a young leader,[7] William Booth wrote: "Making saints must be *our* work, that is *yours* and *mine*. G.S.R. [George Scott Railton] and others are all for converting sinners and making *workers*. We want *saints*."[8] He can scarcely contain his delight, when a month later he commented on Bramwell's reply:

> He wrote me last week saying that it is the *experimental realisation* and *definite teaching* of the blessing of holiness that alone can make us different from the other organisations around us. I say *Amen*. And only this, it seems to me, can justify us in having any separate existence at all.[9]

This "experimental realisation" and "definite teaching" which lay at the heart of the identity of Booth's mission and "alone" justified its existence as an "organization," can only be appreciated in a brief review of both his Methodist and holiness revivalist origins, in order that their influence on The Salvation Army's emerging ecclesiological convictions and practise may be charted.

William and Catherine Booth as Methodists

Though christened in an Anglican parish church in Sneinton, Nottingham, William Booth (1829–1912) experienced little religious influence at home or religious training at church. After his father died, the impoverished family was forced to move to the Goose Green area. A middle-aged couple took a special interest in him and introduced him

6. Rader, "Holiness, Revival and Mission," 74.

7. See Bramwell-Booth, *Bramwell Booth*.

8. Cited in ibid., 143. See Watson, *Soldier Saint*.

9. Cited in Bramwell-Booth, *Bramwell Booth*, 142.

to the Broad Street Wesley Chapel, where he attended Sunday services, became a member of Brother Henry Carey's midweek class, and in his early teens experienced a life-changing conversion. It propelled him into active evangelism with his boyhood friend, Will Sansom. They "conducted religious meetings on the streets, and led processions on Sunday evenings from street meeting to indoor meeting."[10] When in 1849, at the age of nineteen, he moved to London to find work in the familiar pawnbroker's trade in Walworth, he threw himself into the life of Wesleyan Methodism as a lay preacher.

It was a period of turmoil within Wesleyan Methodism. The so called "Fly Sheet" controversy came to a head in that year.[11] The annual Conference expelled three Ministers, one of whom was Samuel Dunn, Booth's Minister at Broad Street Chapel in Nottingham. Considerable unrest followed from what was considered a heavy-handed response. One hundred thousand Methodists, in sympathy with the reformers, found their membership tickets were not renewed, and were effectively expelled to join congregations with reforming sympathies. One of these members in London was Catherine Mumford (1829–1890). Her biographer records that, "the outspoken manner in which Miss Mumford had expressed her condemnation of the Conference and sympathy with the Reformers was naturally objected to by her class-leader, who remonstrated with her on the folly of her course, reminding her that in identifying herself with the malcontents she would not only forfeit her position in the church she loved, but seriously injure her worldly prospects."[12]

Equally, when William Booth resigned his appointment as a lay preacher with the Wesleyans in the Lambeth circuit, so that he could "better serve my generation by preaching in the streets" his superintendent minister, John Hall, most likely suspecting that he may have sympathies with the reformers, "without reply . . . withdrew my ticket of membership."[13] Mr. Rabbits, a wealthy businessman impressed by his preaching, decided to sponsor him. He preached his first sermon in the Walworth Road Chapel, which had gone over to the Wesleyan Reform movement. In the congregation that day was Catherine Mumford. They

10. Green, *The Life and Ministry of William Booth*, 13.

11. See Chadwick, *The Victorian Church: Part One*, 380–86.

12. Booth-Tucker, *The Life of Catherine Booth*, 49.

13. Stead, *General Booth*, 37.

soon became engaged to be married and together began a search for a spiritual home through a variety of early Methodist splinter groups. Booth's affections never lay heavily with the reformers and even more so when his opportunities for preaching were limited due to the democratic nature of the reformers belief that "priest and people were one in the sight of God."[14] There followed, at Catherine's suggestion, a brief flirtation with Congregationalism, in spite of what she describes as her husband's love for Methodism "that amounted almost to idolatry."[15]

It did not take Booth long to discover that his theology was out of harmony with a Congregational emphasis upon election.[16] He had never been quite as certain as his fiancée about this venture. He wrote to Catherine:

> It is one thing to forsake Methodism. It is quite another to abandon a doctrine which I look upon as a cardinal point in Christ's redemption plan—His universal love, and the possibility of all being saved who will avail themselves of His mercy.[17]

Within a week of leaving the Cotton End Congregational College,[18] he found his way back into the Wesleyan Reform movement, and was invited to become the minister of a Church in Spalding, Lincolnshire.

After eighteen months in this circuit, he joined the Methodist New Connexion, which in 1797 had been the first of the splinters from Wesleyan Methodism. Booth struggled with what he considered the Reformers' disorganization and democratic inclinations in making decisions that affected his ministry, as indicated by his fiancée Catherine:

> There is not the least security for the future, & the spirit of some may spread & become the spirit of many, and to be dependent on the will of a disorganized society for your position & bread will not be at all congenial to a temperament like yours . . . they are generally so democratical [sic], nay, absurdly, extravagantly so.[19]

---

14. Hattersley, *Blood and Fire*, 48.

15. Begbie, *William Booth*, 1:139.

16. Ibid., 1:139–40.

17. Booth-Tucker, *The Life of Catherine Booth*, 1:74.

18. The six months spent at this college represent the full extent of his formal theological education.

19. Bennett, *The Letters of William and Catherine Booth*, No. CM72, 184. Hereafter *Letters*.

This move is difficult to understand in that the New Connexion had seceded from Wesleyanism largely on the grounds of demanding greater
local autonomy and congregational participation. Catherine argued:

> The Reform Movement is no home and sphere for you; whereas
> the principles of the Connexion you live in your very soul. I be-
> lieve you will be satisfied, when once from under the influence of
> your Spalding friends.[20]

The Wesleyan community was principally divided by theological
issues of authority and governance, inherited from Wesley. The Booths
eventually left the Methodist New Connexion to become independent
itinerant evangelists, frustrated by the Conference decision that William
should remain a circuit minister in Gateshead, when his talents clearly
lay in itinerant revivalist preaching. The decision launched them into an
independent campaign, based largely on Methodist chapels that would
welcome them. They finally settled in London in 1865, and joined the
Special Services Committee's mission work in the East End. It was their
Methodism that doctrinally shaped their understanding of that mission.
A comparison of the twelve doctrines of the Methodist New Connexion
(1838), the seven doctrines of the East London Christian Revival Society
(1865), the ten doctrines of the Christian Mission, (1870) and the eleven
doctrines of The Salvation Army (1878),[21] shows a remarkably close
alignment. In John Rhemick's estimation they were "essentially the same
statements of faith,"[22] bearing in mind that more of the New Connexion
doctrines were added with each revision. Roger Green confirms that:

> One of the great faults of some of the previous biographies of
> Booth is that they have failed to understand that he was driven by
> a particular theological vision . . . not merely broadly Protestant
> or even generically Evangelical. It was Wesleyan, and Booth's the-
> ology of redemption—including his understanding of sin, grace,
> salvation, holiness—can be understood only if this is taken into
> account.[23]

20. Booth-Tucker, *The Life of Catherine Booth*, 1:109.

21. See Murdoch, *Origins of The Salvation Army*, 173–75; Rhemick, *A New People of God*, 30–34.

22. Rhemick, *A New People of God*, 34.

23. Green, *The Life and Ministry of William Booth*, 1. See also Green, "William Booth and Methodism"; Green, "The Salvation Army and the Evangelical Tradition," 51–69. See in particular Green's opposition to Murdoch, "Evangelical Sources of Salvation

Booth later revealed the depth of his own admiration for John Wesley:

> I worshipped everything that bore the name of Methodist. To me
> there was one God, and John Wesley was his prophet . . . and all
> that was wanted, in my estimation, for the salvation of the world
> was the faithful carrying into practice of the letter and the spirit
> of his instructions.[24]

When Booth addressed the Wesleyan Conference in 1880 he confidently informed them that The Salvation Army was, "the continuation of the work of Mr. Wesley, for we have gone on, only a great deal further, on the same lines which he travelled."[25]

Nineteenth-Century Trans-Atlantic "Holiness Revivalism"

If their Methodist roots offer little surprise to Salvationists, the foremost influence upon the young teenage convert in Nottingham was the visiting American Methodist and holiness revivalist preacher James Caughey. His influence on Booth has not escaped the attention of Salvation Army historians, but his brand of holiness revivalism and the tension that it precipitated amongst the Methodist churches in Britain, who eventually asked him to leave, has not been fully acknowledged. To appreciate the nature of this tension, it is necessary to understand the nineteenth century trans-Atlantic movement of holiness revivalism.

Wesley sent ten of his itinerants between 1769 and 1774, including Francis Asbury in 1771, to largely respond to the unofficial exploits of Methodist settlers in America. Asbury was made "General Assistant" for America in September 1783 and urged by Wesley to "keep to the British standards of the *Notes, Sermons and Minutes*."[26] According to Timothy Smith, despite Asbury's best efforts, Wesley's doctrine of Christian perfection "did not occupy a chief place in early Methodist preaching in the New World . . . The moral needs of rural and Western America directed attention to the more elemental work of saving sinners."[27] The rise of interest in holiness in urban America may have been sparked by the publi-

---

Army Doctrine," 235–44, a view later modified in Murdoch, *Origins Of The Salvation Army*, 65–66. See also ibid., 173–75, appendix A.

24. Booth-Tucker, *The Life of Catherine Booth*, 1:52.

25. Booth, "The General's Address at the Wesleyan Conference," 1.

26. Rack, *Reasonable Enthusiast*, 409.

27. Smith, *Revivalism and Social Reform*, 115.

cation in 1825 of Timothy Merritt's *Treatise on Christian Perfection, with Directions for Obtaining That State.* Merritt was a well-known minister in the New York City District, and his book appeared in 33 editions by 1871. A wave of other publications followed. The General Conference of 1832 called for a revival of holiness, and in 1841 Luther Meyrick and the Wesleyan Methodists seceded from the parent body citing both their objection to compromises on the issue of slavery, which they were against, and the neglect of Christian perfection teaching. In 1842 the Methodists and Oberlin College, where Charles Finney was Professor of Theology and Asa Mahan was President, combined in holiness conventions around the New York City and New England area, where both James Caughey and Phoebe Palmer were active in Methodism. Finney, Mahan, Caughey and Palmer were four leading personalities in holiness revivalism, who each made a significant impact across the Atlantic, an impact that did not escape the attention of William and Catherine Booth, eager to absorb revivalist influences that would further their cause.

Melvin Dieter, in *The Holiness Revival of the Nineteenth Century*, describes a developing synthesis between American revivalism and Wesleyan perfectionism that he believes can only be understood by looking back to both Jonathan Edwards and John Wesley for inspiration. Jonathan Edwards with his revival theology and methods shaped American revivalism in a way that his successors carried into the renewed search for holiness in the 1830s. Edwards' basic principle of evangelism was that the moment of salvation was "now." The gospel message was urgent and it was the immediate duty of everyone who heard its call to repent and be saved. The synthesis developed as Methodists translated this current sense of immediacy in the expectation of conversion, into the sphere of sanctification, or Christian perfection. As Dieter explains:

> To the Wesleyan perfectionists who believed that the sinner's response to the revivalist's appeal for justification by faith still left him, as a Christian convert, short of a life of uninterrupted love for God and man; it was but a short step given the prevailing mood and methods of American revivalism, to move in with the 'second blessing' message . . . of a second crisis in the Christian's life . . . The sense of immediacy was also there; the time to enter the "higher life" was "now."[28]

28. Dieter, *The Holiness Revival*, 19.

Dieter finds clear testimony to this development in the writings of Harriet Beecher Stowe who commented,

> that pressing men to an immediate and definite point of conversion produced immediate and definite results and so it may be found among Christians pressing them to an immediate and definite point of attainment (i.e. entire sanctification) will, in like manner, result in marked and decided progress.[29]

Holiness revivalism, as practiced by the Booths, is crucial to an understanding of the Salvationist ecclesiology that has emerged, especially in regard to an emphasis on individual salvation, a subjective focus on the conditions that the individual must fulfill in their "attainment" of personal justification and sanctification and the pragmatic methods that this revivalism espoused. Many of the itinerant or lay revivalists that most influenced the Booths, visited churches, but were not themselves primarily focused upon the life of the community. Their concern was the personal salvation and sanctification of individuals. These key individuals and their influence require introduction, before examining the outworking of this American synthesis in the ministry of William and Catherine Booth.

James Caughey

James Caughey was a Methodist minister, yet more pertinently a product of what Dieter describes as, "all that was American in the nineteenth century promotion and practices of the Wesleyan emphasis."[30] He was a leading exponent of this American synthesis of holiness revivalism—its message of entire sanctification and its pragmatic methods geared towards an immediate response. In his campaign in Britain (1841–1847), he brought both a renewed emphasis upon Wesleyan perfectionism to a Methodist tradition that had begun to lose its focus upon a second work of grace, and a new sense of urgency and immediacy in receiving it.

Born on 9th April, 1810, in the north of Ireland, he emigrated with his family to America, grew up in New York State, and became a Methodist, turning away from his family's Calvinism. He was caught up in the local revival, in 1830. Within two years he was a preacher on probation, in a further two years a deacon and by 1836 an ordained el-

29. Cited in ibid., 20.
30. Ibid.

der. Caughey became a successful preacher and a prolific writer, with dramatic appeals for the blessing of holiness. He arrived in England in July 1841, and at the Manchester Wesleyan Methodist Conference was offered a pulpit in Dublin by Thomas Waugh. His first sermon led to a five-month revival with seven hundred converts recorded. Not all in the Conference approved of his methods, but he was welcomed in particular by the Wesleyan Reformers, one of whom was the Rev. Samuel Dunn, minister of Broad Street Wesley Chapel in Nottingham, where Booth was a teenager. Caughey spoke in Nottingham and made a profound and lasting impact upon the young William Booth.[31] Whilst Booth's conversion pre-dated by two years his introduction to Caughey,[32] he recalled Caughey's immense impact upon him:

> He was an extraordinary preacher filling up his sermons with thrilling anecdotes and vivid illustrations, and for the straightforward declaration of scriptural truth and striking appeals to the conscience, I had up to that time never heard his equal . . . Multitudes were saved, many of whom became the most useful members of the society. All this had a powerful effect upon my young heart. The straightforward conversational way of putting the truth . . . the common-sense method of pushing the people up to decision . . . the corresponding results that followed, in the conversion and sanctification of hundreds of people, made an ineffaceable impression on my mind, filling me . . . with confidence in the power and willingness of God to save all those that come unto Him.[33]

Richard Carwardine records that "after nearly six years of revivals . . . including two trips to the Continent, Caughey could claim to have been instrumental in over twenty thousand conversions and to have brought nine thousand to experience 'entire sanctification.'"[34]

Booth witnessed and approved the dramatic, if divisive impact of holiness revivalism in Caughey's ministry, fresh as it was from the cauldron of New York State's "burned-over" district.[35] Carwardine suggests that whilst British Methodism instinctively understood revivalism, pos-

31. Sandall, *The History of The Salvation Army*, 1:3; Kent, *Holding The Fort*, 38; Dieter, *The Holiness Revival*, 60; Carwardine, *Trans-Atlantic Revivalism*, 102.

32. See Green, *The Life and Ministry of William Booth*, 237 n. 36.

33. Booth, "How We Began," 8.

34. Carwardine, *Trans-Atlantic Revivalism*, 111.

35. See Cross, *The Burned-Over District*, 173–84.

sessing "an Arminian theology that sanctioned an unrestricted appeal to all men,"[36] American Methodism was in Caughey's estimation "clearly more emotional, revival-centered, and tolerant of innovation than that of British Wesleyans."[37] He notes the measure of distrust that lingered in British Methodism against American revivalism and its camp meetings, from the earlier influence of Lorenzo Dow and the emergence of the Primitive Methodist movement with which he was associated:

> Dow and camp meetings had not inoculated Wesleyan Methodists against revivalism as such, but they had injected them with a fear of the schismatic tendencies of revival and a sense that American evangelicalism was less well disciplined than it ought to be . . . When . . . James Caughey, arrived to give them effect, he would find a residue of distrust for things American that no amount of practical success could ever remove.[38]

Despite the impressive statistics of those converted and sanctified,[39] Caughey's critics detected something new in his methods. In contrast to the spontaneity of previous revivals, such as those of the English Methodist, William Bramwell (1759–1818), "Caughey's meetings . . . were premeditated, part of a preconceived campaign to stir a religious awakening, more or less without regard to the initial receptiveness of the audience."[40] Carwardine comments that, "with James Caughey the day of the revival technician who was paid for his services had arrived."[41] Amongst the many elements in Caughey's preaching were methods he learned in the revival fervour of 1830s America, such as "knee work" (prayer meetings after preaching), and the altar call, where Caughey would invite people to move forward to either the communion rail or the "penitent's form" to make an immediate response. This method, Carwardine explains, was seen as "the 'most remarkable' feature of his

---

36. Carwardine, *Trans-Atlantic Revivalism*, 103.

37. Ibid.

38. Ibid., 107.

39. See the statistical list given in defense of Caughey in 1847 by a Wesleyan Methodist, cited in Kent, *Holding the Fort*, 312; and in Carwardine, *Trans-Atlantic Revivalism*, 4, 112–14.

40. Ibid., 127.

41. Ibid., 128.

work, for although an integral part of American services, it was not universally employed in British Methodism."[42]

Recalling his teenage "cottage meetings," Booth remembers, "we had lively songs, short and sharp exhortations insisting upon decision for Christ upon the spot, which was to be signified by coming out and kneeling at the round table that stood in the middle of the room."[43] The "mercy seat," as it became enduringly known in The Salvation Army, was a central feature of Booth's revivalism.[44] Norman Murdoch suggests:

> Booth was Caughey's heir. Caughey convinced Booth that converting the masses was possible through scientific, calculated means. Revivals which were planned, advertised, and prayed for would succeed.[45]

In Booth's own words:

> I saw as clearly as if a revelation had been made to me from Heaven that success in spiritual work, as in natural operations, was to be accounted for, not on any mere abstract theory of Divine sovereignty . . . but on the employment of such methods as were dictated by common sense, the Holy Spirit, and the Word of God.[46]

Caughey, this most influential influence upon the Booths, baptized their son Ballington in Sheffield, and Catherine remarked to her parents:

> After almost adoring his very name for ten years past, to be thus privileged was well nigh too much for me. When he took leave of me, I pressed one fervent kiss on his hand, and felt more gratified than if it had been Queen Victoria's.[47]

Charles Grandison Finney

The re-emphasizing of "Christian perfection" in American Methodism was paralleled by a movement that had its origin at Oberlin College,

---

42. Ibid., 120.

43. Booth, "How We Began," 9. See Booth, "Fifty Years' Salvation Services," 1–9, for his assessment of this early ministry as "a miniature Salvation Army."

44. See Bovey, *The Mercy Seat Revisited.*

45. Murdoch, *Origins Of The Salvation Army*, 12.

46. Booth, "How We Began," 8.

47. Booth-Tucker, *The Life of Catherine Booth*, 1:219.

Ohio, where the Professor of Theology, Charles Finney and the President, Asa Mahan, were the two leading proponents of what came to be known as "Oberlin perfectionism." Finney, born in 1792, converted on 10th October 1821, licensed to preach on 30th December 1823, was ordained as a Presbyterian minister on 1st July 1824. His successful revivalism in New York State led in 1835 to the publication of *Lectures on Revivals of Religion*,[48] (first published in Britain in 1837). Keith Hardman suggests that:

> The theology of revivals held both in the Old World and in eastern Massachusetts was that awakenings would come only at God's pleasure. The prevailing Calvinist concept of election had a massive dampening effect: people must simply wait, perhaps all their lives, and if they were of the elect, in God's own time salvation would surely come. Individual initiative was therefore discouraged.[49]

Hardman suggests this was first questioned in New England by Jonathan Edwards' grandfather, Solomon Stoddard, who asked the question, "To what extent can clergy and laity be partners with the Almighty in the bringing of awakenings?"[50] Finney represents the culminating force in promoting the potential for human cooperation in the effecting of revivals.

Converted under the ministry of Rev. George Gale, whom Finney admired, he nevertheless in Hardman's view found that Gale's Calvinism "overly demeaned human motivation and action" and that in this he was unconsciously "voicing the concerns of many Americans at that period who were abandoning Calvinism and predestination, or at least rejecting the very elements that were most repellent to the unconverted, the ideas that they were mired in sin and unable to exert moral choice."[51] Finney became armed with the New Divinity theology that emerged from the followers of Jonathan Edwards, through such men as Joseph Bellamy (1719–1790) and Samuel Hopkins (1721–1803), who sought to improve upon Edwards' ideas by developing a theology that resisted "original sin," placing responsibility upon the individual with the innate

---

48. Finney, *Lectures on Revivals of Religion*.
49. Hardman, *Charles Grandison Finney*, 19.
50. Ibid.
51. Ibid., 47.

ability to exercise free will in making good choices. Timothy Smith summarizes this New Divinity:

> By grafting onto covenant theology the doctrine of the moral nature of divine government, which required the consent of the human will to all that God provided or demanded; by locating depravity not in our natures, as Jonathan Edwards had, but in our dispositions our selfish wills; and by adopting Samuel Hopkins' idea that disinterested benevolence, or unselfish love towards God and man, was the sum of the Christian's duty [Nathaniel] Taylor and [Lyman] Beecher transformed Calvinist dogma into a practical Arminianism, without having to jettison Calvinist verbiage.[52]

This freedom and optimism in the human condition opened the way for a greater sense of human participation in the course of revivals. Finney confidently explained that a revival "is not a miracle, nor dependent on a miracle, in any sense," but "a purely philosophical result of the right use of the constituted means."[53] In his lecture on "Measures to Promote Revivals" Finney argued:

> Under the gospel dispensation, God has *established no particular system of measures* to be employed and invariably adhered to in promoting religion . . . our present forms of public worship, and every thing, so far as *measures* are concerned, have been arrived at by *degrees*, and by *a succession of New Measures* . . . It was left to the discretion of the church to determine, from time to time, what *measures* shall be adopted, and what *forms* pursued, in giving the gospel its power'. (Finney's emphasis).[54]

In this respect Finney was an admirer of John Wesley, whom he suggested "introduced so much of new measures, as to fill all England with excitement and uproar and opposition, and he was everywhere denounced as an innovator and a stirrer up of sedition, and a teacher of new things which it was not lawful to receive."[55] In the matter of preaching Finney declared:

---

52. Smith, "The Doctrine of the Sanctifying Spirit," 93. See Finney, "Natural Ability," in *Finney's Systematic Theology*, 303–21.

53. Finney, *Lectures on Revivals of Religion*, 13.

54. Ibid., 250–51.

55. Ibid., 260. Hardman, *Charles Grandison Finney*, 84, suggests that most of Finney's new measures came from Methodism.

> Look at the Methodists. Many of their ministers are unlearned, in the common sense of the term, many of them taken right from the shop or the farm, and yet they have . . . won souls every where . . . their plain, pointed and simple, but warm and animated mode of preaching has always gathered congregations.[56]

Hardman calls Finney "the 'pragmatist's pragmatist,'" a man who "did his best to remove the unpredictability in God's working, and operated on what John Calvin's followers would have called Pelagian principles."[57] Finney was himself clear that God remained central to the enterprise, willing to work in partnership with people of good faith:

> I said that a revival is the result of the *right* use of the appropriate means. The means which God has enjoyed for the production of a revival, doubtless have a natural tendency to produce a revival. Otherwise God would not have enjoined them. But means will not produce a revival, we all know, without the blessing of God. No more will grain, when it is sowed, produce a crop without the blessing of God.[58]

Whether or not Pelagian, Finney could be mistaken for implying that God responded to human initiative rather than *vice versa*. Catherine Booth's biographer reveals that she read church history and theology. "Wesley, Finney, Fletcher, Mosheim, Neander, and Butler were taken up, in turn, and in some cases carefully epitomized" and "Finney's lectures on theology she specially appreciated."[59] As Finney's *Lectures in Systematic Theology* were only published in Britain in 1851, it is most likely that it was his *Lectures on Revivals of Religion* that she was reading at this time. The Booths' intimate personal letters are littered with references to Finney, jealous as they were for the inheritance of John Wesley and his evangelistic success in their own day. Catherine wrote to William: "It would be a good plan to read Finney's tenth, eleventh & 12th lectures on revivals."[60] On the subject of excitement and shouting, Catherine, having spoken of "Caughey's silent, soft, heavenly carriage . . . he did not shout, there was no necessity," urged William to read

56. Ibid., 273.

57. Hardman, *Charles Grandison Finney*, 100. See Warfield, "Oberlin Perfectionism," 1–63.

58. Finney, *Lectures on Revivals of Religion*, 13.

59. Booth-Tucker, *The Life of Catherine Booth*, 1:39.

60. *Letters*, No. CM98, 243.

Finney, where her views are found, "*exactly* [her emphasis] in Finney's *Lectures on Revivals*, which I consider the most beautiful & common sense work on the subject I ever read."[61] She also encouraged William to "read Finney's directions for the treatment of penitents; they are excellent, the best part of the work. If you are not well acquainted with them, be sure to read them. They are in his *Lectures on Revivals*."[62] Equally Catherine reveals her sermon preparation: "I have now to *begin* to think about a subject for Sheriff Hill in the morn'g. I think I shall take, 'Be filled with the Spirit', but I can only find one lecture in Finney's on it & that treats more on the *hinderances* (sic) to being filled with the spirit."[63] For his part William informed Catherine on one occasion that, "other matters of a more important kind and character demand my attention; Finney's Moral Theology for instance,"[64] on another, "our love has not been merely an emotion, but it is indeed of truth an *affection* . . . Bear in mind Finney's distinction between the two words,"[65] and on yet another, "' am reading Finney . . . on election and final perseverance, and I see more than ever reason to cling to my own views of truth and righteousness."[66] Catherine entitled one of her later addresses, "Adaptation of Measures"[67] in which, following Finney, she found six texts from the Bible that all exhibited this principle of adaptation, declaring, "While the Gospel message is laid down with unerring exactness, we are left at perfect freedom to adapt our measures and modes of bringing it to bear upon men to the circumstances, times, and conditions in which we live — free as air."[68] She did not refer directly to Finney but her claim to draw her convictions from, "some of the most thoughtful and spiritual men of this age,"[69] is unmistakable.

In spite of his evangelistic success, Finney recorded in his *Memoirs* that "on looking at the state of the Christian church as it had been revealed to me in my revival labors, I was led earnestly to inquire whether

61. *Letters*, No. CM29, 87.
62. Ibid.
63. *Letters*, No. CB152, 331.
64. *Letters*, No. WB6, 10.
65. *Letters*, No. WB145, 351.
66. *Letters*, No. WB8, 11.
67. Booth, *Papers on Aggressive Christianity*, 41.
68. Ibid., 50.
69. Ibid., 47.

there was not something higher and more enduring than the Christian church was aware of."[70] At Oberlin College, together with Asa Mahan and the other staff and students, a deepening search for this Christian life ensued. In 1839 Finney's *Memoirs* record that a student rose one day to ask, "whether sanctification was not attainable in this life, that is sanctification in such sense that Christians could have unbroken peace, and not . . . have the feeling of condemnation or a consciousness of sin."[71] Convinced that the answer was "yes," they began publishing this belief in *The Oberlin Evangelist* and *The Oberlin Quarterly*, and in 1840 Finney himself published his book *Views of Sanctification*. In an age in which the issue of slavery divided whole denominations, the founder of Oberlin College, Arthur Tappan, insisted that Finney, his New York City Pastor, be drafted in for six months each year as Professor of Theology, to develop an ideology of Christian perfection that would be the basis of a higher Christian life, capable of inspiring and reforming American society away from such evils as slavery and the growing urban culture.

Timothy Smith defends Finney against accusations of Pelagianism, suggesting that his mature covenant theology saw "entire sanctification," through the baptism of the Holy Spirit, as a sovereign work of grace, a new covenant outworking of God's promises, rooted in the OT covenant of holiness, in an unbroken chain from Abraham to Christ. Smith even suggests that "his covenant theology . . . opened the door to the evangelical unity for which Wesley and Whitfield prayed but were never able to grasp."[72] Nevertheless, in denying total depravity, he expressed this covenant in highly subjective terms that problematically emphasized human ability and initiative. Nevertheless, Catherine confided in William: "I often wish I could have an hour's talk with Finney. I think he would be able to advise me. He would understand me."[73] Finney's writings, including his autobiography, were reproduced in the *Christian Mission Magazine*, and as late as 1895 *The Officer* magazine declared that, "there are no books, other than our own publications, which we can recommend more heartily than those of Finney."[74]

---

70. Finney, *The Memoirs of Charles G. Finney*, 391.

71. Ibid., 409.

72. Smith, "The Doctrine of the Sanctifying Spirit," 103.

73. *Letters*, No. CM45, 126.

74. The Salvation Army, "Our Library—Finney's Works," 12.

Phoebe Palmer

Phoebe Palmer was born in 1807 in New York City, where she lived most of her life. In 1835 her sister, Sarah Lankford, formed the "Tuesday Meeting for the Promotion of Holiness" when she combined two ladies' prayer meetings from local Methodist congregations.[75] Phoebe Palmer was in 1837 "sanctified" at these meetings and became the leader.[76] In 1839 Thomas Upham joined the group, opening it to men, and Timothy Merritt launched a new monthly magazine called *The Guide to Christian Perfection*. (The name later changed to *The Guide to Holiness*). Palmer herself wrote extensively. *The Way Of Holiness*, published in 1849, sold 24,000 copies by 1851, appearing in 35 editions by the American Civil War, and *Faith and Its Effects* was published in its twenty-fourth edition by 1859. Palmer had an immense stature in the holiness movement, a direct influence on the Booths, and the many Christian leaders who passed through her Tuesday night meetings. J. Edwin Orr calls her a "Priscilla who taught many an Apollos the way of God more perfectly."[77]

Charles Edward White accepts Dieter's explanation that Palmer, a Methodist, "was applying 'all that was America in the nineteenth century' to Wesley," but suggests that she was also attempting to carry "Wesleyan doctrines to their natural conclusion; she was working out their inner logic."[78] He lists six ways in which he suggests Palmer modified John Wesley's doctrine of entire sanctification. Firstly, she followed John Fletcher, Wesley's preferred successor until his untimely death, in identifying entire sanctification with the baptism of the Holy Spirit. Whilst this was true, Wesley never endorsed his use of this term in the context of entire sanctification. He published Fletcher's *Last Check to Antinomianism* in 1775, with these references unedited, yet his final and definitive revision of *A Plain Account of Christian Perfection* in 1777, did not alter his view that the baptism of the Holy Spirit related to justification. McGonigle is clear that the emphasis on the baptism in the Spirit "arose in American, rather than British Methodism,"[79] a lead that Palmer followed, aware of Fletcher's use of the term. Smith insists that "being so

75. Smith, *Revivalism and Social Reform*, 105.

76. Kent, *Holding the Fort*, 313.

77. Orr, *The Light of the Nations*, 208.

78. White, "Phoebe Palmer," 204.

79. McGonigle, "Pneumatological Nomenclature," 71.

deeply involved in the elaboration of John Wesley's language of Calvary" she was actually "one of the last to adopt the new terminology . . . in the fall of 1856, after a summer of immense spiritual refreshing in camp meetings in Western New York,"[80] an emphasis made clear in her book *Promise of the Father.*[81]

Donald W. Dayton identifies the source of references to the baptism of the Holy Spirit in relation to entire sanctification, as probably arising within Oberlin perfectionism,[82] and in particular in John Morgan's essay "The Gift of the Holy Spirit."[83] Finney and Mahan in turn took up this terminology. It is commonly held that this identification of the baptism of the Holy Spirit with entire sanctification eventually gave rise to the Pentecostal Movement.[84] Both William and Catherine Booth adopted this language in speaking of entire sanctification, and it became a prominent feature of one of the most prolific writers on holiness in The Salvation Army, Samuel Logan Brengle.[85]

Secondly, White suggests Palmer linked entire sanctification with divine power, from the promise in Acts 1:8, "ye shall receive power, after that the Holy Ghost is come upon you," (KJV) but the same argument follows, in that the phrase "power from on high" was used extensively by Charles Finney, and is clearly evident in the *Christian Mission Magazine* reports and articles of the 1860s and 1870s. Perhaps her most distinctive contribution was, thirdly, what she called "a shorter way" of being sanctified. Charles Edwin Jones comments that "the genius of Mrs. Palmer's message and methodology was that it spoke to the dilemma faced by many in the second and third generations who believed themselves incapable of realizing, in the same manner as their parents, the witness of the Holy Spirit that they had been made perfect in love."[86] Kent agrees that "something had gone wrong with the Wesleyan Methodist tradition . . . men struggled to approach the divine source of the power of holiness but they still found themselves yielding to temptations, and they did not

---

80. Smith, "The Doctrine of the Sanctifying Spirit," 106.

81. Palmer, *The Promise of the Father.*

82. See Dayton, "Asa Mahan," 61.

83. See ibid., 62.

84. See for example: Dieter, "The Development of Nineteenth-Century Holiness Theology"; Dayton, "Asa Mahan."

85. See, for example, Brengle, *When the Holy Ghost Is Come.*

86. Jones, "The Inverted Shadow," 124.

seem able to attain the kind of subjective experience which they could interpret as evidence that 'holiness' had been given them."[87] Palmer moved the focus from waiting for a deeper assurance of holiness, to simply claiming and possessing this gift by faith. Dieter sees in this development a clear continuum with American revivalism from Edwards to Finney. "The call of the revivalist to the sinner, for an immediate faith decision for his evangelical conversion, was paralleled by the holiness evangelist's call to the Christian for an immediate faith decision for his entire sanctification."[88] This call did not heed what Kenneth Collins outlines as Wesley's careful *via salutis,* his structured steps towards sanctification, within an overall gradual process of transformation.[89] Wesley was mainly insistent that sanctification was a late reality in the life of a believer approaching death, but sufficient intimation in his writings exists to suggest that he believed that God could "'cut short his work,' in whatever degree he pleases, and do the usual work of many years in a moment."[90] This encouraged Palmer to develop her own teaching in a way that she believed was still faithful to Wesley.

This note of immediacy in Palmer's writing, fourthly, shifted entire sanctification from a goal to the beginning of the Christian life, not long after justification. Wesley had been reluctant to put down a precise timetable that limited God's sovereignty, preferring to keep the focus on God's initiative, rather than on any human reckoning:

> God's usual method is one thing, but his sovereign pleasure is another. He has wise reasons both for hastening and retarding his work. Sometimes he comes suddenly and unexpected; sometimes, not till we have long looked for him.[91]

In order to "cut short" God's work, Palmer fifthly, developed a methodology that incorporated her "altar phraseology." Firstly, entire consecration was characterized by a full surrender "of body, soul, and spirit; time, talents, and influence; and also of the dearest ties of nature," all placed as a "living sacrifice" on Christ's altar, in which, following

---

87. Kent, *Holding the Fort,* 320.

88. Dieter, *The Holiness Revival,* 61.

89. Collins, *The Theology of John Wesley.* See in particular 307–12.

90. Wesley, *The Works of the Rev. John Wesley,* 11:423.

91. Ibid., 11:407.

Matthew 23:19, "the altar sanctifies the gift" (KJV).[92] Secondly, sanctification was then to be received in faith and, thirdly, testified to. She was convinced that people could be sanctified if and when they willed it, an emphasis very much in keeping with Finney's New Divinity. Palmer's sixth emphasis was therefore the assurance of faith, rather than feeling. Wesley was equivocal in his presentation of assurance, announcing on the one hand that "none . . . ought to believe that the work is done, till there is added the testimony of the Spirit, witnessing his entire sanctification, as clearly as his justification,"[93] whilst in the same account conceding that "the witness of sanctification is not always clear at first; (as neither is that of justification;) neither is it afterward always the same, but like that of justification, sometimes stronger and sometimes fainter."[94] Ultimately he confessed that in the matter of knowing whether someone has been sanctified "we cannot infallibly know one that is thus saved, (no, nor even one that is justified,) unless it should please God to endow us with the miraculous discernment of spirits."[95] Palmer was unequivocal that if it was promised in scripture and claimed in faith through full consecration, it could be trusted to be assuredly given, regardless of feelings.

This teaching directly assisted Catherine Booth in claiming entire sanctification, as revealed in a letter to her parents from Gateshead, dated 11th February 1861, just prior to leaving the Methodist New Connexion. She had struggled for some time to secure this experience, had spent a whole day in prayer, and was joined by William, who had claimed the experience in the previous week:[96]

> When we got up from our knees I lay on the sofa exhausted with the excitement and effort of the day. William said, "Don't you lay all on the altar?" I replied, "I am sure I do." Then he said, "And isn't the altar holy?" I replied in the language of the Holy Ghost, "The altar is most holy, and whatsoever toucheth it is holy." Then he said, "Are you not holy?" I replied with my heart full of emotion and with some faith, "Oh I think I am!" Immediately the word was given me to confirm my faith, "Now are ye clean

92. Palmer, *Way Of Holiness*, 26–27.
93. Wesley, *The Works of the Rev. John Wesley*, 11:402.
94. Ibid., 11:420.
95. Ibid., 11:398.
96. See Booth-Tucker, *Life of Catherine Booth*, 1:271.

through the word which I have spoken unto you." And . . . from that moment I have dared to reckon myself dead indeed unto sin, and alive unto God through Jesus Christ my Lord.[97]

As well as Palmer's "altar phraseology," she had been reading William Edwin Boardman's *The Higher Christian Life*, published in 1858 at the height of the revival in America. Boardman was a regular member of Palmer's Tuesday night meetings, and present at the Oxford and Brighton Conferences to promote Holiness, which led to the Keswick Convention.[98] He aimed to appeal to those within denominations that might not have previously associated with either the Methodists or Oberlin. The book proved hugely successful on both sides of the Atlantic. Catherine mentioned to her parents that she had been "reading that precious book 'The Higher Life,'"[99] and her letter continued:

> I perceived that I had been in some degree of error with reference to the nature or rather manner of sanctification, regarding it rather as a great and mighty work to be wrought in me through Christ, than the simple reception of Christ as an all-sufficient saviour dwelling in my heart and thus cleansing it every moment from all sin.[100]

Catherine grasped from Palmer and Boardman that entire sanctification was not a great act of God to wait for, but something to receive. Kent suggests that Palmer appealed to a more Calvinist understanding of God's sovereignty,[101] yet the receiving was still cast in the subjective guise of naming, claiming and attaining, in which the individual's initiative in placing herself upon Christ's altar, called for God's agency. As Palmer expressed it: "He will cause the fire to descend . . . [and] . . . will not delay to do this for every waiting soul, for He standeth waiting, and the moment the offerer presents the sacrifice, the hallowing, consuming touch will be given."[102] The Booths, as will be demonstrated, followed Palmer's urgent subjective emphasis upon immediately claiming this blessing through their own simple steps. As late as 1896, William Booth

97. Ibid., 1:273.

98. See Pollock, *The Keswick Story*.

99. Booth, "Letter of Catherine Booth to Her Parents, 11 February 1861."

100. Ibid.

101. Kent, *Holding the Fort*, 321.

102. Cited in Dieter, *The Holiness Revival*, 27. See footnote on page 72 which does not clarify the source.

penned words that are still sung by contemporary congregations, the last verse of which continues to echo Palmer's "altar phraseology":

> To make our weak hearts strong and brave, send the fire!
> To live a dying world to save, send the fire!
> Oh, see us on Thy altar lay
> Our lives, our all, this very day;
> To crown the offering now we pray, send the fire![103]

It is beyond the scope of this introduction to the origins of Salvation Army ecclesiology, to fully explore the interrelated influences that were awash in holiness revivalism. Dieter's proposal of an American synthesis may clearly be supported, "by which American revivalism, in the tradition from Jonathan Edwards to Charles Finney, and Wesleyan perfectionism, in the tradition of the American Methodists, each took up the emphasis of the other to form a new blend of American revivalism and Wesleyan perfectionism" requiring that "the wedding of these two forces"[104] is acknowledged in understanding this period. The Booths left the Methodist New Connexion soon after claiming entire sanctification, for an independent itinerant ministry. They took the "higher life" message and pragmatic methods of holiness revivalism with them. The next two sections will demonstrate, firstly, their pre-occupation with this understanding of holiness revivalism, in view of many historians having missed its full significance and secondly, the specific ecclesial consequences that ensued, in which a focus upon the Church was overwhelmed by a postmillennial vision of their mission, to usher in the kingdom of Christ. It will ultimately be demonstrated that the consequences of holiness revivalism continue to shape the ecclesial identity of the contemporary Salvation Army, and sustain competing tensions within it.

The Booths' Holiness Revivalism

William and Catherine Booth were never content for long in any denomination of which they were a part. It is little wonder that they founded their own. They were motivated by an evangelistic impulse, imbibed in Methodism from the inspiration and example of Wesley, to seek the sal-

---

103. The Salvation Army, *The Song Book of The Salvation Army*, No. 203, 165.
104. Dieter, *The Holiness Revival*, 61.

vation of all people. Yet they left the Methodist New Connexion in 1861, directly inspired by the American interpretation of those Wesleyan and Methodist roots, for a life of independent itinerant revivalism, following the example of Finney, Caughey and Palmer.[105] They had earlier sought Caughey's advice as to whether to leave the New Connexion, and heeded his suggestion that William continue until he had at least secured his ordination. When they left, they wrote to Caughey for advice, and still bruised by his own dealings with the Connexion, he did not reply.[106] Catherine wrote to Phoebe Palmer to inform her of their decision, and with her husband ill and preaching commitments to fulfil, Palmer wrote to them in St. Ives:

> My object in writing to you now is to ask whether your devoted husband and yourself will be able to come and take our place. I have sometimes thought that we might in some way be permitted to work into each other's hands.[107]

They did not take up the offer, but were clear that holiness revivalism was the spiritual answer to Britain's woes. J. Edwin Orr's insistence that Britain experienced a second evangelical awakening[108] that spread from America via Ireland to the rest of the United Kingdom has been challenged by John Kent,[109] a view that Catherine Booth would have supported. Speaking in hindsight of the American revival of 1858 and the subsequent 1859 revival in Ireland, she revealed to a London congregation that:

> Some years ago, when the wave of revival was sweeping over Ireland and America, you know the Churches in this country held united prayer-meetings to pray that it might come to England; but it did not come, and the infidels wagged their heads, and wrote in their newspapers: "See the Christians' God is either deaf or gone a-hunting, for they have had prayer meetings all over the land for a revival, and it has not come."[110]

---

105. See Chadwick, *The Victorian Church, Part Two*, 286–99. Chadwick describes Booth as "the most remarkable revivalist of the age" (ibid., 287).

106. See Murdoch, *Origins of The Salvation Army*, 36.

107. Cited in Booth-Tucker, *The Life of Catherine Booth*, 1:320–21.

108. Orr, *The Second Evangelical Awakening*.

109. Kent, *Holding the Fort*, 111–12.

110. Booth, *Papers on Godliness*, 74.

Catherine revealed her indebtedness to Finney when she put this lack of revival down to the fact that God's "people asked amiss" for God answers the prayers of "God's saints . . . those who keep His commandments, who walk in the light and have fellowship with Him through the Holy Spirit."[111] To her mind, revivals were the conditional result of entirely sanctified saints who employed the right means and methods.

Some disagreement lingers about the consistency of the Booths' holiness revivalism. Both Kent and Murdoch[112] have suggested that they only took up this emphasis in the mid to late 1870s, after the visit to Britain of two more Americans, Hannah and Robert Pearsall Smith. The evidence, however, is that the making of entirely sanctified saints was a consistent focus from the moment they claimed the experience in 1861, both in their ministry in Gateshead with the Methodist New Connexion,[113] and in their subsequent independent itinerant holiness revivalism in Cornwall, where Booth regularly sent reports and statistics to *The Revival* of those saved and sanctified, in the same manner as Caughey. Equally, Booth's earliest London periodicals, *The East London Evangelist* and *The Christian Mission Magazine* reveal a constant focus. In the first issue of *The East London Evangelist*, in October 1868, Booth wrote: "We also propose devoting a large portion of our space to the topic of Personal Holiness. The importance of this theme nor tongue nor Pen can possibly overrate."[114] Palmer's "altar phraseology" persisted:

> We have an altar! Hast thou offered thy sacrifice upon it? Dost thou remember what a complete sacrifice it requires? . . . Our altar is CHRIST . . . As whatever touched the Jewish altar was Holy—not because of any merit in the offering, but the altar—so when we present ourselves "a living sacrifice, the altar sanctifies the gift."[115]

Booth left this doctrine out of the East London Christian Revival Society's 1865/6 list of seven doctrines, but this is easily explained. He pragmatically decided not to court dissent over his controversial claim

111. Ibid.

112. See Kent, *Holding the Fort*, 327–29; Murdoch, *Origins of The Salvation Army*, 66.

113. See Pentecost, "William Booth," 116f. See also Booth-Tucker, *Life of Catherine Booth*, 1:281–83, for Catherine's holiness preaching in Hartlepool, 1861.

114. Booth, "Dedication," 2.

115. Ibid., 10.

that believers could be perfectly without sin, if not sinlessly perfect. Not all of his early followers and financiers approved. Catherine Booth's biographer, Booth-Tucker, suggested that:

> The Christian helpers who had at first gathered round him had almost all forsaken him and fled . . . Some of them objected to his holiness teaching. Others considered that he laid too much stress upon repentance and works, and too little upon bare faith. Not a few grew weary of the ceaseless open-airs and processions, with the mobbing and mockery of the crowd . . . They did not like the penitent form.[116]

This was a description of Booth's holiness revivalism. Its emphasis on the eradication of sin and its aggressive methods had created significant tension in some English denominations. David Bebbington explains that amongst some strands of holiness teaching within the Wesleyan tradition in the nineteenth century, there was in part a move to completely eliminate the moment of crisis in sanctification, and in part a complete loss of the distinctive Methodist teaching on holiness altogether. He cites, for example, an article in *The Methodist New Connexion Magazine*, "The Law of Holiness,"[117] written at the same time as Booth experienced dissent, in which there was "no trace of the Wesleyan tradition whatsoever."[118]

Booth's mission gathered a wide variety of independently minded people in the cause of Christian mission, and disunity over holiness revivalism's promotion of entire sanctification was a major concern, which *The Revival* regretted:

> It is a great mercy to be able heartily to rejoice in the labours of any dear servant of God; and far from being disposed coldly to criticise any individuality of manner or matter, to regard it, on the contrary, as a happy privilege to give him the right hand of fellowship, and bid him God speed. We make this remark because we fear that in no small degree has the blessing which many have sought been hindered by a narrow-minded, judg-

---

116. Booth-Tucker, *The Life of Catherine Booth*, 1:403–4. Catherine Booth is a clear source for Tucker's comments. See Booth, *The Diary and the Reminiscences of Catherine Booth*, 90. See also Sandall, *The History of The Salvation Army*, 1:46.

117. "The Law of Holiness," cited in Bebbington, *Holiness in Nineteenth-Century England*, 67.

118. Bebbington, *Holiness in Nineteenth-Century England*, 67.

ing disposition—a sore evil of this present time as regards the church.[119]

As Booth's leadership became secure, he became more confident in shaping the movement, which included a formal institution of his doctrine of holiness. In 1870, not 1876 as suggested by Murdoch,[120] and prior to the Pearsall Smith's visit to England, Booth revised the doctrinal statement of the Christian Mission to include: "We believe that it is the privilege of all believer's to be 'wholly sanctified' and that 'their whole spirit and soul and body' may 'be preserved blameless unto the coming of our Lord Jesus Christ' (1 Thess. 5:23)."[121] The 1870 Conference Minutes outlined that:

> Meetings for the promotion of entire sanctification shall be held weekly if possible at all our stations and to which none but members shall be admitted and those only by showing their tickets.[122]

The first *Constitution of The Christian Mission* published in 1870 carried some pertinent "Conditions of Membership," in an effort to ensure a peaceful emphasis on holiness:

> (11) Any members guilty of . . . propagating any doctrine or opinion which is calculated to hinder the work of God and divide the Society, or for the breach of any of our rules, shall for the first offence be reproved . . . [and]

> (16) A person shall not necessarily be disqualified for membership by differing with us on minor questions of doctrine, unless such difference, in the judgement of the elders' meeting, is likely to hinder the usefulness and mar the peace of the Society.[123]

The arrival of Robert and Hannah Pearsall Smith in Britain in 1873, heightened interest and the Brighton and Oxford conferences in 1874 and 1875 paved the way for the founding of the Keswick Convention. Murdoch's reference to Booth taking up this message in 1876, more accurately refers to the Conference minutes of 1876, which merely clarified what Booth meant by the doctrine he had formally instituted in 1870:

119. "The Reverend W. Booth in Whitechapel," 59–60.

120. Murdoch, "Evangelical Sources of Salvation Army Doctrine," 235–44.

121. Christian Mission, *Minutes of the First Conference of the Christian Mission*.

122. Ibid., section XXVIII.

123. Sandall, *The History of The Salvation Army*, 1:279–80.

We believe that after conversion there remains in the heart of the believer inclinations to evil or roots of bitterness, which, unless overpowered by Divine Grace, produce actual sin, but that these evil tendencies can be entirely taken away by the Spirit of God, and the whole heart thus cleansed from everything contrary to the will of God, or entirely sanctified, will then produce the fruits of the Spirit only.[124]

The 1878 Foundation Deed of The Salvation Army confirmed it as its tenth doctrine.[125] In 1881 *The Doctrines and Discipline of The Salvation Army*, gave an extensive account of the doctrine, including an emphasis on sin's potential eradication.[126]

The Ecclesial Consequences of Holiness Revivalism

It is essential for Salvationists to fully understand the nuances of their holiness revivalist origins, if they are to adequately reflect upon their ecclesiology. William Booth was clear that he did not set out to form a new church or denomination, but to engage in aggressive evangelistic Christian mission. This is the first ecclesial strand in what is here described as a tangled cord of mission, army and church. When, in 1878, on the cusp of the Christian Mission being renamed The Salvation Army, Booth explained the nature of this mission: "It was not my intention to create another sect . . . we are not a church. We are an Army—an Army of Salvation."[127] Booth was less interested in the nature of the community than he was in the demands of the missional task, a pre-occupation born out of his frustration with the ambiguous ecclesial splintering of Methodism. John Coutts observes that "Booth became the founder of a new denomination, while believing—like most founders of new denominations—that he was doing nothing of the kind."[128] This observation was made much earlier by Cardinal Manning,[129] a critical admirer of Booth:

124. The Christian Mission, *The Christian Mission Conference Minutes*, 1876.

125. See Sandall, *The History of The Salvation Army*, 1:287–91.

126. See The Salvation Army, *The Doctrines and Discipline of The Salvation Army*, 60–91.

127. Cited in Wiseman, "Are We a Church?," 438.

128. Coutts, *The Salvationists*, 15.

129. See McClelland, *Cardinal Manning*, 207–9, for his biographer's comments on his support of the Salvation Army's social response.

> Mr. Booth declares his firm resolve that the Salvation Army shall
> never become a sect. He cites the failure of John Wesley in his
> attempt to maintain an unsectarian position. The meaning of
> this would seem to be that the aim of the Salvation Army is to
> promote general and personal religion apart from all bodies, and,
> above all, apart from all controversies . . . a spirit, which, like the
> four winds, may blow upon all in the valley of dry bones—men,
> women, children, sects, communions, and, as he perhaps would
> say, Churches, quickening and raising them all to a higher life . . .
> Nevertheless we have a conviction that the Salvation Army will
> either become a sect, or it will melt away. This world is not the
> abode of disembodied spirits.[130]

Manning's shrewd insight reveals the Booths' disregard for the doctrine of the Church. Their holiness revivalism was pre-occupied with, firstly, a doctrine of the individual's full salvation, and in particular a subjective emphasis on the required human conditions of justification and entire sanctification. Secondly, it emphasized the necessary pragmatic methods of an aggressive style of Christian evangelism. Booth never explicitly articulated a doctrine of the Church. It did not exist in the Methodist New Connexion's doctrines that he borrowed. Inevitably he founded a new denomination whilst denying that this was his purpose. In this respect, the first consequence of the Booths' holiness revivalism must be understood to be a lack of focus on the Church in favour of aggressive non-denominational mission.

Aggressive Non-Denominational Mission

From the influence of Finney and Caughey, in particular, the Booths were following a movement that was attempting to abandon conventional ecclesial terminology and practice, in favor of mission. Nineteenth-century holiness revivalism was a missionary movement, independently minded, itinerant and reluctant to be confined by denominational boundaries. Revivalist campaigns were seldom a formal denominational call, and more the individual inspiration of keen supporters. Booth wrote to *The Revival* from St. Ives in Cornwall and confirmed that "the work has been, to a very delightful extent, unsectarian; all the chapels in the town, with one exception, being thrown open to us; and wherever we preached Jesus to the multitude, Wesleyans, New Connexion

---

130. Manning, "The Salvation Army." See also Begbie, *Life of William Booth*, 31.

Methodists, Primitives, and Bible Christians flocked around us, pleading with God for further outpourings of the Spirit."[131]

This apparent harmony, almost exclusively conducted amongst churches of a Methodist persuasion with holiness revivalist sympathies, masked the tension that was growing between denominational structures and itinerant revivalists. *The Revival* reported with regret the outcome of a Methodist Conference:

> The president said that . . . the first thing he had to do in one of his circuits was to tell some very influential men who waited upon him for the purpose of requesting that an American Revivalist should occupy a chapel for a month, that as long as he was superintendent of that circuit, the Revivalist should not place his foot in any of the pulpits—and he heard no more about it. If all ministers would act likewise towards those ambiguous people it would save a great deal of trouble.[132]

Even in view of the recorded success of the Booths' campaign, with an estimated 7,000 converts,[133] Orr notes that in the same year, 1862, the June Methodist New Connexion Conference at Dudley, accepted his resignation "disapproving his Revivalism."[134] The Primitive Methodist Conference in the same month in Sheffield urged all its pastors "to avoid the employing of Revivalists so-called,"[135] and the Wesleyan Conference in Camborne in July directed its superintendents to close their chapels to "continuous services by outsiders."[136] *The Revival* exclaimed, "surely John Wesley would have blushed for those who thus rule in his name."[137]

Dieter, in relation to American revivalism, notes what he calls "revivalism's paradox":

> Holiness evangelists . . . representing several denominations, became increasingly active and aggressive in their evangelism . . . Their very efforts to refrain from taking on the nature of a second church—their members, in the early period, were all

131. *The Revival*, No. 135, Saturday February 22, 1862. See also *The Revival*, No. 110, Saturday August 31, 1861.

132. *The Revival*, No. 163 Thursday September 4, 1862.

133. Booth-Tucker, *Life of Catherine Booth*, 1:255.

134. Orr, *The Second Evangelical Awakening*, 116.

135. Sandall, *History of The Salvation Army*, 1:11.

136. Ibid., 1:16.

137. *The Revival*, No. 163 Thursday September 4, 1862, 111.

members of some other regulated religious body—prejudiced the groups against any tight internal control. It allowed free spirits, who sometimes were escaping to the group from discipline in some other religious society, or were feeding their own sense of individuality, to readily find a home and an outlet for their ambitions.[138]

This created the "paradox" of increasingly tense relations between holiness revivalism and the denominations, in the context of the revivalists' message of Christian unity, "perfect love" and holiness. Dieter comments that "it was against this background of growing strife, resulting from the aggressive efforts of the holiness associations and bands to win the churches to their holiness reform, that their equally perfectionist statements concerning Christian unity sounded so contradictory to some."[139]

The Booths were not alone in being influenced by American holiness revivalism. Kent notes the growing number of British lay revivalists during the 1850s, and comments that:

> All these men were committed to an aggressive evangelical way of life long before the Ulster Revival of 1859. American influence mattered more than Irish, for the publication of Finney's *Lectures* in England, and James Caughey's long visit in the 1840s, helped to stimulate the group's development.[140]

With the London City Mission as an example in mind, Kent suggests that whilst "the Oxford Movement was re-emphasizing the doctrine of the Church, the reverse process went on among evangelicals, who measured the high claims made for the Church against this institutional failure to support their schemes."[141] These evangelicals freed themselves from "traditional ecclesiastical restraints, while inventing a new, looser and more relevant urban structure in which revivalism could operate happily."[142]

Many of these lay revivalist evangelicals met in 1861, in the wake of the 1859 Ulster revival, under the auspices of the newly created Home Mission Movement. Reginald Radcliffe, a Liverpool lawyer, called a meeting at Sussex Hall, Leadenhall Street, London on 23rd January 1861,

138. Dieter, *The Holiness Revival,* 238.

139. Ibid., 240.

140. Kent, *Holding the Fort,* 101.

141. Ibid., 103.

142. Ibid.

attended by about two hundred people, where Rev. Baptist W. Noel (St. John's Baptist Chapel, John Street) declared, "I believe we are on the eve of a greater work than England ever saw; and the East of London is the place to begin."[143] They met to discuss urban mission, and they formed the East London Special Services Committee. William Booth first met Radcliffe in Chester in 1857, and in the summer of 1861, prior to his withdrawal from the Methodist New Connexion, visited London to investigate Home Mission work opportunities. He wrote to Catherine: "My name had been before them. They were very much interested in me, and wished me to take part in the service at the [Garrick] theatre tomorrow night. To this I consented."[144]

Booth found this experience amongst London's urban poor hugely challenging and unconvinced that he was suited for it, returned to Gateshead in a "final effort to reconcile the demands of the New Connexion Conference with the line of duty to which his convictions directed him."[145] When he returned to London three years later from his itinerant campaigns, the Special Services Committee, whose members included Richard Morgan and Samuel Chase, publishers of *The Revival*, invited him to temporarily take charge of a mission they had started in Whitechapel in a tent, on an old Quaker burial ground. Booth claimed that it was only to be for two weeks.[146] In spite of his misgivings about his suitability for this work, he later admitted that:

> Before the fortnight had passed I felt at home; and more than this I found my heart being strongly and strangely drawn out on behalf of the million people living within a mile of the tent—ninety out of every hundred of whom, they told me, never heard the sound of the preacher's voice . . . And so the church and chapel congregation somehow or other lost their charm in comparison with the vulgar East-enders.[147]

The mission became known as the East London Revival Association and then the East London Christian Mission, and after establishing an evan-

---

143. Sandall, *The History of The Salvation Army*, 1:21.

144. *Letters*, No. WB 130, 345. See *Letters*, No. WB 131, 345, for his comments after the visit, and Booth, "How We Began," 18, for his expression of inadequacy at knowing how to reach these people.

145. Sandall, *The History of The Salvation Army*, 1:22.

146. Booth, "How We Began," 18.

147. Ibid. See Booth, *The Diary and the Reminiscences*, 88, for her recollections.

gelistic center and society in Croydon and other parts of London beyond the "East End," it was renamed The Christian Mission, before becoming The Salvation Army in 1878.

The Salvation Army began as an initiative of the Special Services Committee, itself partly inspired by holiness revivalism, the product of lay evangelical efforts to evangelize Britain, and in particular those growing urban areas untouched by effective Christian mission of an evangelical kind. It began outside of denominational boundaries, amongst laity disenchanted by what was perceived to be the failure of the churches to evangelize the nation. John Rhemick asserts: "The Salvation Army was born in a time when a cold intellectualism was pervading many of the churches of England . . . there was no time to talk about fine points of doctrine while millions were dying and going to hell."[148] Writing about life in the late Victorian City, McCleod maintains:

> It was a measure of Evangelical achievement that for much of the century so many members of the upper and middle classes felt bound to attend church regularly, to observe Sunday and to censor their conversation. It was a sign of the limits of this achievement that so much of this was hypocrisy.[149]

Wilson Carlile, who founded the Church Army, was clear that "in my view, the problem of indifference [within the Church of England] was even greater then than it is now; and yet, inside the Church, any enthusiasm or really aggressive effort was speedily crushed by excessive respectability."[150]

Booth's determination to evangelize the urban poor received many commendations, and undoubtedly renewed an understanding that the Church was called to mission. It was a measure of his success that Dr. Lightfoot, the Bishop of Durham, urged his congregation to greater efforts in evangelism:

> Shall we be satisfied with going on as hitherto, picking up one here and one there, gathering together a more or less select congregation, forgetful meanwhile of the Master's command, "Go ye into the highways and hedges, and compel them to come in?" The Salvation Army has taught us a higher lesson than this. Whatever may be its faults, it has at least recalled us to this lost

148. Rhemick, *A New people of God*, 4.

149. McLeod, *Class and Religion in the Late Victorian City*, 152.

150. Carlile, "The Church Army," 36.

ideal of the work of the Church—the universal compulsion of the souls of men![151]

Nevertheless, in terms of ecclesiological reflection, Salvationists should recognise the independent and individualistic elements of Booth's enterprise. In an interview in 1894 Booth reflected on God's leadings in his life: "I went to God—not to the Church, nor to the Bible, nor to my feelings, but to Himself—and I have ever since been sending people who have desired mercy to the same source."[152] This individualistic sense of an immediacy in God's dealings with individuals that bypassed the life of the community was further affirmed in Booths 1881 publication of his *Doctrines and Discipline*. In answer to the question "what do you mean by the Spirit speaking DIRECTLY to the hearts of men?," the reply reveals an individualistic interpretation of God's action to individual souls, in that "He does not confine Himself to sending messages to men through His *people*, or through *books*, but He, Himself, goes straight to people's hearts and so influences them as to make them feel what He wants them to do."[153] The Salvation Army, as will be outlined more fully in the next chapter, was in large part a product of this individualistic effort, independent of existing church structures, to save souls.

The Pragmatic Nature of the Booths' Aggressive Christianity

If the foundations of The Salvation Army as a Christian denomination emerge, firstly, from within an evangelical missionary movement disaffected by the church's apparent failure to evangelize the nation, it is instructive for Salvationists, secondly, to examine the nature of what the Booths termed "aggressive Christianity."[154] In 1874, several years before the "Salvation Army" gained its name, Catherine Booth, with ideas inspired by Finney, stated that "the only law laid down in the New

151. Cited in Booth Tucker, *The Life of Catherine Booth*, 2:280. See also Inglis, *Churches and the Working Classes*, 188.

152. The Salvation Army, "Fifty Years' Salvation Service," 6.

153. The Salvation Army, *The Doctrines and Discipline of The Salvation Army*, 39. See in this respect Volf, *After Our Likeness*, 161f, in relation to John Smyth's similarly individualistic expression, and its currency in both Free Church circles and Protestantism in general.

154. See Booth, *The Salvation Army in Relation to the Church and State*, 73, where she claims to have "coined" this term, though holiness revivalism was commonly known as an aggressive approach to evangelism.

Testament for the prosecution of this aggressive warfare is the law of adaptation,"[155] in which Christ's commission was "go ye, not build temples or churches, and wait for them to come to you, but go ye, run after them, seek them out, and preach my Gospel to EVERY creature."[156]

In the preaching of this gospel, Catherine sought to be faithful to Wesley's *via salutis*, yet with her ear clearly tuned to the urgency and immediacy of holiness revivalism's insistence on instant results in both justification and entire sanctification. Unlike Finney, she started from a clear position on original sin, that "man is fallen, and cannot himself obey even his own enlightened intelligence" in which "there must be an extraneous power brought into the soul."[157] In this respect she held Wesley's concept of God's prevenient grace, in which "conscience is an independent witness standing as it were between God and man; it is in man, but for God."[158] Furthermore, "conscience is the reigning power of the soul, the will is the executive, and in order to keep a pure conscience the will must act out its teaching."[159] She therefore understood their mission amongst sinners as one of "working together with the Holy Ghost to deepen conviction and drive them to real submission to God."[160]

Nevertheless, whilst she understood that "the only power that can really affect and transform the soul is the Spirit of God," she was not content to leave the Spirit to accomplish this work, for "we do not attach much importance to people merely receiving the truth!"[161] Rather, the difference between "a self consuming, soul-burdened Holy Ghost, successful ministry, and a careless, happy-go-lucky, easy sort of thing, that just rolls it out like a lesson, and goes home, holding itself in no way responsible for the consequences," was not to just "deliver" the gospel, but "to get the truth HOME to the HEART ... to drive it home—send it in—make it FELT."[162] This ministry involved such close co-operation between her and God that often it was difficult to discern the difference between divine and human agency, in which "there is a sense in which

---

155. Booth, "Aggression," 206.

156. Ibid., 205.

157. Booth, *The Salvation Army in Relation to the Church and State*, 11.

158. Booth, *Popular Christianity*, 130.

159. Ibid., 135.

160. Booth, "Dealing with Anxious Souls," 57.

161. Booth, *The Salvation Army in Relation to Church and State*, 39.

162. Booth, *Papers on Godliness*, 87.

the spirit of the man, as well as the Spirit of God, infuses itself into the spiritual progeny."[163]

This high regard for human agency was apparent when she explained the problem of godless youths without much evidence of conscience, in which "there seems nothing back in their minds on which to rest any appeal, on which to put the lever by which you are to civilize, refine and exalt them. We have to make this".[164] "Levering" these young people involved "the most personal, practical, and pungent appeals . . . to the individual conscience . . . to show them that they are wrong . . . to press in upon their souls the conviction of their guilt."[165] Such was her aggressive Christianity. It was the employment of the most effective language, methods and measures in humanly persuading people of their guilt, in order to reach their conscience and effect the exercise of their wills towards repentance and rebirth by the Holy Spirit. The synergy of this co-operation was close enough for her on one occasion to call upon mothers "to train their children so that they shall be SAVIOURS OF MEN."[166] Whilst often there was an attempt to distinguish between divine and human agency, listeners could be forgiven for thinking that God responded to human initiative rather than *vice versa*. Booth suggested that "it takes God and man to make a potato, and it takes God and man to save a soul . . . let man do his part and God will do His part" for "God is waiting; and when man does his part then souls will be saved."[167] The Booths lacked an explicit and sustained theology of covenant that might have kept the focus more fully on divine initiative, grace and calling.

This almost synergistic expression of co-operation in the Booths' aggressive Christianity with its "adaptation of measures," had critical ecclesial consequences for the movement that they founded, in terms of its visible form. In response to the criticism that she was "reducing religion to mere machinery," Catherine argued simply that she was "only providing a machinery through which the Holy Spirit of Christ can operate," for "Jesus Christ and His apostles left us free as air as to modes and measures, that we may provide that kind of organization most suited to

---

163. Booth, *The Salvation Army in Relation to Church and State*, 58.

164. Ibid., 9.

165. Ibid.

166. Ibid., 13.

167. Booth, "The General's Address at Exeter Hall on Monday Evening," 9.

the necessities of the age."[168] She went as far as to suggest that "God does not care about the *forms* or modes," so long as "we have the living spirit in them."[169] On another occasion she insisted that: "God says 'GO AND DO IT: compel them to come in. *That* is your work. I have nothing to do with the measures by which you do it, providing they are lawful.'"[170] The foundation was in place for the Booths to visibly develop their organization, without cause for theological reflection upon its visible form, so long as the Holy Spirit could be infused into human work. The next chapter will examine the human machinery—The Salvation Army—which developed out of the pragmatism of aggressive Christianity.

The Ethical Demands of the Booths' Concept of "full salvation"

The loss of objectivity in the Booths' individualistic and pragmatic focus upon the human work of aggressive Christianity was further supported by their emphasis upon the conditional rather than unconditional nature of what they commonly termed "full salvation." They were thoroughly Wesleyan in their extreme fear of any taint of antinomianism in the preaching of the gospel. Catherine confided that she received "many letters . . . congratulating us that we do not teach the Antinomian doctrines of a great deal of the evangelistic teaching of this day, that we don't preach the 'only believe gospel,' but that we preach repentance towards God, as well as faith in Jesus Christ, and a life of OBEDIENCE to God."[171] Aggressive preaching of this kind would ensure that "the Lord shall honour us to bring into His family . . . not . . . stillborn ghosts of a sinewless sentimentalism; but strong, hardy, cross-bearing, Christ honouring, soul-winning men and women, able to open heaven and shake hell by their faith and zeal and effort in our Redeemer's kingdom."[172]

The consequences of the subjective nature of this conditional emphasis are most apparent in the Booths' outlining of what they perceived as God's "second blessing," or full salvation. For fear of any suggestion of an unconditional work of grace not requiring an ethical human response, the Booths, unlike Wesley, yet in keeping with holiness revival-

---

168. Booth, *The Salvation Army in Relation to Church and State*, 51.

169. Ibid.

170. Booth, *Papers on Godliness*, 88.

171. Booth, *The Salvation Army in Relation to Church and State*, 39.

172. Booth, "Dealing with Anxious Souls," 90

ism, almost lost sight of imputed righteousness from Christ as a free gift of grace in justification. They concentrated on the immediacy of entire sanctification as a second imparted moment of "full salvation" to be subjectively claimed.[173]

Wesley wrestled all his life between the claims that a Christian could be delivered from sin as against the belief that "sin remains but no longer reigns."[174] In 1763 and 1767, he added two sermons *On Sin in Believers* and *The Repentance of Believers* to, as Outler suggests, "counter the distortions and bring the controversy [over Christian perfection] more nearly back to balance."[175] These sermons gave renewed focus on the on-going work of sanctification in a justified believer, in which the sin that is in us, "does not imply that it has possession of our strength . . . The usurper is dethroned. He *remains* indeed where he once reigned; but remains *in chains*."[176] In this respect, Wesley concluded that "the term sanctified is continually applied by St. Paul to all that were justified" for "by this term alone, he rarely, if ever, means 'saved from all sin'" and that "consequently, it is not proper to see it in that sense, without adding the word wholly, entirely, or the like." Rather, "the inspired writers almost continually speak of or to those who were justified, but rarely of or to those who were wholly sanctified." It therefore "behoves us to speak almost continually of the state of justification; but more rarely . . . at least in full and explicit terms, concerning entire sanctification."[177]

In contrast, the Booths interpreted virtually all biblical references to sanctification as meaning the "higher" state of entire sanctification, as opposed to "those texts which recognise or depict the lower grade of experience" and which "are by no means to be taken as denoting a state either safe for the believer or satisfactory to God," for they were "an imperfect initiatory or backslidden stage of experience."[178] Their aggressive Christianity was designed to urgently persuade people to claim

173. See The Salvation Army, *Doctrines and Discipline*, 74–83; Booth, "The Holy Ghost," 340, 342.

174. Wesley, *The Works of John Wesley*, 1:317.

175. Ibid., 1:316.

176. Ibid., 1:331.

177. Wesley, *The Works of the Rev. John Wesley*, 388, although he adds the 1777 edit note "more rarely, I allow; but yet in some places very frequently, strongly and explicitly."

178. Booth, *Address on Holiness*, 3. Also Booth, "Holiness: An Address at the Conference," 194, on the dubious nature of partial sanctification.

the experience, in faith, now, and it broke with the gentle continuum of Wesley's *via salutis*.[179] His advice to be "always drawing, rather than driving,"[180] equivocally rested on the timing of God's sovereign will:

> I believe this instant generally is the instant of death, the moment before the soul leaves the body. But I believe it may be ten, twenty, or forty years before. I believe it is usually many years after justification; but that it may be within five years or five months after it, I know no conclusive argument to the contrary.[181]

Catherine Booth informed a congregation that provided they met the conditions "you shall have it . . . and this Exeter Hall will be consecrated to soul-saving and to soul-sanctifying power today.[182]

With regard to what entire sanctification meant, the 1876 *Christian Mission Conference Minutes* explained that the "roots of bitterness" can be "overpowered by Divine Grace" and that sinful "tendencies can be entirely taken away through a cleansing that allows the heart only to produce 'the fruits of the Spirit.'"[183] The 1881 *Doctrines and Discipline*, in answer to the question "What is entire sanctification?" further clarified that "sin is destroyed out of the soul, and all the powers, faculties, possessions, and influences of the soul are given up to the service and glory of God."[184] Dieter terms this "an absolutist-static concept of grace,"[185] in which sin was a material substance to be removed from the heart and destroyed, a concept that was certainly evident in Wesley's writings on Christian perfection. Richard Cope Morgan, the Booths' long-time supporter at the *Revival*, ultimately expressed his dismay at this doctrine. He illustrates an argument that raged in nineteenth-century Holiness teaching between an expression of "eradication," of being set free from sin, against the more moderate Keswick doctrine of being set free from the dominion of sin. Morgan wrote to Booth:

---

179. See Yuill, *We Need Saints!*, 101–19.

180. Wesley, *The Works of the Rev. John Wesley*, 387.

181. Ibid., 446.

182. Booth, *Papers on Godliness*, 170. See also Booth, *Address on Holiness*, 21.

183. The Christian Mission, *Christian Mission Conference Minutes*, 1876.

184. The Salvation Army, *The Doctrines and Discipline*, 62. See also Booth, "Mrs. Booth's Address at Exeter Hall," 2.

185. Dieter, "The Wesleyan Perspective," 42.

> My dear Brother, I believe that Jesus can and does save and keep
> us as we trust Him. But that is very different from saying that all
> sin is gone—gone by the roots—nothing of it left . . . Our motives
> are all pure . . . Oh, brother, think of the havoc this profession of
> sinlessness must make and is making.[186]

Whilst the Booths may not have maintained Palmer's altar terminology, they were equally methodical in outlining the conditions upon
which this experience could be immediately enjoyed.[187] This required
firstly, a "definite idea of the blessing,"[188] as an actual and obtainable
experience of being "delivered from *all sin*, and enabled to do the will
of God *continually* in this life;"[189] secondly, "a godly sorrow for all sins
of backsliding,"[190] including tobacco, alcohol, worldly dress and entertainments, which were "unworthy of a follower of Christ;"[191] thirdly an
entire consecration, or living sacrifice upon God's altar; fourthly faith
"that the blood cleanses, and the Spirit fills;"[192] fifthly assurance and
testimony. William Booth advised, "Keep your offering on the altar . . .
He will surely claim, fill and satisfy His own" for "if God be not a liar all
things are yours; *believe* this, *rest* upon it, and you will soon *feel* it."[193]

Most notably, in the Booths' understanding of human co-operation
with God in entire sanctification, God's free grace had become wrapped
up in subjective human expectations about an individual's particular
lifestyle, that were projected on to God's will. Catherine fiercely con-
demned alcohol in her sermon "Strong Drink versus Christianity," in
which "the drink, not the abuse of it, but the drink itself, is an evil thing,"[194]
where "to trim on this drink question is the highest treason to the cause
of Christ."[195] The terrible consequences of addiction in London's urban

186. Morgan, "Letter to William Booth, 11 June 1881." See also Booth, "Unpublished
Letters by the Army Mother," 8; Bramwell-Booth, *Catherine Booth*, 226.

187. See Booth, *A Ladder to Holiness.*

188. Booth, *Address on Holiness*, 17; Booth, *Purity of Heart*, 88.

189. The Salvation Army, *Doctrines and Discipline*, 60.

190. Booth, *Address on Holiness*, 17; Booth, *Purity of Heart*, 92.

191. The Salvation Army, *Doctrines and Discipline*, 75.

192. William Booth, *The East London Evangelist, April 1, 1869*, 105; see also
Bramwell Booth, "Sanctification," in *The Christian Mission Magazine*, February 1878,
32; Booth, *Papers on Godliness*, 169.

193. William Booth, *The East London Evangelist*, April 1, 1869, 105.

194. Booth, *Papers on Practical Religion*, 27.

195. Ibid., 36.

slums provided much needed context to these comments, but equally she remonstrated with her wealthier middle class audiences over "the Paris-born frivolities . . . of a glass of wine," shaming them with her denunciation: "Very well, you can have it; but you shall not have the wine of the Kingdom."[196] With regard to fashionable dress she suggested, "professors will dress like the prostitute of Paris. Very well; but they shall not be the bride of the Lamb."[197] Furthermore, "worldly amusements and entertainments," such as "Shakespearian readings" and "popular and worldly novelists," she judged to be "utterly antagonistic to the spirit of Christ."[198] Whilst many of these intensely subjective lifestyle convictions have waned, the subjectivism persists in the expectation that Salvation Army soldiers of Jesus Christ, in God's Church, must be teetotal to maintain their sanctity. This will be taken up more fully in the next chapter.

Lay Participation and the Role of Women

If the Booths' aggressive holiness revivalism contributed unhelpful individualistic, pragmatic and subjective elements to the emerging ecclesial convictions of their movement, more positively it renewed the vital role of the laity, and in particular of women. Walter and Phoebe Palmer were both high profile lay members of the Church, as were Robert and Hannah Pearsall Smith. The Booths often compared their followers to the humble nature of the first disciples—ordinary people who could be empowered by the Holy Spirit to achieve extraordinary things. Their theology was optimistic in its high view of the possibilities of grace in the ordinary believer, to deliver them from sin and to restore in them God's image. Catherine's sermons held aloft, "how much like God we can be—how near to God we can come on earth preparatory to our being perfectly like Him,"[199] for God "proposes to restore me—brain, heart, soul, spirit, body, every fibre of my nature—to restore me perfectly, to conform me wholly to the image of His Son."[200] This restoration of God's image in the believer was an embodiment of Christ in the world: "These are the sort of words the world wants—the living words, living embodi-

196. Booth, *Papers on Godliness*, 95.
197. Ibid.
198. Booth, *Papers on Practical Religion*, 41–42.
199. Booth, *Papers on Godliness*, 143. See also ibid., 6–7.
200. Ibid., 165.

ments of Christ . . . *living epistles* . . . We want JESUS TO COME IN THE FLESH AGAIN."[201]

Their mission was a movement of the people for the people. After his dealings with the respectable church people that he met on his revivalist tours, it took Booth time to adjust to the population of East London. Whitechapel, Bethnal Green and Poplar, gave evidence of the greatest poverty and depravity, and he and his followers soon realised that the most effective communicators were those who had come to faith from within the community. Booth suggested:

> The idea never dawned on me that any line was to be drawn between one who had nothing else to do but preach and a saved apprentice lad . . . I have lived, thank God, to witness the separation between layman and cleric become more and more obscured, and to see Jesus Christ's idea of changing in a moment ignorant fishermen into fishers of men nearer and nearer realisation.[202]

Equally Catherine remarked:

> We are teaching the Churches that others besides clergymen, ministers, deacons and elders can be used for the salvation of men . . . As a clergyman said to me the other day, "There are 35,000 souls in my parish, what can one do?" What indeed! Set the carpenters and the washerwoman on to them, saved and filled with the Spirit.[203]

George Scott Railton noted that Booth at first "had little knowledge of the way to get at those who lay outside the spheres of existing religious organizations. All was to be learnt."[204] By 1877 Railton declared: "We have found out how to do it now." He affirmed that "what . . . we delight in, is the growth of that all-pervading, all-consuming love to God and souls amongst our people, which fits humble and uneducated men and women to go and seize any town for their Lord."[205] The "all-consuming love to God and souls" was his expression of the fruits of holiness revivalism. The "humble and uneducated men and women" were not

201. Ibid., 166. See also Bramwell Booth, "Sanctification," 30.

202. Cited in Railton, *The Authoritative Life of General William Booth*, 17. See also Booth, *Talks with Officers of The Salvation Army*, 14.

203. Booth, *The Salvation Army in Relation to Church and State*, 75. See also Booth, "Aggression," 207.

204. Railton, *Heathen England*, 3rd ed., 27.

205. Ibid., 37.

college-trained clergy, but ordinary people able to communicate within the language and culture of Britain's poor, a powerful demonstration of the "priesthood of all believers" in action. The ability to "seize any town" was a direct result of their having found the right methods and means, liberated as they were from what they perceived as alien and ineffective church traditions.

Many active in the movement were women. Catherine Booth must take credit for this. William admitted to Catherine in 1855, a few months before their marriage:

> I would not stop a woman preaching on any account. I would not encourage one to begin . . . I would not stay *you* if I had power to do so. Altho', *I should not like it.* It is easy for you to say my views are the result of prejudice; perhaps they are. I am for the world's *salvation*; I will quarrel with no means that promises help.[206]

Four years later in Gateshead, the Palmers were touring nearby in Newcastle. Phoebe Palmer was attacked for her preaching as a woman by Arthur Augustus Rees, an Independent Minister in Sunderland, who produced a strongly worded denial from Scripture that this was permissible.[207] Catherine wrote to her parents:

> It was delivered in the form of an address to his congregation, would you believe that a congregation half composed of ladies would sit and hear such self-deprecatory nonsense? They really don't deserve to be taken up cudgels for.[208]

But she defended them, and Phoebe Palmer, in the form of a pamphlet which she published as *Female Teaching,*[209] claiming, "whatever may be its merits it is my own, and far more original, I believe, than most things that are published, for I could get no help from any quarter."[210] It remains a remarkable pioneering document of the period. She was building upon the momentum gained in Methodism and in the growing American holiness revivalism.[211] Finney encouraged women in Christian ministry,

206. Cited in Begbie, *Life of William Booth*, 1:259.

207. Rees, *Reasons for Not Co-Operating.*

208. Booth-Tucker, *Life of Catherine Booth*, 1:243.

209. The first edition of this pamphlet is not available, but she published an enlarged second edition in 1861, Booth, *Female Teaching.*

210. Booth-Tucker, *Life of Catherine Booth*, 1:244.

211. See Hardesty, *Your Daughters Shall Prophesy.*

through the example of his wife. Hardman suggests that together they developed "her public leadership and personal growth while encouraging the perception that she was not merely his support but a real adjunct to his ministry."[212] He further notes that "Finney's understanding of theology and the activism of each Christian meshed so well with the developing mood in Jacksonian America, so the part played by women in the nation was broadening significantly at this time, and Lydia Finney was among the first to exemplify the changes."[213] Whilst she played a significant part in leading and mobilizing women in prayer and home visitation, there is no record of her taking a public role in speaking. This example was given by Palmer, who was the more celebrated speaker in her partnership with her husband, Dr. Walter Palmer, and whose influence as a woman was significant in challenging prejudice, custom and tradition.

Catherine Booth was an altogether more militant influence for the rights of women to play an equal role with men. When she sent her thirty-two page pamphlet to her mother for her comments, she remonstrated:

> A church with one wing folded cannot fly; with one foot paralysed, cannot walk; with one arm motionless can do but half its work . . . We plead for more labourers in the world's great harvest, but they must be *men*! If the Holy Ghost sends troops of inspired women, the fields of more than half Christendom are fenced with thorns to prevent their entrance, though the crops fall rotting on the ground and the multitudes are famishing within sight and reach of plenty![214]

There were of course those who saw the value of women in ministry, provided it was the appropriate sphere of service, and did not encroach St. Paul's injunction that women keep their silence in Church. Catherine was disdainful of male prejudice:

> How preposterous is it to suppose that He would have pursued so obviously self-contradictory a course as to gift woman with peculiar powers and in the same breath forbid their use! . . . this pious fraud of man on woman's rights is defended and concealed with mis-applied passages of Scripture.[215]

212. Hardman, *Charles Grandison Finney*, 101.

213. Ibid.

214. Booth-Tucker, *Life of Catherine Booth*, 1:244.

215. Ibid., 245.

Shortly after publishing her pamphlet, Catherine, under shaking conviction presented herself at the pulpit and asked her husband if she might be allowed to speak. Her subsequent preaching ministry drew thousands in the fashionable areas of London's West End, whilst her husband was engaged in the slums of the East End. Her pamphlet prophesied: "Whether the Church will allow women to speak in her assemblies can only be a question of time; common sense, public opinion, and the blessed results of female agency will force her to give an honest and impartial rendering of the solitary text on which she grounds her prohibitions."[216]

Bramwell Booth reflected some years later that "the Army Mother herself had never quite contemplated placing women in positions which would involve *their authority over men.*"[217] Yet after initial hesitation and internal debate, the rapid growth of the movement led to women being placed in leadership of congregations. One of the first was Kate Watts, who at the age of nineteen was sent by Booth to Merthyr Tydfil in South Wales. She recalled him saying "I do not know whether they will give you anything to eat, for they are starving (coal mines had been closed for several years)." She concluded: "In five and a half months we registered more than five hundred converts."[218] William and Catherine Booth's daughter Evangeline was elected by her peers to be the fourth General of the International Salvation Army, in 1934. The next chapter will examine the development of the Booths' concept of the Christian saint, whether woman or man, as a soldier of Christ, "with some muscle and pluck."[219]

Postmillennialism, Social Holiness, and Social Action

If Wesley's concept of "perfect love" did not prompt the Booths to reflect deeply upon the shape of God's love as gathered Christian community, they nonetheless applied aggressive Christian mission to their postmillennial vision and its predisposition towards social action and service—the social dimension of "perfect love" for one's neighbor.[220] In

---

216. Booth, *Papers on Practical Religion*, 110.

217. Booth, *Echoes and Memories*, 178.

218. Watts, *Fighting in Many Lands*, 29.

219. Booth, "The Past of the War," 242. See also Booth, "A General Order Against Starvation," 317.

220. See Booth, *In Darkest England*; Sandall, *The History of The Salvation Army: Volume III, 1883–1953, Social Reform and Welfare Work*; Coutts, *Bread for my Neighbour*;

outlining Finney's postmillennialist credentials, Keith Hardman suggests that "most Protestants then were postmillennialists, which meant that they had been taught to dream that, theologically, their efforts for the kingdom of heaven were helping to bring in the thousand years of the golden age foretold by Isaiah and other Old Testament prophets and Revelation."[221] Finney gave leadership to this dream, boldly declaring in his *Lectures on Revivals* that "if the church will do all her duty the millennium may come in this country in three years."[222] Whilst his postmillennialism, and its accompanying reformist activity in the realm of alcoholism and the abolition of slavery, predated the development of his views on perfection, they dovetailed naturally into this new vision. Hardman illustrates this marriage succinctly in Finney's statement that the "great business of the church is to reform the world—to put away every kind of sin."[223]

The postmillennial vision of the thousand year reign of Christ was a far more compelling priority for Booth than a theological reflection upon the nature of the church and the ecclesiology of his own movement. Booth had from the outset, amidst the poverty and squalor of London's urban slums, along with many similar missions, offered relief to the poor through a myriad of initiatives such as soup kitchens and "farthing breakfasts." Yet the vision of the potential for his growing mission movement to assist in the ushering in of the imminent Millennium captured his imagination. Shortly before the publication of his famous blueprint for a social revolution, *In Darkest England and the Way Out,* he published an article which outlined his dream, entitled "The Millennium; or, The Ultimate Triumph of Salvation Army Principles." Critical to the realization of this vision was the proclamation of his holiness message throughout the land.

> Without this inward purification—this root holiness—no matter how favourable the circumstances of men, outward rightness of conduct is simply impossible . . . for, unless the springs of action are clean, the conduct which proceeds from them cannot be pure. But in those days, by the power and operation of the Holy Spirit, the purpose of Christ, which is the destruction of the works of

---

Fairbank, *Booth's Boots*; Unsworth, *Maiden Tribute*; Redwood, *God in the Slums*.

221. Hardman, *Charles Grandison Finney*, 152; Wilson, *Religious Sects*, 62.

222. Finney, *Lectures on Revivals*, 306.

223. Finney, "The Pernicious Attitude of the Church," 11.

the devil will be accomplished; men will be entirely sanctified, and the prophecy will be fulfilled which says, "Thy people shall be all righteous."[224]

Confirming his postmillennial rather than premillennial convictions, Booth confessed:

Some say that the general triumph of godliness will be ushered in by the personal reign of Christ. We Salvationists, however, expect it to be preceded by further and mightier outpourings of the Holy Ghost than any yet known, and reckon that the war will, thereby be carried on with greater vigour.[225]

Booth's aggressive war metaphor was well suited to postmillennialism. He saw his aggressive movement as a tool in the creation of a better world to usher in the reign of Christ. Catherine was equally confident: "The Salvation Army deserves and demands the careful and patient study of all who would learn how best to follow God and hasten the coming of His kingdom."[226] Central to the ushering in of Christ's kingdom was their message of holiness. Booth wrote to Salvationists, "If you are a holy man or woman . . . you will help forward the War . . . far more effectively than you will if you are not fully saved. Holy people are the great need of the world."[227]

When Booth published *In Darkest England and the Way Out*, in 1890, it was the final statement of a picture he had painted as a young man preaching in the streets, of a salvation lifeboat, an emergency service, being launched into a sea of drowning people to rescue and pull them to safety. Now it was not just a picture of personal salvation, but of social redemption as well. In 1889 Booth had published his belief that salvation meant being saved from both the misery of damnation in the next world, and of salvation from the miseries of the present world. This meant that he had a gospel for both worlds: "it came with the promise of salvation here and now; from hell and sin and vice and crime and idleness and extravagance, and consequently very largely from poverty

---

224. Booth, "The Millennium," 338.

225. Ibid., 337.

226. Booth, *Popular Christianity*, 197. See also Booth, "The Kingdom of Christ"; Booth, *The Salvation Army in Relation to Church and State*, 15; Cadman, "The New Kingdom."

227. Booth, *Purity of Heart*, 71–72.

and disease, and the majority of kindred woes."[228] The frontispiece to *In Darkest England and the Way Out* contained a diagram showing the route by which lost and drowning souls, were rescued by Salvationists in their lifeboat, dragged ashore, and led into the City Colony, where a host of social schemes provided, accommodation, rehabilitation, training, and employment. The journey took them from there to the Farm Colony outside the city and ultimately overseas to expanding new colonies to start a new life. Roger Green dryly comments, that Booth's vision was "an expression of the perceived natural result of the methods of revival coupled with an English version of ruling the world."[229]

Conclusion

Holiness revivalism, the combination of American revivalism and Wesleyan perfectionism, carried to Britain by, amongst others, Caughey, Finney and Palmer, had a decisive impact upon the theology and practice of William and Catherine Booth. More specifically, their aggressive Christianity had consequences for The Salvation Army's emerging ecclesial convictions and practice, which remain embedded in a contemporary reflection upon Salvationist ecclesiology. The Booths founded an aggressive evangelistic Christian mission. Whilst this mission subjectively focused on the life of the individual, and laid relatively little emphasis upon the shape of "full salvation" in the community life of the church, it unmistakably recalled the Victorian church to the priority of mission.

The next chapter will examine how this pragmatically took the form of a second ecclesial strand; an army. Equally it renewed an understanding of the crucial role of the laity and in particular of women, in a church that was overly clericalized as a male preserve for ordained ministry. Significantly, it envisaged sacrificial engagement in social reform and welfare towards a better world, in a church that could appear indifferent to the marginalized. Serving as they were amongst the squalid conditions of the newly urban poor in London's East End, and with the insight of holiness revivalism's emphasis upon God's redemptive power in human life, they developed a holistic appreciation of the

228. Booth, "Salvation For Both Worlds: A Retrospect." See also Smith, "The Battle-Cry of the Social Reform Wing."

229. Green, *The Life and Ministry of William Booth*, 206.

poor, whom they served wholeheartedly in body, mind and spirit. Most notably in ecclesial terms, the subjective picture of a lone, living sacrifice upon God's altar, paved the way for the abandonment of the symbols of bread, wine and water, that would have objectively emphasized God's initiative in drawing God's people into the Trinitarian life of God. This must be addressed in the next chapter.

2

The Establishing of The Salvation Army

Introduction

The Booths' Christian Mission, inspired as it was by nineteenth-century trans-Atlantic holiness revivalism, took a significant step forward in its ecclesial identity, when in 1878 it was renamed The Salvation Army. This renaming was a logical progression given the aggressive nature of holiness revivalism. In that the Booths had an individualistic emphasis on the priority of "saving souls," and a subjective focus on the human conditions of full salvation, the military form that they chose was pragmatically designed to further this task, rather than to theologically express the nature and visible form of God's Church, as the historical record suggests. Nevertheless, in time, the visible metaphor of an army itself proved a powerful source of understanding for Salvationists, on what it meant to be a gathered community. To the Booths' non-denominational, laity focused, female ministry affirming, "higher life" raising, postmillennial Christian mission, engaged in social action—all ecclesial characteristics influenced by holiness revivalism—was added the very specific denominational identity of an Army, with autocratic governance, hierarchy, Officer leaders, the regulated and disciplined lifestyle of the Soldier, and in 1882, the abandonment of sacramental rituals and forms that were an integral part of the ecclesiology of virtually all churches and denominations.

Gathered in May 1878, in William Booth's bedroom, his eldest son and successor, Bramwell, and his key "lieutenant," Railton, reviewed a printer's draft of the Christian Mission's 1878 Annual Report, in which

Railton had entitled the Christian Mission a "Volunteer Army." He had used the idea previously in *Heathen England*:

> We are not, and will not be made a sect. We are a corps of volunteers for Christ, organized as perfectly as we have been able to accomplish, seeking no church status, avoiding as we would the plague every denominational rut, in order . . . to reach more and more of those who lie outside every church boundary.[1]

Booth changed the term "volunteer army" in the Annual Report and replaced it with "salvation army." In Railton's third edition of *Heathen England*, published in 1879, the phrase "a corps of volunteers for Christ" was changed to, "we are an army of soldiers of Christ,"[2] and in the fifth edition (no fourth edition is available) he added Booth's reasoning that "we are not volunteers, for we feel we must do what we do, and we are always on duty."[3] The "Volunteers" were at that time an auxiliary and part-time citizen army, instituted by George III and re-organized in 1863, (later to become the Territorial Army), but a figure of humor and fun.[4] The Christian Mission's annual conference held in August 1878 was dubbed "Our War Congress" and at Bramwell Booth's instruction, a sign painted in large letters "The Salvation Army" was hung over the platform. The *Christian Mission Magazine's* September edition carried a report of the Congress and announced that "it has organized a salvation army to carry the blood of Christ and the fire of the Holy Ghost into every corner of the world."[5]

The *Christian Mission Magazine* was renamed, and in an article in the first edition of *The Salvationist* Booth explained that:

> We are a salvation people—this is our specialty—getting saved and keeping saved, and then getting somebody else saved, and then getting saved ourselves more and more, until full salvation on earth makes the heaven within, which is finally perfected by the full salvation without, on the other side of the river.[6]

1. Railton, *Heathen England*, 3rd ed., 144.
2. Ibid., 145.
3. Railton, *Heathen England*, 5th ed., 29.
4. Sandall, *The History of The Salvation Army*, 1:230.
5. *The Christian Mission Magazine*, 225.
6. Booth, *Salvation Soldiery*, 15.

Despite his understanding that they were a "people," his individualistic expression of salvation made clear his focus on personal salvation, purity and mission. Despite Booth's minimizing the change of name,[7] hindsight reveals the extent to which this simple renaming of newspaper and mission had immediate consequences, and assisted just one of a multitude of similar missions active in the 1860s, the vast majority of which no longer exist, to survive and extend into an international movement. There were 30 stations and 36 evangelists at the beginning of 1878, and at the conclusion 75 stations and 120 evangelists.[8] In 1886, just eight years later, there were 1,749 Corps (previously stations) and 4,192 Officers (previously evangelists).[9] Railton declared in 1887 that "all we have written as to The Army has had a wonderful confirmation in the fact that it has grown during its 22nd year half as large again as it was when this book was written."[10] The official historian confirms that in 1887 these totals were in actual fact 2,262 Corps and 5,684 Officers.[11] The journalist and close friend of the Army, W. T. Stead, reflecting on the change of name wrote in 1891, "From the moment that the Army had received its title its destiny was fixed. The whole organization was dominated by the name."[12]

Aggressive Christianity and The Salvation Army

The change of name from Christian Mission to Salvation Army should be viewed as the logical outcome of an aggressive holiness revivalism, set as it was in London, in the prevailing popular culture of Victorian Britain, at the heart of the British Empire. There were many influences upon the development of an aggressive Salvation Army, but four are of particular note. Firstly, the Booths held a firm belief in a personal Devil. Satan was the enemy who had recruited his own opposing army and held multitudes captive. Booth maintained,

> how much we see in the present . . . to justify the assertion of Satan that he is really and truly *in possession of the bodies and*

7. Ibid., 15.

8. Sandall, *The History of The Salvation Army*, 2:5.

9. Ibid., 2:338.

10. Railton, *Twenty One Years Salvation Army*, 5.

11. Wiggins, *The History of The Salvation Army*, 4:184.

12. Sandall, *The History of The Salvation Army*, 2:1.

souls of men and of the very world they dwell in . . . and we have the most striking justification of the assertion, that Satan is really and truly now, as then, in an awefully solemn sense, *the God of this world'*.[Italics original][13]

Secondly, in keeping with contemporary evangelical belief, the Booths maintained a vivid description of hell as the destination of those held captive by Satan. They called it a place of "endless punishment," with the same phrase used in the doctrines of the Methodist New Connexion (1838), the Evangelical Alliance (1846), and the Salvation Army (1878).[14] Booth was not averse to using the fearsome rhyming phrase "turn or burn" in his evangelistic appeals[15], and was prepared to confirm in an article called "Hell!" that "of course there is a hell—a lake that burns with fire and brimstone, whose worm dies not, and where the fire is not quenched . . . where there is weeping and wailing and gnashing of teeth, and where the smoke of their torment ascendeth up for ever and ever."[16] *The Doctrines and Discipline of The Salvation Army*, discounted any suggestion of the annihilation of the wicked, and confirmed in answer to the question "Do you believe that this punishment will last for ever?," "Yes, for ever."[17] In view of this conviction Booth urged his followers to "give yourself body and soul, time and strength, to the great task of saving people from going there 'by any means,' 'in season and out of season' . . . let all your words and ways tell everybody that you believe in hell."[18]

Thirdly, in the matter of acting "by any means," Booth had seen the influence of Finney's new means and measures in action in the ministry of James Caughey. He and Catherine fully subscribed to Finney's view in *Lectures on Revivals of Religion* that revivals resulted from "the right use of the constituted means,"[19] and that "it was left to the discretion of the church to determine, from time to time, what *measures* shall be

---

13. Booth, *Salvation Soldiery*, 49.

14. See Rhemick, *A New People of God,* 33–34.

15. Booth, *Salvation Soldiery*, 47.

16. Booth, "Hell!," 169.

17. The Salvation Army, *The Doctrines and Discipline of The Salvation Army*, 100.

18. Booth, "Hell!," 171. See also, Booth, *Salvation Soldiery*, 22: "Shake *them* up. Startle them with apparitions of death, and judgment, and devils, and hell. What matters taste and propriety to you?"

19. Finney, *Lectures on Revivals of Religion*, 13.

adopted, and what *forms* pursued, in giving the gospel its power."[20] Elijah Cadman, described by Sandall as "a one-time sweep's climbing boy and drunken pugilist," had joined the Mission, and, given charge of the work in Hackney reported: "We are making a powerful attack upon the devil's kingdom . . . King Jesus is our great Commander . . . We have an army here that will face the world, the flesh and the devil."[21] In 1877 Booth assumed total control of the Movement, and informed Conference at its 1878 "war congress" that, "We have been called by the arrangement of Divine providence to be officers and leaders in His Army, and we are met to consider how we can best advance the interests of that army."[22]

Writing to the members of the "war congress" Catherine counseled those gathered to "cast off all the bonds of prejudice and custom, and let the love of Christ which is in you have free course, to run out in all conceivable schemes and methods of labour for the souls of men," for "whatever measures are needful for the salvation of men, it is His will that we should adopt them, and His pleasure to succeed us *in* them."[23] In an 1881 address entitled "Conquest" she remarked, "We have done with civilian measures . . . and we have come to military measures . . . we will send these Soldiers after the sinners, and we will harass the life out of them, till they get saved . . . it is the spirit of conquest in the hearts of our people."[24]

William Booth was equally pragmatic. If the task of taking the message of "full salvation" was urgent and in the hands of God's human partners to prosecute as aggressively as love of God and fear of hell demanded, then he should utilize that most aggressive and militant of human forces—an Army. He explained to his troops in *The Salvationist*, that "if it be wise and lawful and desirable for men to be banded together and organized after the best method possible to liberate an enslaved nation, establish it in liberty, and overcome its foes, then surely it must be wise and lawful and desirable for the people of God to join themselves together after the fashion most effective and forcible to liberate a captive world, and to overcome the enemies of God and man."[25] The metaphor

20. Ibid., 250–51.
21. Sandall, *The History of The Salvation Army*, 1:202.
22. *Christian Mission Magazine*, June 1877.
23. Booth, "Letter From Mrs. Booth," 181. See also Booth, "Wake Them Up!," 2.
24. Booth, "Conquest," 2.
25. Booth, "The Salvation Army," 291.

came to dominate. All the regular military language of an army was employed in the vision of waging war on the Devil. Booth informed his followers of God's revelation:

> In the name of the great Three in One . . . recruits are flowing in. Drilling, skirmishing, fighting, advancing, are going on. Some territory has been won, some captives have been liberated, some shouts of victory have been raised . . . Does all this sound strange . . . not sacred, not ecclesiastical, not according to the traditions of the elders, and after the pattern of existing things and institutions? Is it something new? It may be so, and yet it may be none the less true and scriptural, and none the less of divine origin, and made after some heavenly pattern for all that.[26]

Fourthly, in his thesis of the feminizing of piety after 1800, with the resulting perceived loss of piety within masculinity, Callum Brown argues that in an age of growing empire that worshipped force, discernible experimentation was attempted to construct a moral masculinity, and a muscular Christianity, that could inspire the ailing religious fortunes of men. He refers to such movements as the Volunteers after 1860, the Boy's Brigade and The Salvation Army. He argues that the Army attempted "to utilize a curbing of manhood as an evangelizing strategy."[27] Equally Brown details the aggressive nature of the evangelism that emerged in the century's growing evangelical movement, and the major influence of Thomas Chalmers and the "aggressive system" which he popularized, in reaching the rapidly expanding urban communities with the gospel.[28] Many organizations and agencies emerged in this period of evangelical fervor, inspiring the Sunday School movement, home visitation, church building and educational schemes.

Christian hymns were an indication of the popularity of the metaphor of spiritual warfare. It was Rev. S. Baring Gould, not a Salvationist, who penned the words of the fighting hymn 'Onward Christian Soldiers', published in 1865, with the familiar words of the third stanza, "Like a mighty army, moves the Church of God", just as the Booths arrived from their provincial tours, to take up mission work in the East End of London. Moody and Sankey's London Campaign hymn, "Hold the Fort"[29] was

---

26. Ibid., 29–30.

27. Brown, *The Death of Christian Britain*, 88.

28. Ibid., 22–25.

29. Sandall, *The History of The Salvation Army*, 1:227.

aired in 1875. Railton had just published "Our War-Song" in *The Christian Mission Magazine* to the tune of "Men of Harlech" with the opening lines, "Soldier, rouse thee! War is raging; God and fiends are battle waging."[30] In 1875, a "Salvation Battle Hymn" was published to the tune of the Battle Hymn of the Republic, with the chorus, "Glory, glory, hallelujah! Salvation's flowing on." [31] Even the Archbishop of Canterbury, Archibald Tait, caught the mood of the moment and declared his belief that "the only way we shall be able, in the enormous population of this ever-growing country, to maintain the cause of our Lord and Master" is "to welcome every volunteer who is willing to assist the regular forces; and to arm, so far as we can, the whole population in the cause of Jesus Christ."[32]

Much as people came to admire the Army's attempt to reach the poor, the extreme examples of this aggressive evangelistic spirit drew outspoken criticism. Three articles in *The Contemporary Review* during 1882 from Cardinal Henry Manning, Rev. Dean Randall Davidson and the Irish writer, social reformer and feminist, Frances Power Cobbe illustrate, amongst their positive comments, their deep bewilderment and censure. Cobbe recognized that there was "no attempt on the part of the leaders to soften the fact that 'Aggressive Religion' involves compelling the attention of the unconverted, whether they will hear or whether they will forbear."[33] She complained that "to such of us as can recall the profoundly solemn spirit which characterized the old Evangelical type of piety, there is something more than painful, even abhorrent, in the irreverence which now confronts us,"[34] and "the question is whether, in thus despoiling religion of reverence, these well-intentioned people are not destroying *the thing itself?*"[35]

In his list of concerns, Randall Davidson considered this irreverence to be the greatest danger that was "inherent in the system pursued . . . in the excitement of a great meeting, when the rough audience has caught the enthusiasm of the speakers, and is joining vociferously in doggerel hymns or songs, to the noisy accompaniment of a great brass band, irreverence—gross irreverence in the view of every thoughtful Christian

30. *The Christian Mission Magazine*, February 1874, 6.

31. *The Christian Mission Magazine*, January 1875, 5.

32. Sandall, *The History of The Salvation Army*, 1:229.

33. Cobbe, "The Last Revival," 185.

34. Ibid., 186.

35. Ibid., 187.

man—is, to say the very least, perilously imminent."[36] Cardinal Manning was prepared to recognize that The Salvation Army "could never have existed but for the spiritual desolation of England,"[37] but was bewildered by its methods:

> St. Paul did not go in array, nor with pomp and circumstance of war . . . It is hardly the advent of "the Son of Peace;" and its sounds are rather of the whirlwind than of the still small voice . . . It is one thing to rebuke sinners . . . and another to challenge opposition by military titles and movements with drums and fifes. These things seem not only unwise for the Salvation Army, but dangerous to souls. The "offence of the Cross" is inevitable if we preach "Christ and Him crucified;" and both wisdom and charity lay on us an obligation not to add to it by any needless provocation.[38]

All three spoke of their concern that the search for startling methods with which to gain attention was accelerative, and could only lead to greater and more severe excesses in search of livelier and more vulgar means. Manning concluded, "such are some of our fears for this zealous but defiant movement. Our fears greatly overbalance our hopes."[39]

Booth was nonetheless confident that his pragmatism was legitimate. He told the 1878 "war congress":

> Methodism became part of my very blood. I have had much to unlearn, and it is very difficult to unlearn being a Methodist. But I think I have almost got out of my last skin. I see the land.[40]

His "unlearning" of Methodism, in the popular culture of Victorian Britain, led to the pragmatic metaphor of an army, the logical outcome of holiness revivalism's aggressive Christianity in its determination to employ the most effective methods and means to rescue souls from the clutches of Satan and from the everlasting torment of hell. The ecclesial strand of "army" is therefore the second, in a tangled cord of mission, army and church. Salvationists reflecting upon their ecclesiology should

---

36. Davidson, "The Methods of the Salvation Army," 195.

37. Manning, "The Salvation Army," 335.

38. Ibid., 338–39.

39. Ibid., 342.

40. Booth, "The Past of the War," 237. See also Ocheltree, "Wesleyan Methodist Perceptions of William Booth," 262–76, in which she records both positive and negative Methodist reaction to Booth and The Salvation Army.

consider the reality that the metaphor of an army, like its forerunner, aggressive evangelistic Christian mission, emerged with an ear more tuned to the task of efficiently reaching the "lost" and lone individual than to the life and shape of the gathered community.

The Principle of Autocratic Governance

The first feature of this army was strict submission to authority. If Booth perceived that he was "unlearning" Methodism, he saw himself in one respect to be keeping faith with John Wesley. The leadership of an army required a supremely powerful General, which suited his autocratic temperament, and became one of the most controversial aspects of his new movement.[41] He had established the governance of his Christian mission, from Methodist example, upon Committee lines with an Annual Conference. The first Conference of the Christian Mission in 1870 outlined Booth's responsibility as General Superintendent and his "power of confirming or setting aside all decisions and resolutions of any of the Official, Society, or other meetings held by the Mission, which in his judgement may be in any way prejudicial to the object of which the Mission was first established."[42] With regard to the Mission's property, however, twelve Trustees were to be chosen by the General Superintendent. Equally provision was made, in the event of the General Superintendent's death, resignation or incapacitation, for the "duties, powers and responsibilities"[43] of the office to pass into the hands of the Conference, although he was given the right to appoint a successor to be approved "by at least three-fourths of the Conference."[44]

The constitution of The Christian Mission, registered by deed-poll in 1875, stated that it was "hereafter for ever under the oversight direction and control of some one person" whose powers of veto were extended to cover "all or any of the decisions and resolutions of any Conference."[45] A proposal to make total abstinence a requirement for all members was voted down by Conference in 1876, and a frustrated delegation headed

41. See Bramwell Booth's positive reflections on his father's controversial autocracy in Booth, *These Fifty Years*, 141–51.

42. The Christian Mission, *Minutes of First Conference of The Christian Mission*.

43. Ibid.

44. Ibid.

45. Sandall, *The History of The Salvation Army*, 1:182.

by Bramwell Booth and Railton, pleaded with Booth to assume full control. In January 1877 the Conference Committee unanimously agreed Booth's proposals to scrap the Conference as a legislative assembly, and create a council of war.[46] Booth was left to explain this decision to the Conference due to meet in June 1877. In a review of the mission's work in the March edition of the *Christian Mission Magazine* he stated:

> We have been trying and, we thank God, with no little success, to break loose from all the trammels of custom and propriety which may in any degree have hindered or hampered us in the past. The dreadful tendency to settle down is apparent in connection with all religious work . . . and we are more than ever determined that no conformity to any Church forms or ideas shall hinder us.[47]

He explained the dissatisfaction expressed at "so large a portion of time being consumed in discussion on trifling matters, while the mightier and practical questions, which intimately concern the work of God and the souls of our people, were left partially neglected," and admitted: "I launched the Conference on a sea of legislation which all came to nothing." When it met, he explained to his "council of war" how it would work:

> The Commander-in-chief calls the principal officers around him to receive information and counsel from all. Each brings his facts and expresses his judgment as to what is necessary and important to do, and then in view of all this he resolves upon a programme of operation. This is our council of war . . . This is a question of confidence as between you and me, and if you can't trust me it is of no use for us to attempt to work together. *Confidence in God and in me are absolutely indispensable both now and ever afterwards.*[48]

These pragmatic rather than theological proposals were accepted on 12th June 1877. The General Superintendent effectively became the General. The 1875 constitution was revoked and a new 1878 constitution gave Booth and his successors, whom the incumbent could choose, power as sole trustee, "to acquire or dispose of property and to set up or

---

46. Ibid., 198.

47. *Christian Mission Magazine*, March 1877, 176.

48. *Christian Mission Magazine*, July 1877, 147.

revoke trusts."[49] Furthermore, it was agreed that the constitution could no longer be altered without the consent of an Act of Parliament.[50]

Randall Davidson, the Archbishop of Canterbury's representative on a committee investigating the work of the Army, made his own thoughts public. He criticised "the *Autocracy of the General in Command*" as a particular feature that would "impair its usefulness as a permanent agency for God's glory and man's good." He added:

> Few outsiders, probably, are aware how absolute is his rule. He is the sole trustee for all the buildings and property of the Army; he is empowered to nominate his successor in the trust; and he can by his mere fiat dismiss any officer in the service, or transplant him to another station or to new work.[51]

Davidson commented further upon the hereditary nature of the General's power to appoint his successor:

> It is understood, if not yet definitely enacted, that "General" Booth is to be succeeded by his eldest son ... If the system of arbitrary generalship is—judging by the experience of history— a dangerous one for the common good, the danger in the case of a religious organisation is certainly not diminished by introducing the notion of hereditary rule ... I doubt whether an analogous system can be found in any religious community in the world.[52]

Those comments were prophetic.[53] In 1929, when Booth's son, Bramwell, had become an elderly, increasingly ill and autocratic General, the majority of the Commissioners rebelled against his rule. They used Booth's later 1904 Supplementary Deed Poll, which allowed for the calling of a High Council, and the right of a majority of three quarters of the gathering to vote to depose the incumbent General in the eventuality of incapacity or illness. It was a damaging public spectacle, in which the Booth family lodged a legal challenge to the High Council's powers.[54] Nevertheless, whilst the significant powers of the General were largely

49. Sandall, *The History of The Salvation Army*, 1:235.

50. For a full discussion of these constitutional arrangements and their significance, see Larsson, *1929*, 15–23.

51. Cited in Bell, *Randall Davidson*, 1:48.

52. Ibid.

53. Ibid. See his biographer's comments in this respect.

54. See Larsson, *1929*, 326. Two other contrasting accounts of this episode are given in: Mackenzie, *The Clash of the Cymbals*; Smith, *The Betrayal of Bramwell Booth*.

maintained, the Booth dynasty was broken. In 1931, an Act of Parliament withdrew the General's power to nominate a successor, and transferred the General's powers as sole Trustee to the newly formed Salvation Army Trustee Company.[55] In the following year, 1932, it was agreed that the General would retire at seventy-three (this reduced to seventy in 1953, and continues to be periodically reviewed). Nevertheless, Salvationists reflecting on the important matter of church governance should note that the powers of the General, which remain largely intact, were adopted not from theological reflection upon the nature and form of God's church, but as a pragmatic tool for effective and aggressive mission. Catherine Booth defended this pragmatic approach, stating that "we are just as safe with one man at the helm as with twenty, and far more likely to get the ship into port."[56] Nevertheless, she betrayed an individualistic and voluntaristic understanding of the organization when, in relation to her husband's autocracy, she suggested that "nobody is bound either to join the Army or stay in after they have joined."[57]

Negotiations with the Church of England

Booth's autocratic powers were at the heart of the eventual failure of negotiations with the Church of England, which in 1882 officially assessed the practicality and desirability of some form of co-operation with The Salvation Army that could ultimately have led to it becoming a Religious Order within Anglicanism. The Army was rapidly multiplying its Citadels or Corps, and establishing a significant yet polarizing impact upon public opinion. The Church of England, urged on by many of its clergy, could not afford to ignore these developments. The Archbishop of York, Dr. William Thomson (1862-90), wrote to Booth in a letter dated April 18th, 1882, confirming:

> Some of my clergy have written to me to beg that I would ascertain how far it was possible for the Church to recognize the work of The Salvation Army as helping forward the cause of Christ consistently with our discipline . . . Some of us think that you are able to reach cases, and to do so effectually, which we have great difficulty in touching. They believe that you are moved by zeal for

---

55. See Thompson, "The Salvation Army Act, 1931," 242–44.

56. Booth, *The Salvation Army in Relation to Church and State*, 82.

57. Ibid.

God, and not by a spirit of rivalry with the Church . . . and they wish not to find themselves in needless antagonism with any in whom such principles and purposes prevail.[58]

The Lower House of Convocation petitioned the Upper House to investigate The Salvation Army, to establish whether there were grounds for co-operation, and a fact-finding committee was formed for this purpose.[59] It was chaired by Dr. Benson, Bishop of Truro (afterwards Archbishop of Canterbury), and comprised Canon Westcott of Westminster, (afterwards Bishop of Durham), Dr. Lightfoot, Bishop of Durham, Canon Wilkinson, (afterwards Bishop of Truro), and Randall Davidson, Dean of Windsor (later Archbishop of Canterbury), representing Dr. Tait, Archbishop of Canterbury. The distinguished nature of this committee indicates the seriousness with which this fledgling movement was viewed. Booth, constantly aware of the need to find financial support for his work, was visited by members of this committee, and entered into correspondence with them.[60]

Bramwell Booth later reflected: "We were aware that some kind of union with the Church of England would enhance our position in the eyes of the public, and that it would not only clear our financial skies in the immediate present, but probably enormously increase our resources for the future."[61] He suggested that it was Dr. Benson who was "the moving spirit" in the negotiations for, "there had evidently come a revelation of the new strength which the Church of England would acquire with the Army as its fighting auxiliary."[62]

During these negotiations Benson succeeded Tait as Archbishop of Canterbury. On 5th January 1883 Booth wrote and assured him of his determination to prove "the groundlessness of all fears that have been expressed as to our becoming sectarian by the heartiness with which we shall hail every fresh advance against the common enemy by all true godly men."[63] He alluded to the negotiations with the committee and confirmed: "We have held back our notes on the list of queries with

58. Begbie, *Life of William Booth*, 2:9.

59. Booth, *Echoes and Memories*, 74.

60. Ibid. Bramwell Booth discusses some of the motivation for discussions. See 73–85.

61. Ibid., 84.

62. Ibid., 77.

63. Begbie, *Life of William Booth*, 2:15.

regard to the Army sent to the Clergy, thinking it improbable that the Committee would endeavour to complete their report much before the reassembling of Convocation."[64] Meanwhile, the Committee visited various centres, and secured reports from a variety of quarters. Benson, writing to Davidson during Tait's last illness at the end of 1882 remarked that, "Our Salvation Army Committee went through many letters and accounts of the work—which is more favourably reported from the north than from the south—and settled to have a report drafted and brought before them to discuss when they meet again."[65]

By April 1883 Booth had still not responded to the Committee's enquiries. When the Bishops of Oxford and Hereford expressed concern in the Upper House of Convocation about alleged immorality within some branches of The Salvation Army, Booth wrote to Archbishop Benson in dismay: "It seems to me very hard that the outrageous statements constantly made with regard to us should be credited without our having an opportunity to reply to them."[66] Davidson, in a reply dated 13th April 1883 on behalf of the Archbishop, reminded Booth that he had still not responded to the Committee's questions, even though "nearly a year ago, you were so kind as to offer, for the information of the Committee, to send full answers to the circular of enquiry addressed to clergy and others who had experience of the working of the Salvation Army."[67] Booth's office had apparently lost the original list of questions. They requested a copy which was sent and remained unanswered. There is no evidence that a reply was ever forthcoming and the negotiations stalled.[68]

These brief negotiations ultimately amounted to little, but are instructive for what they reveal of the ecclesial nature of the movement being established. In his study, *The Victorian Church in Decline*, of Archbishop Tait and the Church of England, 1868–1882, Peter Marsh refers to Tait's interest in exploring the possibility "of bringing the Army under the aegis of the established Church," but explains "the Army's enthusiastic eccentricities, shocking in their novelty, and, more significant,

---

64. Ibid.

65. See Benson, *The Life of Edward White Benson*, 540. See also Davidson, *Life of Archibald Campbell Tait*, 510–12.

66. Ibid., 18.

67. Ibid., 20.

68. Frederick Coutts judged the fault to have lain with both sides. See Coutts, *The Salvation Army in Relation to the Church*, 9.

its own insistence on a free hand, made union impossible, though relations between the two became amicable."[69] Booth offered his own later reflection:

> Some of the leading Dignitaries of the National Church were loudly controverting the wisdom of the course pursued by their forefathers in allowing Wesleyan Methodism to drift away from the Establishment, and wondering whether a little patient manoeuvring might not have been successful, not only in retaining the Wesleys . . . within its Fold, but of securing to the Episcopacy the influence and direction of the immense multitudes who have since grown up under the Methodist Banner . . . [and asking] . . . can we not avoid the mistake of the past?[70]

He confirmed that the meeting which took place in his office with Dr. Benson and Dr. Westcott, by their own request, was to discuss, "the possibility of a union between the Salvation Army and the Church, or the attachment of the Army to the Church in some form."[71]

Begbie is clear that both Bramwell Booth and Railton were insistent that William Booth should not relinquish control of The Salvation Army.[72] Bramwell, on reflection, gave his perception of the motives of each member of the Church of England committee. In particular he noted that Dr. Davidson, whilst "very urbane and considerate throughout the negotiation" showing "real ability in fastening upon essentials," he nevertheless grasped that Booth

> was not willing to relinquish his full control, no matter what advantages might be secured from the inclusion of himself and his Organization under the wing of the Church of England. So far as Dr. Davidson was concerned, this was, I am afraid, from the beginning, fatal to the project.[73]

Bell's biography of Davidson mentions briefly his "full appreciation of 'the straightforward ability and earnest zeal of the leaders of the Army,'"[74] but equally his concern as to the autocratic nature of Booth's

69. Marsh, *The Victorian Church in Decline,* 248.

70. Cited in Begbie, *Life of William Booth,* 2:33–34.

71. Ibid., 34.

72. Ibid., 32.

73. Booth, *Echoes and Memories,* 75.

74. Bell, *Randall Davidson,* 1:47.

leadership. Bramwell Booth, clearly aware of Davidson's view, as expressed in *The Contemporary Review*, made his own feelings clear:

> Just as Dr. Davidson felt that the question of authority was the real difficulty, so we saw on our side that the absence of authority was a grave weakness of the Church of England, and that its sacrifice on our part would involve the ruin of the Army . . . the so-called autocracy, although it might lay us open to misunderstanding, was necessary for the effectiveness of our War.[75]

William Booth, in his own reflection revealed that whilst wishing

> to avoid the establishment of another separate Religious Organization, with which I heartily concurred, I was afraid the Union we had been discussing was simply impossible at the present date . . . that the spirit of union—which was the next best thing to actual Union itself—would be most effectually attained by the two Bodies continuing to live and work apart, their labours and influences flowing on side by side, like two distinct streams, with bridges connecting each at frequent intervals.[76]

In effect this decision clearly signalled the identity of The Salvation Army as an autonomous denomination, rather than what might have been a Religious Order in Anglicanism. Yet there is some merit in Salvationists reflecting upon the suggestion that the Booths' Salvation Army developed in character as a quasi-missionary religious order; a special service within the wider church, in which women and men voluntarily signed up to a human religious rule. It is a suggestion that will be revisited shortly.

An Army with Soldiers and Officers

The matter of Booth's autocracy, the subsequent "military" nature of the movement that he established as a highly visible and independent entity, free from the supposed inhibiting influence of the Church of England, is of crucial importance to any understanding of The Salvation Army's developing ecclesial identity. Booth, and his colleagues, fully exploited the potential of the military metaphor in establishing its identity, at the expense of the predominant Biblical pictures of the church that might have added richer, and more rounded dimensions. A convert or disciple

75. Booth, *Echoes and Memories*, 84.
76. Cited in Begbie, *Life of William Booth*, 2:37.

of Jesus Christ became a Christian soldier, fighting within a disciplined and strictly regulated army, hierarchically structured with continents, territories (national boundaries), divisions (regional boundaries) and corps (local congregations). Each soldier was required to obey a stringent set of orders and regulations, in order to ensure the full effectiveness and efficiency of the fighting force, so that they might "seize the slaves of sin and not only set them free and turn them into children of God; but as far as possible in each case to make them soul winners."[77] Booth asked Railton to construct the first "orders and regulations" and commented in the introduction that, "It is a remarkable fact that our system corresponds so closely to that of the Army and Navy of this country, that we have been able to use even the very words of many of their regulations, and of Sir Garnet Wolseley's Soldier's pocket-book."[78] He suggested, "strange indeed that the people of God should never have fully recognized the fact that if they have to fight the world they must fight in the same systematic way that any of the world's armies fight, and this all the more, instead of the less, because our weapons are not carnal, but spiritual."[79] Railton urged the erasing of all lingering memories of Methodist governance:

> There are still some here and there who would like to have business meetings and determine by vote what shall and shall not be done. But every officer and man must be made to understand that anything of the sort would utterly ruin our Army and render it useless. We are not and will not be made a church. There are plenty for anyone who wishes to join them, to vote, and to rest.[80]

Railton saw the Army, not as a church but an aggressive spiritual force, imprinting "military principles in every mind and heart,"[81] and exuded pride in the Army's assumption of God's authority on earth:

> The advantages of an Army over any other organisation of a religious kind need scarcely be explained to those who have long been within it or who know anything of the Churches. Here is the only religious power which takes hold of a man or woman utterly without education or training of any kind, and opens before

77. The Salvation Army, *Orders and Regulations for The Salvation Army*, 1
78. Ibid., 9.
79. Ibid., 1–2.
80. Ibid., 3.
81. Ibid., 4.

him or her the way to carry the salvation of God to thousands of others every day . . . [and] . . . puts this Army utterly beyond comparison with any Church.[82]

Roland Robertson studied The Salvation Army in the 1960s,[83] and offered what Bryan Wilson described in *Patterns of Sectarianism*, "perhaps the most emphatically sociological treatment of all the movements discussed."[84] Robertson commented on what he called the "voluntary subjection to discipline" and "the *voluntaristic-totalitarian* involvement of thousands of British Salvationists."[85] Whilst he suggested the various sociological reasons for the willingness of people to voluntarily embrace totalitarian rule, such as the poverty of its recruits and "familial socialisation," he did not acknowledge the subjectivism of the Army's holiness teaching in the success of this military enterprise. In Booth's aggressive Christianity there was little discrepancy between being holy and being obedient to the General as a soldier in the Army. In his preface to *Orders and Regulations*, Booth declared that they were "not only to be carefully studied and strictly observed by all Commanding Officers, but no effort is to be spared to ensure their circulation in every Corps . . . so that every Corps and man may be brought up as quickly as possible to the highest standard of perfection."[86] Equally, Railton recognised that the Army's teaching on "practical holiness" was the central reason why anyone would wish to submit themselves to such strict discipline in the cause of Christ. He explained that, "the teaching and enjoyment of this great blessing, with all the deliverance from self-seeking and pride which it brings, has made it possible to go on imposing more and more of regulation and discipline on all sorts of men and women without either souring their spirit or transforming the Army's system into mere machinery."[87]

It could be argued that The Salvation Army followed the example of Wesleyan Methodism in expecting "perfect love" to be accompanied by a life of Christian discipline. Wesley, himself autocratic in his leadership style, expected members to conform to set standards of practice and

82. Ibid., 10.

83. Robertson, "The Salvation Army."

84. Wilson, *Patterns of Sectarianism*, 5

85. Robertson, "The Salvation Army," 82

86. The Salvation Army, *Orders and Regulations of The Salvation Army*, ii.

87. Railton, *The Authoritative Life*, 71.

behavior. But, the extreme metaphor of the Christian soldier, so vividly enacted in The Salvation Army, took this discipline to new levels as holy love was translated into very specific, practical standards of behavior and obedience. Unable to secure total abstinence as a standard for all members under the Conference system, Booth was successfully able to insist upon it under the terms of the new constitution, as the absolute General. Railton confirmed that, "to teach practical holiness is to teach abstention from drink, and tobacco, and showy dress, and worldly books and amusements."[88] These ethical demands were enshrined in the *Articles of War*, a covenant with God and the Army that all soldiers signed.[89] With glorious understatement Railton commented: "The Articles simply required everyone to give up the use of intoxicants; to keep from any resorts, habits, company or language that would be harmful; and to devote all their leisure time, spare energy and money to the War."[90]

Not only did the identity of an Army subjectively raise the high standard of a soldier as the bar for membership, it also raised the authority of those Evangelists who were now called Officers. Railton confirmed in *Orders and Regulations* that "this system . . . makes every officer possessed of power equal to the combined power of all his men," for:

> Only with this absolute power over men can there be regularity. If the people . . . had power to vote . . . no officer, however zealous, could be sure of carrying on the same services all year round. But with people who are always under the same control, it is possible, no matter who the officer may be, for the services to be continued day after day, and year after year, without a break or a hitch. This is militarism—a settled, absolute, regular system . . . to accomplish a common settled purpose.[91]

In this efficient and utilitarian army, the officers became vital components, for:

> The work must, of course, depend mainly upon the officers. If these all set themselves to adopt and to carry out day by day the system laid down, no matter whether every part of it seems to them to be the best possible or not, we shall very speedily see so enormous an improvement in the work . . . and every improve-

88. Ibid., 146 .
89. See Sandall, *The History of The Salvation Army*, 2:312–13.
90. Railton, *The Authoritative Life*, 79.
91. The Salvation Army, *Orders and Regulations for The Salvation Army*, 5.

ment in the system will make it easier to carry out further im-
provement still.[92]

Booth saw the danger of officers exercising unbridled power, and
spoke clearly to them about the nature of their leadership in a priesthood of all believers:

> [T]here is a fundamental principle that has to do with the very ex-
> istence and working of the Army, in which it widely differs from
> most, if not all, of the Christian organisations round about us, and
> this is THAT THE FIGHTING IS DONE BY THE SOLDIERS,
> the Officers, leading, guiding, encouraging, and showing the way.
> With other organisations the very opposite is the rule with them;
> it is a principle that the fighting shall be done by the officers.
> They are set apart, ordained, and maintained, and looked up to,
> to maintain the fight. The responsibility for success with them is
> . . . upon the character of the ministry and the ministrations and
> ceremonials, that are managed and conducted by the responsible
> leaders; whereas with us we publicly and most emphatically avow
> that the whole Corps ought to do the fighting.[93]

The necessity of such firm guidance reflected the reality that secular
hierarchical military language and governance was in danger of competing against a servant theology of leadership. Booth, who himself held
absolute sway, challenged his officers:

> You are not their masters. You must not count yourselves such
> for a moment. I give no authority nor encouragement to any such
> notion, and yet I must say that now and then I do hear expres-
> sions and see actions on the part of some of our Officers that lead
> me to fear that now and then they forget themselves.[94]

In 1886 he published the six hundred page *Orders and Regulations for
Field Officers* (as opposed to Headquarters or Staff officers), covering
every conceivable aspect of the organization and its warfare. Despite
Booth's insistence that officers were not "masters," he pronounced that
the Field Officer,

> by virtue of his position stands out before his Soldiers more
> prominently than any other man. To them he is the Ambassador
> and Representative of God. He is their Captain, their brother,

92. Ibid., 8.

93. Booth, "The General's New Year Address to Officers," 4, col. 3.

94. Ibid.

and friend. Their eyes are on him night and day. They regard him as the pattern expressly set for them to copy, the leader who at all times it is their bounden duty to follow.[95]

The movement had from its early recognition of the priority of lay ministry, from Booth's declaration that "the Holy Ghost is just as willing and just as able to speak through a washerwoman as through a bishop,"[96] begun a process of institutionalization and clericalization that increasingly viewed the priority and hierarchy of Officership, in clerical terms. The shift from Booth's conviction of "the separation between layman and cleric become more and more obscured" was evidenced by his later charge to Bramwell:

> It is the Officer upon whom all depends. It has always been so. If Moses had not made a priesthood there would have been no Jewish nation. It was the priesthood of the Levites which kept them alive, saved them from inherent rottenness . . . here is where I think your great work for the next ten years will lie.[97]

Robertson suggests that Booth "came round to the conclusion that the priesthood of all believers, although already effectively dropped in practice, had to be attenuated even as an ideal."[98] The process of routinization and clericalization has been fully addressed in Harold Hill's *Leadership in the Salvation Army: A Case Study in Clericalisation,* in which he details the contradictory rejection by Booth of ordination for his officers and any suggestion of their status as clergy, set against the movement of priority given to them within such a hierarchical movement. He concludes:

> In attempting to maintain a sectarian equality of believers, [the Salvation Army] resisted the idea that its officers were clergy like other clergy. At the same time, because of the autocratic temperament of its founder, it adopted a military, hierarchical structure which served to expedite the process of clericalisation.[99]

95. The Salvation Army, *Orders and Regulations for Field Officers*, part I, chapter I, section I, no. 4.

96. Booth, "The General's New Year Address to Officers," 4, col. 3.

97. Begbie, *Life of William Booth*, 2:306.

98. Robertson, "The Salvation Army," 80.

99. Hill, *Leadership in the Salvation Army*, 73.

Booth's son Bramwell, fought, and eventually secured for Salvation Army Officers, during the First World War, the same opportunities and rights of clergy as other denominations, to be exempted from military service and to be used in chaplaincy roles. Bramwell stated:

> We believe that our Lord Jesus Christ has called us into His Church of the redeemed, that our call has not been by man or the will of man, but by the Holy Spirit of God . . . and that our officers are equally . . . ministers in the Church of God, having received diversities of gifts, but the one Spirit—endowed by His grace, assured of his guidance, confirmed by His word and commissioned by the Holy Ghost to represent Him to the whole world.[100]

Nevertheless, there has been surprisingly little theological reflection by Salvationists on the appropriateness of the military style of Salvation Army governance in relation to the servant nature of ministry. This will be examined further in the next chapter.

The Booths' aggressive Christianity, in the culture of jingoistic Victorian Britain, established an independent and autonomous denomination called The Salvation Army, with highly disciplined and regulated members who were called "soldiers," quasi-clergy who were military styled officers and a polity that was autocratic and hierarchical. Controversially, in 1882, the nature and identity of this army was further established by Booth's decision to dispense with the use of those sacraments of baptism and the Lord's Supper, which had up until that point been an assumed part of the Christian Mission. In view of the investigation of this study into the Army's emerging ecclesiological convictions and practice, in relation to the nature, form and mission of God's Church, it is essential that this decision is fully understood and assessed, both in its historical context and in the next chapter in its contemporary expression.

The Sacraments

The Booths abandoned the Sacraments of baptism and the Lord's Supper for both theological and pragmatic reasons. Firstly, the Booths held no conception of them as means of grace. Their use was not considered to be an essential condition of either justification or sanctification; of the individual fully consecrated and immediately and entirely sancti-

---

100. Booth, *Echoes and Memories*, 82.

fied upon God's altar. Secondly, their use was divisive and therefore pragmatically ineffective and inefficient for Booth in getting people saved and sanctified. They were viewed as culturally bound practices that could be adapted or dispensed with. Thirdly, they had no conception that the sacraments were constitutive for God's church in the way that they established fellowship. The Booths adopted new practices that lacked the same theological character. Fourthly, in view of their aggressive convictions, and with the help of Quaker arguments, they could not interpret the sacraments as biblical commands from Christ. In all these ways, the abandonment of the sacraments illustrated the nature of the Booths' aggressive Christianity, and of The Salvation Army that was its logical outcome.

Booth announced his decision at a meeting of his officers at the end of 1882. His speech was serialized in the *War Cry* during January 1883. The timing was significant in that it coincided with the stalled negotiations with the Church of England. He summarized:

> If the Sacraments are not conditions of Salvation; if there is a general division of opinion as to the proper mode of administering them, and if the introduction of them would create division of opinion and heart burning, and if we are not professing to be a church, nor aiming at being one, but simply a force for aggressive Salvation purposes, is it not wise for us to postpone any settlement of the question, to leave it over to some future day, when we shall have more light, and see more clearly our way before us?[101]

In articulating a provisional position, which he never reversed, Booth offered insight into the four aspects of his rationale.[102]

The Sacraments and Full Salvation

Booth believed that the sacraments were not essential to the gift and experience of salvation as means of grace:

> *The Sacraments must not, nay they cannot rightly be regarded as conditions of Salvation.* If you make them essentials, if you say that men cannot get to Heaven without being baptised with

101. Booth, "The General's New Year Address to Officers," 4, col. 3.

102. See Booth, *Echoes and Memories*, 201–4, for a clear account that Booth was not contemplating the "introduction" of sacraments, but abandoning them from their previous use.

> water, or without "Breaking bread" as it is called, where there is
> opportunity of doing so, then you shut out from that holy place
> a multitude of men and women who have been and are today
> sincere followers of the Lord Jesus Christ.[103]

Booth had in mind the Society of Friends, whose position he took an
interest in. Equally, some years later in an interview with Sir Henry
Lunn, published in 1895, he revisited his decision and re-iterated his
fundamental belief:

> We do not consider that the Sacraments are essentials of salva-
> tion, and in this matter, as I know quite well, I have with me some
> of the most eminent members of the English Episcopal bench,
> who have admitted to me, in conversation, that they would never
> dare to say that a man who had not been baptized, and not re-
> ceived the Lord's Supper, could not enter Heaven.[104]

Booth did not clarify who he was referring to, nor did he give evidence
of an understanding of the nuances of differing sacramental theologies.
He met many of the leading Anglican clergymen of his day. In Booth's
own words, Bishop (later Archbishop) Benson, had remarked on the
Lord's Supper that "the sincere Churchman derived a great blessing from
joining in that particular service." When Booth pressed Benson further
on "whether this blessing was not consequent upon the exercise of faith
in the sacrifice of the Cross which it set forth," and whether this blessing
"could be traced to the fact that a peculiar measure of faith and devotion
was called forth by that particular ceremonial," he recorded Benson's
remark, "that apart from any such special exercises on the part of the
worshipper, God, he thought, had connected a special impartation of
His presence and blessing with this particular service."[105]

Archbishop Thomson, on the other hand, in his 1853 Bampton
Lectures, made clear his view that "a sacrament is an act in which spiritual
blessings are at once represented by and conferred through some visible
thing, according to a positive intuition of God, to those who receive it
by faith."[106] They were "not magical but moral; the sacraments *confer* the
grace of God, they do not *contain* it; they are channels, not fountains.

---

103. Booth, "The General's New Year Address to Officers," 4, col. 3.

104. Cited in Begbie, *Life of William Booth*, 1:468.

105. Ibid., 2:35–36.

106. Thomson, *The Atoning work of God*, 226.

Nor are they the sole or the peculiar means of conveying to believers the effects of our Lord's Incarnation."[107] His biographer confirms that "the sacrament occupied quite a secondary place in his conception of the duties and privileges of the Christian life. It was not the Church's central act of worship, the *sine qua non* of all her devotions."[108]

There is little evidence, in early Salvationist accounts of the sacraments, of a nuanced understanding of differing sacramental theologies within the church. Catherine Booth and George Scott Railton raised the strongest objections to them. Bramwell recalled his mother's deep misgivings and suggested that "her knowledge of the low tone of spiritual life in the Churches . . . made her look with dread upon the possibility that our people, most of whom were very ignorant and simple, might come in time to lean upon some outward ceremonial instead of upon the work of the Holy Spirit as witnessed in a change of heart and life,"[109] a view forcibly expressed in one of her sermons:

> Another mock salvation is presented in the shape of *ceremonies and sacraments*. These were only intended as outward signs of an inward spiritual reality, whereas men are taught that by going through them or partaking of them, they are to be saved . . . What an inveterate tendency there is in the human heart to trust in outward forms, instead of seeking the inward grace! And where this is the case, what a hindrance, rather than help, have these forms proved to the growth, nay, to the very existence, of that spiritual life which constitutes the real and only force of Christian experience![110]

Begbie suggested, however, that Railton was the more extreme of the two:

> He had at his side young men . . . whose impatience with anything in the nature of priest-craft, magic, or sacerdotalism, was akin to passion. They were reformers . . . with little but disdain for traditionalism . . . For George Railton . . . there was only one baptism—the baptism of the Holy Ghost; only one communion

107. Ibid., 227.

108. Kirk-Smith, *William Thomson*, 33.

109. Booth, *Echoes and Memories*, 202.

110. Booth, *Popular Christianity*, 42.

with Christ—the communion of a cleansed heart devoted to his service.[111]

Bramwell Booth confirmed that his mother, whilst not feeling "so strongly as Railton on the subject,"[112] was nevertheless the leading influence.[113] Together they encouraged Booth to focus on the priority of holiness revivalism, the "inward spiritual reality" and the "communion of a cleansed heart" over the outward ceremonial of sacraments, unwilling as they were to believe that the two could successfully combine. Bramwell spoke of his mother's "deep horror of anything which might tend to substitute in the minds of the people some outward act or compliance for the fruits of practical Holiness."[114] This, together with his father's "utilitarian" approach "particularly as related to questions not necessary to Salvation," won the day, and Bramwell, reluctantly, "completely concurred in the decision to which the Founder had come."[115] If sacraments were not essential to salvation, they were equally not essential to The Salvation Army.

This did not signal a completely dualistic "spiritualization" of Salvationist faith, for dramatic new symbols substituted for the loss of water, bread and wine. With regard to conversion, the "mercy seat" or "penitent form," an aggressive method of calling sinners to the condition of repentance, developed from holiness revivalism. The drum substituted as a penitent form in "open-air" meetings, where adult conversion was perceived as an instant and dramatic experience, far removed from the sprinkling of water on babies. Bramwell admitted that in the decision to abandon infant baptism, "I do not think that any of us were much troubled."[116] Infant baptism had been assumed in the Christian Mission from what Booth described as his "sixteen years' experience as a Methodist minister," but his experience in establishing mission work amongst the abject poverty and debauchery of London in the pragmatic mode of holiness revivalism had clearly been instructive for he admitted

---

111. Begbie, *Life of William Booth*, 1:461.

112. Booth, *Echoes and Memories*, 204.

113. Ibid., 202.

114. Ibid., 203–4.

115. Ibid.

116. Ibid., 201.

that, "during those years we have had to unlearn and learn a great deal."[117] Catherine was more expansive:

> Oh the thousands of souls who are resting their hopes of salvation on the fact that they have been baptised, not only such as believe in the palpable delusion of baptismal regeneration, but amongst ordinary church and chapel going people. As I look at our Army congregations in Rinks, Theatres, and other similar places, and note the signs of sin, debauchery, and crime on many of their faces, I say to myself, I suppose all these people have been baptised; but I do not think there are many thieves, or harlots, or drunkards, or openly immoral people who claim baptismal regeneration. Thank God! It is only genteel sinners who can bring themselves to believe in such a palpable sham.[118]

Referring to the 1859 revival in Ireland Catherine remarked, "When I was in Ireland, some of the oldest and most experienced Christians who took part in that great revival some twenty-five years ago told me that a great proportion of the results of that wonderful work of God were lost, in consequence of a controversy about water baptism."[119] David Bebbington confirms that for evangelicals, the relation of baptism to conversion "probably qualified as the chief theological controversy of the early and mid-nineteenth century,"[120] due to the Church of England's *Book of Common Prayer* declaring at the end of the baptismal ceremony that an infant was regenerate and the Catechism's further insistence that baptism was the occasion of new birth. In this respect, any suggestion that adult baptism be instituted in place of infant baptism was likely to be equally controversial.

Booth confirmed the priority of his holiness revivalism when he informed his officers in 1882 that "there is one baptism on which we are all agreed—the one baptism of the Bible—that is the baptism of the Holy Ghost, of which baptism John spoke as vastly superior and far more important than the baptism of water ... be sure you insist upon that baptism."[121] As an alternative to infant baptism, he published a Service of Dedication in which "Soldiers can introduce their children to the Army,"

---

117. Booth, "What Is The Salvation Army?," 175.

118. Booth, *Popular Christianity,* 42.

119. Ibid., 46.

120. Bebbington, *Evangelicalism in Modern Britain,* 9.

121. Booth, "The General's New Year Address to Officers," 4, col. 3.

but only on the basis that they "explain it to the parents, and show them that unless they are willing to bring up their children as Soldiers and Officers in the Army, they cannot have any part in it."[122]

Equally, where water baptism ironically gave way to the dramatic use of the mercy seat as an individual symbol of God's immediacy, and to baptism in the Holy Spirit, so in sustaining the Christian life, the Lord's Supper was overshadowed by the dramatic nature of the Holiness meeting, as events at the 1878 war congress demonstrate:

> The usual intoxicating wine not having been prepared for sacrament, we managed uncommonly well with water, and in fact everybody seemed to have got into a condition in which outward circumstances are scarcely noticed, and the soul feasts on God, no matter what passes outside. We had been drinking the best wine for hours.[123]

Not only does this report confirm the usual practice of observing the Lord's Supper, but that it was most often associated with the Holiness meeting and all-night prayer meeting. On this occasion the *Christian Mission Magazine* reported that:

> Big men, as well as women, fell to the ground, lay there for some time as if dead, overwhelmed with the Power from on High . . . to confound the wicked one and to raise many of His people into such righteousness and peace and joy in the Holy Ghost as they never had before, and thousands if not millions, of souls will have to rejoice for ever over blessings received by them through the instrumentality of those who were sanctified . . . between the 8th and 9th of August, 1878.[124]

Moving from wine to water was incidental and ultimately irrelevant to what they perceived as the experience of the far more immediate and powerful reality of the transforming work of the Holy Spirit, which did not depend upon the observance. The move to no physical elements was incidental within the context of the holiness meeting, where ironically, the individual was encouraged to kneel at the Holiness table to be symbolically consecrated upon God's altar and to receive the "blessing of holiness." The sacraments became expendable church tradition within

---

122. Ibid.

123. *The Christian Mission Magazine*, September 1878, 252.

124. Ibid.

the context of holiness revivalism's aggressive means and measures, and the immediacy of God's grace.

In *Sacraments and the Salvation Army,* David Rightmire argues that the Booths abandoned baptism and the Lord's Supper as traditionally prescribed sacraments, yet substituted the new methods to visibly demonstrate the importance of the sacramental life:

> Rather than viewing the sacraments as "dramatic symbols" capable of mediating the presence of Christ in any real sense, the individual believer is the locus of the incarnation, mediating the Spirit of Christ as a "parable in action." Thus, the shift in thought is away from any objective understanding of sacramental efficacy to a subjective expression of divine action in sacramental living. The "husk" of material signification is abandoned for the "kernel" of spiritual reality . . . and expressed sacramentally to the world by the power of his Spirit.[125]

Here lay the origins of what has only relatively recently been developed in The Salvation Army as an understanding of the sacramental life, to be explored in the next chapter. Rightmire claims that the implicit "theological rationale for such a position [the sacramental life] was never systematically developed by William Booth."[126] Phoebe Palmer's "altar phraseology'" had assisted the Booths in focussing upon the individual human life consecrated upon God's altar, through a symbolic kneeling at the mercy seat or the holiness table, rather than focussing upon the consecrated communal elements of bread and wine. In the loss of the physical elements of water, bread and wine, Booth's army lost the signs and symbols of an objective theological focus on God's work of grace in God's community, for the subjective and individualistic symbol of the consecrated saint. Booth illustrates this in his remark that:

> Neither water, sacraments, church services nor Salvation Army methods will save you without a living, inward change of heart and a living active faith and communion with God . . . and an active, positive consecration of yourself and all you have got to help Him who hung upon the cross to fill the world with salvation and bring lost sinners to His feet.[127]

---

125. Rightmire, *Sacraments and the Salvation Army,* 196f .

126. Ibid., 205.

127. Sandall, *The History of the Salvation Army,* 2:131.

The Sacraments and Pragmatic Considerations

Booth's underlying theological assumptions were based on a subjective and individualistic focus on the conditional immediacy of God's justifying and entirely sanctifying grace. He was, therefore, pragmatically able to abandon the objective focus which the sacraments gave to God's grace in the face of the divisions they created in the Victorian church. The Church of England was in open warfare over the place of ritual, form, and sacrament. The Ritualists were an extreme response to the "Oxford movement," and made even the Tractarians feel uneasy. Outlining the difficulties which the Ritualists made for both Archbishops Thomson (York) and Tait (Canterbury), and recognizing the extremity of their position, Marsh comments that "the passionate determination with which ritualists upheld their practices made Pusey suspect that they were motivated by ideals different from the Oxford Movement . . . and whereas Tractarians made much of the need to obey the consecrated leaders of the Church, ritualists defied all constituted authority in the Church of England and adopted whatever rites appealed to them."[128]

The birth of The Salvation Army and Booth's subsequent reflection on the place of sacraments fell directly within this larger cauldron of argument and suspicion. It spilled over into his movement, made up of people from a variety of denominational backgrounds and none. His son, Bramwell, remarked that he "saw something at this time of the High Church party in the Church of England, and, though an outsider, I deplored, with some of the Church's own best men, the tendency of that movement to a kind of materialism—the reliance, that is, upon outward and visible signs which so easily become substitutes for inward and spiritual grace."[129]

The burden of this dissension and strife fell heavily upon Archbishop Tait, who at the end of 1882 was close to death. Bishop Benson, who was to succeed Tait, wrote to Randall Davidson, Tait's secretary, about this trouble and suggested, "I can only ask him to feel that his prayers and efforts for Peace in the Church cannot be in vain, and that many feel that while, in his illness he *is shut* out from the counselling which *all—(all of all parties,* I never saw anything like it) were looking to him for, yet they think that his interceding is only counselling in perhaps a higher and

---

128. Marsh, *The Victorian Church in Decline,* 117.

129. Booth, *Echoes and Memories,* 204.

more powerful way." This lack of peace in the church impacted upon the internal life of The Salvation Army, where holiness revivalism's emphasis upon the priesthood of all believers disallowed a concept of a "separate priesthood," or of Episcopal ordination.

Philip Needham suggests that "because laymen with leadership ability were often elevated to officer rank and given appointments with little if any formal training, many officers were not equipped to administer sacraments."[130] Further to this the Army commissioned women officers with equal ministerial responsibility to men, and the idea of women administering the sacraments was unthinkable in Victorian Britain. Even within its own ranks some absented themselves when women administered the sacraments, taking their cue from wider church tradition. Booth, so adept at translating the Christian faith into popular culture, found it increasingly difficult to imagine how this church tradition could be adequately translated into his Army's holiness revivalism.

Whilst at Bishop Benson's suggestion whole Salvation Army Corps were encouraged to go to the local Anglican parish church for communion,[131] this created difficulties. A practical consideration was the serving of alcoholic communion wine in Anglican churches to converted alcoholics. Booth was also alarmed by the response that was sometimes met at the parish church. Bramwell recalled that "fearing opposition of their 'respectable' parishioners" the local clergy "arranged that The Salvation Army visits should be in the night, and as one consequence large crowds generally attended."[132] The reaction of Archbishop Thomson's biographer to this practise illustrates the dissension it provoked:

> A striking illustration of Thomson's doctrine of the Church can be seen in his allowing the indiscriminate admission of 400 Salvationists to Holy Communion at St. Paul's Church, York, early in 1882 ... The Salvationists, gathered chiefly from the most ignorant class of society, had received no instruction in Holy Communion, many were probably unconfirmed and without a desire to be confirmed, and some probably had not even been

130. Needham, *Community In Mission,* 24.

131. For Bishop Benson's letter requesting this see Begbie, *Life of William Booth,* 1:465.

132. Booth, *Echoes and Memories,* 206.

baptised. There could surely be no doubt that a grave scandal had been caused.[133]

Bramwell reported that certain clergy took matters into their own hands,

> publicly announcing their refusal to administer the communion to those who had not been "confirmed" according to the Church of England system. As most of our people, though living godly lives, had not been confirmed, nor, for that matter, their forbears either, the Founder saw that another line of division was likely to develop.[134]

William Booth intimated that some clergy "recommended that that portion of our people who had not been confirmed should go to the dissenters for the ordinance, while the portion who had been confirmed should go to the Church,"[135] and complained that this "would have divided us at the very door of the Church."[136] Booth had anticipated difficulties, but nothing quite so divisive. When Bishop Benson and Cannon Westcott visited him at his office in Queen Victoria Street in May 1882, and requested "the regular attendance by each Corps at the Parish Church" even allowing "for the Army to march up to the Church-doors with bands playing and banners flying," he explained the practical cultural difficulties of a "High Ritual form of service" where

> the bulk of our people would be found totally ignorant of the supposed benefits flowing out of the use of images, candles, crucifixes, vestments, or of almost any of the numerous forms and ceremonials practised in many churches, or they would be found very strongly opposed to them.[137]

In view of his conviction of God's immediacy, conditional upon an individual's entire consecration upon God's altar, and in face of potential division that might tear his fledgling movement apart, Booth felt able to pragmatically retreat from the outward observance of baptism and the Lord's Supper, to focus upon the inward reality, ironically through the use of new visible symbols that his military metaphor afforded.

---

133. Kirk-Smith, *William Thomson*, 32.

134. Booth, *Echoes and Memories*, 206.

135. Booth, "The General's New Year Address to Officers," 4, col. 3.

136. Ibid.

137. Cited in Begbie, *Life of William Booth*, 2:35.

The Sacraments and the Church

Booth's third rationale related to his explicit denial that The Salvation Army intended to be a church. He informed his officers:

> A clergyman said, without being contradicted, that it is evident that the Army is not a Church. That to be a Church there must be the exercise of the sacramental functions, which evidently are not duly appreciated, anyway which are not generally practised by the Army. We are evidently getting further away from the ordinary idea of a Church every day.[138]

Booth's tone suggested he was less than convinced by this clergyman's theology of the Church. There is no evidence as to whether he knew, for example, of either the Augsburg Confession[139] or Calvin's marks of the Church.[140] He implicitly appeared to be re-conceiving the Church through the "experimental" theology and pragmatism of holiness revivalism's aggressive methods, in which sacraments were not required. As he understood them, they appeared to be culturally removed from the poor that he was ministering to, and hopelessly compromised as unifying practices. He was, however, being scrutinized by the Church of England's Salvation Army committee. Randall Davidson had challenged him directly:

> I have precluded myself from reference even to so vital a point as the Army's position with respect to the sacraments of Christ. That question, about which there seems still to be much uncertainty in the Army's councils, must be dealt with soon, and firmly, if the Church is to extend active sympathy to the Army as a whole.[141]

Bishop Benson explained to Booth that the sacraments were essential to the nature and life of the Church, and that since "it is indeed patent that an *Army* is not a whole *Kingdom*—that soldiers have citizens for their object and care—and that the building up of themselves as citizens is a duty which it is not safe for them to forget," it would therefore be essential for the Salvationists to participate in these sacraments, for "it is for her [the Church] impossible to feel that what I have called citi-

---

138. Ibid.
139. See Bettenson, *Documents of the Christian Church*, 295.
140. Calvin, *Institutes of the Christian Religion*, 2:1023.
141. Davidson, "The Methods of the Salvation Army," 199.

zenship can be complete without them."[142] In this respect Benson, with his view of apostolic succession and priestly orders, was pleased that Booth had given him the assurance that he would not set up a rival and sectarian sacramental system:

> I am able to understand how the call you have to make to the dechristianised and degraded may be conducted by you without express teaching on those Institutions, and rejoice that you so firmly hold that it is no business or part of your own system to administer them. Here is to be recognised an immense difference between the Salvation Army and the sects which have adopted an imitation of the Sacramental system.[143]

Booth found himself caught between Davidson's insistence that he value the sacraments, Benson's Episcopal request for him to send his soldiers to the Church of England, a practice that proved so controversial, and significant differences of opinion within his own ranks that reflected the wider division of the Church. Believing fundamentally that they were not essential to his mission, and in view of the prevailing wisdom that he could not be a church without them, he appears to have formally accepted a judgement that consolidated his organisation as an Army, and not a Church. Benson implored him further that his followers, some of whom were undoubtedly Anglicans "should not be debarred by compulsory arrangements of your own from the partaking of the Communion with their brethren . . . not that you should make *positive* arrangements for the communicating of your people, but that counter arrangements should not be made which would render their life of communion impossible."[144] Booth finally instructed his officers to "not prohibit our own people in any shape or form from taking the Sacraments . . . the churches and chapels all round about will welcome you for this, but in our own ranks let us be united, and go on our own way, and mind our own business."[145] Whether or not he held the sacraments to be integral to a doctrine of the Church, Booth confirmed to his officers, that they would be discontinued in The Salvation Army: "It seems as if a voice from Heaven had said, and is still saying, that we are

---

142. Begbie, *Life of William Booth*, 1:466.

143. Ibid.

144. Ibid., 467.

145. Booth, "The General's New Year Address to Officers," 4, col. 3.

to be AN ARMY, *separate from, going before, coming after, and all round about the various existing Churches.*"[146]

Nonetheless, the Booths gave no thought to the ecclesiological significance of baptism and the Lord's Supper. In emphasizing the enjoyment of the spiritual reality without the outward physical observance of sacraments, they were influenced by the Society of Friends, whose views, as expressed by Robert Barclay, whom Bramwell Booth read, owed some debt to Ulrich Zwingli (1484–1531).[147] In his *Commentary on True and False Religion*, Zwingli refuted in turn what he saw as the Roman Catholic, Lutheran and Anabaptist view of the sacraments and wished that "this word 'sacrament' had never been adopted by the Germans without being translated into German." He concluded that "a sacrament is nothing else than an initiatory ceremony or pledging."[148] Sacraments could not "free the conscience from sin," it was not true that "when you perform the sacrament outwardly a purification is certainly performed inwardly" and nor are they given "for the purpose of rendering the recipient sure that what is signified by the sacrament has now been accomplished."[149] On the other hand, unlike the Quakers or Salvationists, Zwingli insisted that their initiatory character was still essential to the church: "The sacraments are, then, signs or ceremonials . . . by which a man proves to the Church that he either aims to be, or is, a soldier of Christ, and which inform the whole Church rather than yourself of your faith."[150] Zwingli concluded:

> In Baptism we receive a token that we are to fashion our lives according to the rule of Christ; by the Lord's Supper we give proof that we trust in the death of Christ, glad and thankful to be in that company which give thanks to the Lord for the blessing of redemption which He freely gave us by dying for us.[151]

Booth gave no indication that he knew of Zwingli's theology, yet he certainly overruled his allegiance to Wesley, who, in the matter of Christian perfection instructed,

146. Ibid.

147. See in particular Barclay and Zwingli on the Latin translation of "sacramentum" for mystery (Eph 5:32) in Zwingli, *Commentary*, 180f.; Barclay, *An Apology*, 411.

148. Zwingli, *Commentary*, 181.

149. Ibid., 179.

150. Ibid., 184.

151. Ibid.

> that not only babes in Christ . . . but those who are "grown up into perfect men," are indispensably obliged, as often as they have opportunity, "to eat bread and drink wine in remembrance of Him" . . . [for] . . . there is no perfection in this life, which implies any dispensation from attending all the ordinances of God.[152]

The Sacraments and the Bible

The Booths perceived holiness revivalism to be an obedient response to scripture, in the making of saints who were entirely sanctified or fully saved. Their motto, "Blood and Fire," at the centre of their tricolored flag, was thoroughly Trinitarian in its focus upon the Father's sending of the Son, the sacrificial atoning and cleansing of Christ's shed blood and the purifying of the Holy Spirit's fire. Nevertheless, their subjective and individualistic theology of God's immediacy could not conceive how baptism and the Lord's Supper could be interpreted from scripture as commands.[153] Their insistence upon new aggressive means and methods interpreted these time honoured actions as expendable church tradition. Booth informed his officers and soldiers:

> Let us remember him who died for us continually. Let us remember His love every hour of our lives, and continually feed on Him—not on Sundays only, and then forget Him all the week, but let us by faith eat his flesh and drink His blood continually.[154]

Booth interpreted the words of John's Gospel non-sacramentally. When asked in 1895 by Sir Henry Lunn, if he substituted anything for the sacraments, he replied, "only so far . . . as to urge upon our Soldiers in every meal they take to remember, as they break the bread, the broken body of our Lord, and as they drink the cup, His shed blood; and every time they wash the body to remember that the soul can only be cleansed by the purifying Blood of Christ."[155] His "spiritualised" holiness revivalism instinctively encouraged him to take baptism and the Lord's Supper

---

152. Wesley, *The Works of the Rev. John Wesley,* 383.

153. This was unusual in that Booth had a high view of Scripture whilst not fundamentalist. See Booth, "What Do We Mean by Inspiration?," 12–14. See also Cunningham, "The Army's Attitude," 163–69.

154. Booth, "The General's New Year Address to Officers," 4, col. 3. Booth is clearly referring to a non-sacramental interpretation of John 6:55, 56.

155. Cited in Begbie, *Life of William Booth,* 1:469.

out of the sanctuary and into the everyday lives of his soldiers, who were, as consecrated living sacrifices, continually laid upon Christ's altar. He wrote to Salvationists explaining that Paul's words "whether therefore ye eat, or drink, or whatsoever ye do, do all to the glory of God [1 Cor 10:31 AV]," meant that "every meal we partake of will become a sacrament, and every duty we perform will be an act of religion, and every day we live will be a sacred day."[156] He asked his officers:

> Are you one with us in the methods and measures we employ; or
> are you still bound hand or foot by the traditions and usages of
> the elders? . . . some of you have grown up amidst the influence
> of forms and ceremonies, which however useful they may be, or
> may have been in other circumstances, only edge in and bar us
> out from the work we want to accomplish.[157]

Anticipating their enquiry as to the authority upon which he relinquished the Church's interpretation of a Biblical command for these practices, Booth confirmed that:

> I cannot accept any obligation as binding upon my conscience,
> neither will I seek to bind any upon yours, to do, or believe, or
> teach anything for which *authority cannot be furnished from the
> Word of God*, or which God Himself does not reveal to us by His
> Spirit, as our present duty to Him or to our generation.[158]

In this respect both he and his son Bramwell suggested, following Barclay, that baptism and the Lord's Supper should be treated in the same way that the church had treated the apparent command of Christ to wash one another's feet in John's gospel.[159] Booth re-iterated the provisional nature of his decision in 1895, when he suggested to Sir Henry Lunn "that this with us is not a settled question," but he never reversed it.[160]

The next chapter will examine contemporary Salvationist reflection on ecclesiology, in which the question will be asked as to whether the Army's holiness revivalist origins and the dramatic imagery and symbolism that it precipitated, in effect created a new ritualism that it had

156. Booth, *Letters to Salvationists on Religion for Every Day*, 1:102.

157. Booth, "The General's New Year Address to Officers," 4, col. 3.

158. Ibid.

159. See Begbie, *Life of William Booth*, 1:468; Booth, *Echoes and Memories*, 205–8; McKinley, "Quaker Influence," 47–56.

160. Begbie, *Life of William Booth*, 1:469. Begbie indicates that Booth remained unsure of his decision until the end. See ibid., 1:201, 461–64.

sought to avoid. Frances Power Cobbe, for example, complained of "the Ritualists, who, while instituting a superfluity of corporeal demonstrations of reverence in worship, have yet, it is to be feared, done somewhat to distract, by 'histrionic' services and the multiplicity of genuflexions, the aim of worshippers from that inward prostration of spirit which Evangelicalism sought alone." Yet she lamented that "far beyond all these, at the furthest swing of the pendulum, we now behold parading our streets the Salvation Army, amongst whom scarcely a vestige of religious awe, or even of decorum in touching things reverenced by their neighbours, can be traced."[161]

From another perspective, Randall Davidson observed "what—for want of a better term—may be called the *ritualism* of the Army, including under that name the adoption of military titles and uniforms, the use of banners and brass bands, and the purposely obtrusive character of its placards and hand-bills."[162] In this respect, Salvationists should reflect on whether Booth's lack of an objective theological compass, aggressively eliminated ritual, form and tradition, only to replace them with methods that were substitutes, that have become as ritualistic and traditionalistic as he viewed the High Church party of his own day. This will be taken up in the next chapter, and discussed further in dialogue with Karl Barth.

The Salvation Army as a quasi-Religious Order in the Church?

William Booth and Catherine, who died prematurely in 1890, led the transition of a relatively small holiness revivalist Christian mission that rapidly extended beyond London's borders, to become a remarkable, international, highly visible and controversial, non-sacramental Christian military organization, The Salvation Army, in a few short years. Its aggressive expression of Christianity, adapted to the task of evangelizing Britain's urban poor, developed an autocratic and hierarchical movement of energetic, colorful, passionate and disciplined, women and men, officers and soldiers, that both shocked and excited many within Victorian society. The Church of England was encouraged by its clergymen to engage with the movement, possibly to harness its rich potential for reaching the poor, possibly to help curb its excesses. Nevertheless,

161. Cobbe, "The Last Revival," 187.
162. Davidson, "The Methods of the Salvation Army," 191.

what were people to make of this Army? What was the nature of this movement in relation to the Church?

Whilst unwilling to be identified as *a* church, both William and Catherine Booth were clear about The Salvation Army's place within the wider church. Mention has already been made of their reluctance to be sectarian in their ministry. Booth informed Archbishop Tait that "we think that we have a claim upon your sympathy, because we do not seek to justify our existence, by finding fault with you."[163] Equally Catherine was clear that "we are one in aim with the Churches," and therefore working in partnership, especially in view of the reality that "the Churches of this land . . . are not keeping pace by a long way with the increase of the population, much less overtaking the lapsed multitudes beyond."[164] In this respect, "surely everybody who believes in any kind of religion, must see the awful necessity for some extraneous and irregular agency, adapted to reach this continent of dark, indifferent, infidel souls."[165] She went as far as to suggest that their missionary endeavor was such that "no people preceding us, so far as Church history shows, have ever conceived of a people who have a more comprehensive idea of their responsibility, both as individuals and as an organization, than ever existed in the world before."[166] This was a huge and unsubstantiated claim, but illustrates her belief that however "irregular," the Army was a special missionary service working within and alongside the churches, and worthy of "donations and subscriptions from the Christian public towards such a movement."[167] Even the Archbishop of Canterbury made a much celebrated donation to this cause.[168] Their son and second General, Bramwell, when he reflected on the negotiations held with the Church of England was adamant that "of this, the Great Church of the Living God, we claim, and have ever claimed, that we of The Salvation Army are an integral part and element—a living fruit-bearing branch in the True Vine."[169]

---

163. Booth, *The Salvation Army in Relation to Church and State*, 28.

164. Ibid., 40.

165. Ibid., 27.

166. Ibid., 31.

167. Ibid., 14.

168. Begbie, *Life of William Booth*, 2:11.

169. Booth, *Echoes and Memories*, 79.

In relation to questions raised about The Salvation Army's relation to the churches, Booth informed his officers:

> We answer, "What is your attitude towards the 'Fire Brigade?' or if you live on the sea coast, what is your attitude towards the 'Lifeboat crew?' or, again, we might say, what is your attitude towards the Volunteers in the killing armies? You cheer them on, encourage them, subscribe to their funds, go to their assemblages and bless them." We say, "DO THE SAME WITH US."[170]

Booth was in the process of conceiving and executing a highly disciplined, militarized, and specialist Christian force of "crack troops," a special service within the Church, such as he envisaged in his social reform plan *In Darkest England and the Way Out*. In terms of his non-denominational, postmillennial vision of the capacity for The Salvation Army to usher in the millennial reign of Christ, he believed that he was "warned by the failure of John Wesley in maintaining his unsectarian position," and was "striving to avoid what we think were his mistakes."[171] In this respect he believed that the rigorous nature of membership of the Army was a safeguard against schismatic sectarianism. "Instead of refusing to complete our organisation, we strive to perfect it more and more, making it, however, step by step, more exacting on all who join, so as to exclude all but real soldiers, leaving to the Churches all who wish mere church life."[172]

Booth expressed his desire not to discount the church, to be divisive or competitive, but to raise a special force to "spread far and wide a spirit of love and hearty co-operation that will do much to lessen the dividing walls of sectarianism."[173] His colleague, Railton, drew the comparison with a religious order: "we have got an organisation . . . formed of people whose devotion, determination and confidence at least equal that of the Jesuits."[174] It was an observation that did not escape the attention of others. Frances Power Cobbe conceded that "first among the elements of

---

170. Booth, "The General's New Year Address to Officers," 4, col. 3.

171. Booth, "What is the Salvation Army?," 175.

172. Ibid., 181.

173. Ibid., 182.

174. Sandall, *The History of The Salvation Army*, 1:237. See also The Salvation Army, *The Salvation War 1884*, 113, in which comparisons with the Jesuits were also rejected, in that "the Army is not, and could never be made a system of slavery to individual rulers."

success is the organization of the 'Army,' which combines the inspiriting military pattern with the rigid discipline and complete autocracy of the great monastic orders," for "General Booth's authority more nearly resembles, I believe, that of a General of the Jesuits or Franciscans, than that of Sir Garnet Wolseley or Sir Evelyn Wood."[175]

In reality The Salvation Army could potentially have become a Religious Order within the Anglican Church if there had been the will on both sides, neither possessing the imagination to surmount the perceived obstacles to such an arrangement. H. B. Workman was critical in his study, *The Evolution of the Monastic Ideal*, of the seeming inability of Protestants to embrace new religious movements. He suggested, that "the Church of Rome would have used Wesley and Booth to found new Orders within herself, whose zeal and enthusiasm would have strengthened rather than weakened the church."[176] On the other hand, the Anglican Church did embrace a number of movements or religious orders in the nineteenth century, and these formed the basis of Michael Hill's study of Weber's concept of the religious *virtuoso*, in which "Virtuoso religion typically refers back to a strongly-valued source of tradition which it restates in its pristine purity and seeks to emulate by means of ethical rigorism."[177]

Hill compared the religious order and the sect, and found many parallels "especially in the area of high commitment and perfectionism," but primarily differentiated them on the grounds that "the sect internalizes its own authority, while religious orders derive their authority ultimately from the parent church."[178] In this respect, having established itself as a completely autonomous movement, The Salvation Army was classified sociologically in Bryan Wilson's analysis of sectarian patterns, as a specific example of a "conversionist" sect[179] that would normally develop into a denomination within one generation. It was possible that this process could be delayed, since "such development depended on the standards of admission imposed by the sect, the previous rigour with which children had been kept separate from the world, and on the point at which a balance was struck between the natural desire of parents to

175. Cobbe, "The Last Revival," 183.
176. Workman, *The Evolution of the Monastic Ideal*, 334.
177. Hill, *The Religious Order*, 3.
178. Ibid., 7.
179. Wilson, *Patterns of Sectarianism*, 27.

have their children included in salvation and their awareness of the community view that any sort of salvation depends on the maintenance of doctrinal and moral standards."[180]

Roland Robertson studied The Salvation Army in the 1960s and concluded that it was "an established sect—a movement which from an essentially sectarian base has, with modifications, persisted well beyond its first generation of members, while retaining sufficient of its pristine characteristics to qualify as a sect."[181] In his final conclusion he did suggest, however, that "whilst it is most appropriate to regard the movement as an established sect, it is also in some respects an order within Anglicanism."[182] Clearly this suggestion is preposterous in relation to any formal link with the Church of England being denied in 1882. Nevertheless, in view of Hill's study drawing close parallels in sociological terms between sects and religious orders, there is some merit in suggesting, that in denying he was sectarian in founding a new church organization, and whilst not formally attached to a parent church, Booth was initially and implicitly attempting to project his Army as a quasi-missionary religious order and a special service within the wider church.

In his study, Hill described ten features of the ideal type of order based on what he perceived to be historically consistent, one of which suggested that the Order, "though originally a lay movement, exists only as part of the church but retains a degree of moral and organisational autonomy."[183] This does appear on the face of it to be what Booth rejected, for he admits that when Bishop Benson and Canon Westcott visited him to discuss some kind of Union, "nothing was asked beyond an open recognition of our connection with the Church, and the regular attendance by each Corps at the Parish Church, or at an authorized service in some other consecrated building."[184] These potential arrangements proved problematic, as already demonstrated. Nonetheless, Booth's attitude was not typically sectarian. Hill makes the comparison when he comments that, while sects very consciously see themselves as an elect 'remnant' set apart from the '*massa damnata*' of the rest of humanity, the religious order must include among the ranks of the potentially saved the ordinary

180. Ibid., 38.

181. Robertson, "The Salvation Army," 56.

182. Ibid., 105.

183. Hill, *The Religious Order*, 29.

184. Cited in Begbie, *Life of William Booth*, 2:34.

lay members of the wider church."[185] Equally Wilson describes the sect as "hostile or indifferent to the secular society and to the state."[186]

Whilst The Salvation Army, in its holiness teaching and strict terms of membership, encouraged its members, like religious orders, to be very separate from society, there is evidence that under Booth's leadership the movement was far more engaged with and referential to both the Church and the State, than is the general characterisation of sects. It is hard to imagine why Booth would have marched his troops to the local Anglican parish church if he was fundamentally hostile or even indifferent. Equally, Robertson was willing to admit that, in relation to the state, there was a "central paradox of the Army—for the welfare work, which it has undertaken from the time of the soup kitchens of the incipient phase through the ambitious schemes launched as a consequence of the Darkest England programme, has constituted its main claim to indispensability" and through this work, "has gained its respect, and the secular honours which its leaders have been accorded." [187]

If there was no significant hostility in Booth's positive appreciation of the role of the Church and the State, then two further insights offered by Hill on the nature of *virtuoso* religion within religious orders, have some bearing on The Salvation Army. He says that "the individual member of a religious order is basically seeking personal perfection, whether such perfection is defined in terms of individual or social goals or of an active or contemplative life."[188] The Army's Wesleyan emphasis on Christian perfection in its aggressive holiness revivalism has already been documented. When this is combined with Hill's third insight that "the order demands considerably more obedience from its members than the wider church demands from either its lay members or its clergy,"[189] an interesting correlation emerges. The emphasis on entire sanctification, coupled with a developing military organization and discipline, constitute two integral features of the Army that correlate with Hill's insight that both a search for perfection and a level of obedience and sacrificial commitment are found within Orders.

185. Hill, *The Religious Order*, 67.

186. Wilson, *Patterns of Sectarianism*, 24.

187. Robertson, "The Salvation Army," 55.

188. Hill, *The Religious Order*, 51.

189. Ibid., 40.

Ultimately, the ecclesial identity of Booth's Salvation Army was an enigmatic legacy that he left subsequent generations to grapple with. Clearly it was an autonomous Christian army, and therefore not technically a religious order. Nevertheless, there was something equivocal about the Booths' ability to imply that it was both attempting to represent the Church and yet not *a* church. Perhaps his clearest statement came in 1894:

> The Salvation Army is not inferior in spiritual character to any Christian organization in existence. We are in no wise dependent on the Church . . . If it perished off the face of the earth tomorrow we should be just as efficient for the discharge of the duties we owe to men as we are today . . . We are, I consider, equal every way and everywhere to any other Christian organization on the face of the earth (i) in spiritual authority, (ii) in spiritual intelligence, (iii) in spiritual functions. We hold "the keys" as truly as any Church in existence.[190]

In this statement lay the seeds of what eventually emerged as a Christian denomination that currently explains its identity as a Christian Church, and will be the subject of the next chapter. However, in view of Booth's initial insistent denials that it was such a church, denials that continued for many decades beyond his death, there is value in Salvationists reflecting upon the nature of Booth's militant, aggressive and disciplined troops as maintaining pristine characteristics of the Church in mission, above and beyond those that were expected within the life of the churches. Railton admitted that "owing to our allegiance to this rigid military system, we are losing almost every year evangelists, as well as people, who, having lost their first love, begin to hanker after the 'rights', 'privileges', 'comforts', 'teaching' or 'respectability' of the churches."[191] Salvationists understood that there was a place for the Church, but were equally clear that in terms of aggressive holiness revivalism and its essential mission to see women and men fully saved and engaged in fully saving others, there was a legitimate place for a *virtuoso* special service within the Church. Such was the passion of this single-minded focus on full salvation that the means justified the end. Even the sacraments, seen by most as essential to the nature of the Church, were expendable in pursuit of this goal.

190. Cited in Booth, *Echoes and Memories*, 82.
191. Railton, *Heathen England*, 3rd ed., 144.

Conclusion

It must be concluded, therefore, that the Booths' holiness revivalism ultimately combined two ecclesial strands. In short, holiness revivalism inspired an aggressive Christian mission that in the culture of Victorian Britain, under the leadership of the Booths, logically led to an autocratic and disciplined missionary army; an army that, in its implementation of the standards and disciplines of practical holiness, called women and men to a special service within the church that required obedience and rules of behavior beyond the requirements of the churches. This development held in tension a non-denominational "higher life" movement, affirming a collegiate sense of lay participation and initiative in Christian mission, as outlined in chapter one, with the very specific denominational identity of The Salvation Army as an autocratic and increasingly clericalized hierarchy, ruling over the regulated and disciplined lifestyle of the Soldier. At the root of both these strands of mission and army, however, were the individualistic and subjective tendencies that emerged from the Booths' early focus on what they articulated as the conditional immediacy of God's entirely sanctifying grace or full salvation. In the midst of exponential international growth, little theological reflection was given to the reality that new visible rituals, traditions and forms had been substituted for those that had been abandoned. This was the highly innovative, effective, but complex legacy that the Booths' bequeathed. The next chapter will detail the development of the third strand, "church," in a tangled cord of mission, army and church.

3

The Salvation Army as a Church

Introduction

William Booth died in 1912, two years after the convening of the historic 1910 World Missionary Conference in Edinburgh, which some argue marked the commencement of the modern ecumenical movement.[1] As concluded in chapter two, he left The Salvation Army with an ecclesial legacy of two entwined strands of aggressive mission and quasi-military army, that, in his ecclesial imprecision, existed as a form of special missionary emergency service both within and alongside the wider church. It was not until 1998 that this Salvationist ecclesial equivocation was formally and explicitly resolved with the publication of the Army's revised *Handbook of Doctrine*, in which for the first time a chapter was included on the doctrine of the Church. "One very important change since the Eleven Articles were formulated and adopted" it argued, "is the evolution of the Movement from an agency for evangelism to a church, an evangelistic body of believers who worship, fellowship, minister and are in mission together."[2]

This bold assertion adds a significant new dimension to any reckoning with the nature, form and mission of the Church, and is the central focus of this investigation. It is the conviction of this book that it also adds a third strand to the complex and tangled Salvation Army

---

1. Pollock, *The Keswick Story*, 173; Neill, *A History of Christian Missions*, 554. See Stanley, *The World Missionary Conference*.

2. The Salvation Army, *Salvation Story*, 100.

ecclesiology of mission, army and now church, the focus of this third chapter. The adoption of this newly acknowledged element is here explored, within an ecumenical context, assessing the extent to which The Salvation Army has reflected adequately upon what it means to be the Church. In this respect there are some critical questions that must be asked. To what extent do the identified threads of mission and army remain a reality for the contemporary Salvation Army? Are they compatible with its conviction that it is *a* church? Does The Salvation Army fully, faithfully and essentially express what God has called, commissioned and ordained God's Church to be? What does The Salvation Army add to an understanding of the Church and what can it learn from wider ecumenical reflection and dialogue upon the nature, form and mission of the Church?

Roger Green suggests that from as early as 1870 when the Christian Mission was formulated, and at least from 1878 when The Salvation Army was named, Booth had an implicit and "simple" ecclesiology, that the Army "was divinely ordained . . . a renewal in the nineteenth century and twentieth century of the Church in the New Testament, the early Church, the Reformation Church, and the Wesleyan revival" a manifestation "of the historic Church from its inception in the New Testament . . . an integral part of that Church on earth."[3] If this truly is the case, and it has already been suggested that the matter is far less straightforward than this, by 1954, Albert Orsborn, the sixth General of The Salvation Army, reveals the continuing ambiguity in a Salvationist articulation of its identity. Writing to Salvationists about the forthcoming World Council of Churches Assembly to be held in Evanston, Chicago, U.S.A., he contends that "we are almost universally recognized as a religious denomination by governments and for purposes of a national emergency—such as war service—or for convenience in designating our officers, they group us with the Churches," but adds:

> This is as far as we wish to go in being known as a Church. We are, and wish to remain, a Movement for the revival of religion, a permanent mission to the unconverted, one of the world's greatest missionary societies; but not an establishment, not a sect, not a Church, except that we are a part of that body of Christ called

---

3. Green, *War On Two Fronts*, 54–55 .

"The Church militant" and we shall be there, by His grace, with "The Church triumphant."[4]

Orsborn's phrase "a permanent mission to the unconverted" was popular with Salvationists who found themselves in ecumenical discussion and increasingly called upon to explain the nature of the movement. One officer, Harry Dean, in 1969 voiced a growing concern that the Army has "no mention of the Church in our eleven points of doctrine."[5] In 1976 the tenth General, Clarence Wiseman, in an article, "Are we a Church?," admits that The Salvation Army has never "developed a theology of the Church . . . we have been too busy doing the Lord's work to take time to think seriously about our precise position in His 'Body' . . . some day someone will tackle the task."[6] Nevertheless he reveals the complexity of the matter when he offers a variety of identities, including "we are more than a mission—we are an *Army*, God's shock-troops . . . a permanent mission to the unconverted . . . a caring social service movement . . . a religious order . . . part of the living Church of God . . . a 'church' in the more circumscribed, denominational sense of the word."[7]

In 1998, just over forty years from Orsborn's equivocal statement, under the leadership of the fifteenth General, Paul Rader, the revised *Handbook of Doctrine* clearly states: "Salvation Army doctrine implies a doctrine of the Church. Each doctrine begins: 'We believe . . .' 'We' points to a body of believers, a community of faith—a church."[8] This conviction is further consolidated in a 2008 ecclesiological statement *The Salvation Army in the Body of Christ*, in which The Salvation Army is no longer simply a "permanent mission to the unconverted" but "a Christian church with a permanent mission to the unsaved and the marginalised."[9] This development can only be fully explored within the context of the growth of ecumenism in the twentieth century, as the essential driving force behind The Salvation Army's confession of its ecclesiological convictions. The influence of ecumenism must briefly precede a presentation of the Army's current ecclesiological convictions,

4. Orsborn, "The World Council of Churches," 73.

5. Dean, "What is the Church?," 697.

6. Wiseman, "Are we a Church?," 435.

7. Ibid., 438.

8. The Salvation Army, *Salvation Story*, 100.

9. The Salvation Army, *The Salvation Army in the Body of Christ*, 10–11.

in order that a judgement may ultimately be formed on the theological implications of such a confession, discerning the extent to which those convictions are theological or sociological in their focus.

Ecumenism and the World Council of Churches

The Salvation Army, whilst wishing to remain autonomous and identifiable as a separate organization, has from its beginnings been open to partnership with other churches, especially in relation to missionary co-operation. Nevertheless, in view of Orsborn's equivocal statement of Salvationist identity, this chapter focuses specifically on the impact of the World Council of Churches upon The Salvation Army's ecclesiological reflection from 1948 onwards. Orsborn was elected as the sixth General after the Second World War, in 1946, and in March 1948, prior to the inaugural August assembly of the WCC in Amsterdam, the Army's representative on the Central Committee of the World Council in Process of Formation, Commissioner Cunningham, wrote to Orsborn: "It seems to me for the Army to take its full place in this great world gathering of the spiritual forces of Christendom is a logical development of the Army's policy of co-operation which has been steadily widening in scope since General Bramwell took office in 1912."[10] He reminded him of the Army's history of cooperation:

> During the Great War the Churches of Britain formed together in 1916 in The Christian Crusade. General Bramwell appointed Colonel Jeffries and myself as the Army's representatives on it . . . General Bramwell appointed Army representatives on other bodies in which all the Churches were united, such as The World Alliance for International Friendship through the Churches, the Christian Organisations Committee of the League of Nations Union, the Temperance Council of the Christian Churches, the Public Morality Council, etc . . . [and when] . . . the two great World Conferences of the Churches at Oxford (Christian Life & Work) and at Edinburgh (Christian Faith & Order) were convened in August 1937, the Army's Leader accepted the invitation to send a representative, who later was appointed a member of the Executive in Britain . . . [Finally when] . . . plans were set on foot to form the World Council of Churches as a permanent body, the Army's Leader formally accepted the invitation for the

10. Cunningham, "Letter to General Orsborn," March 21, 1948.

Army to become a constituent member of the World Council, and it is such, of course, today.[11]

Cunningham exhorted Orsborn to grasp "an altogether unique opportunity for the Army to take its appropriate place among the Churches of Christendom" within "that Spirit of Christian co-operation which has been a growing feature of the life of the Church of Christ during the last quarter of a century."[12] Orsborn was frank in his reply:

> I am not fully convinced that we shall ultimately agree with the objective of the World Council of Churches, inasmuch as this assembly is concerned not only with Faith, but with Order . . . Just let me make this small quotation: ". . . but all churches must realise that in the Council they will be confronted with the unescapable [sic] question: why they remain separated in many ways from churches with which they have actual fellowship in other ways." We do not want this, either now or ultimately, and therefore it occurs to me to wonder why we should participate in an Assembly whose ultimate objective does not commend itself to us.[13]

Cunningham sought to assure Orsborn that "from what I know of the attitude of the Church Leaders in the World Council I am convinced nothing in nature of organic union, or the merging of all the denominations is likely or possible within any foreseeable future—if ever. Unity, not union, is the aim."[14] The Amsterdam assembly gave the same assurance to the churches, that "whilst earnestly seeking fellowship in thought and action for all its members, the Council disavows any thought of becoming a single unified church structure independent of the Churches which have joined in constituting the Council, or a structure dominated by a centralized administrative authority."[15] Nevertheless at its 1950 meeting in Toronto, the WCC Central Committee acknowledged the need to "state more clearly and definitely what the World Council is and what it is not," and gave the further assurance that, "the purpose of the World

---

11. Ibid.

12. Ibid.

13. Orsborn, "Letter to Commissioner Cunningham."

14. Cunningham, "Letter to General Orsborn," April 24, 1948.

15. World Council of Churches, "World Council of Churches, 'Toronto Statement.'" See also, http://www.oikoumene.org/resources/documents/central-committee/toronto-1950/toronto-statement.html.

Council of Churches is not to negotiate unions between Churches, which can only be done by the Churches themselves acting on their own initiative, but to bring the Churches into living contact with each other and to promote the study and discussion of the issues of Church unity."[16]

Orsborn was not convinced, and underlined for the six delegates to the next assembly in 1954 at Evanston

> what we do not want for the Army, and what we will not have
> . . . We do not favour organic unity with the Churches . . . we can
> accept no discussion and no challenge to our position on the
> Sacraments . . . we cannot allow the effective ordination (com-
> mission) of our officers, including the women, to be challenged
> . . . we cannot join anything which may tend to curb our spirit of
> aggression.[17]

Following Orsborn's reticence, his successor, Wilfred Kitching, more positive about ecumenical relations, released in 1961 an engaging article about the WCC, prior to the New Delhi Conference.[18] Nevertheless, when the 1975 WCC Assembly in Nairobi declared the Council's purpose, "to call the churches to the goal of visible unity in one faith and in one Eucharistic fellowship expressed in worship and in common life in Christ, and to advance towards that unity in order that the world may believe,"[19] Salvationist concerns about the potential loss of their distinctive position on the sacraments re-surfaced.

The Army's representative on the Central Committee, Commissioner Harry Williams commented, "99.9% of Christians think eucharistically. We and the Quakers are odd . . . we don't expect to get our own way in such a forum . . . but we clarify our own attitudes and review our practice." In 1978, the anniversary of the name Salvation Army, its retired General, Frederick Coutts, wrote a short booklet *The Salvation Army in Relation to the Church*,[20] to defend the Army's place within the Church and its non-sacramental position. In the same year Nikos Nissiotis and Lukas Vischer, Moderator and Director of the Commission on Faith and

---

16. Ibid.

17. Orsborn, "The World Council of Churches," 77.

18. The Salvation Army, "The Army and the World Council of Churches."

19. World Council of Churches, "World Council Churches Constitution," paragraph 111, 1.

20. Coutts, *The Salvation Army in Relation to the Church*. See also Coutts, "The Salvation Army and Its Relation to the Churches," 649–54.

Order, wrote to Commissioner Williams to try to reassure the Army. Whilst they admitted that "the large majority of churches belonging to the WCC consider the sacraments of baptism and eucharist to be essential for the life of the Christian community" and "cannot share your conviction that the external signs of the sacraments are not necessary," they nevertheless live with you

> in spiritual and fraternal fellowship in the framework of the WCC. They would therefore like you to understand those passages in the New Testament which speak of baptism and eucharist. They would also like to share with you the experience of the sacramental tradition . . . All the Churches would probably agree that God is not bound to the sacraments . . . The Church is called to observe the sacraments which she gratefully receives whereas God is free to act without the sacraments. *Deus non ligature sacramentis.* We feel, that if it is proper to maintain this principle in theology, it is also proper to welcome within the Christian communion a community which grafts this principle into its actual life. Thus, within the ecumenical fellowship, The Salvation Army is a reminder to all churches that God can act outside of the sacraments . . . the witness of a community which seeks to live the experience of the sacraments without the external signs is an invitation to all churches to place the inner reality before the sign.[21]

It is difficult to comprehend why this sensitive and positive statement failed to allay fears, except that other concerns intervened. In 1979 the Army suspended its membership of the WCC and entered into a process of dialogue with regard to future relations. The catalyst for this decision was a grant made by the Programme to Combat Racism (PCR). Launched in 1968 as part of the WCC Programme Unit on Justice and Service, it sought to develop ecumenical policies and programs towards the liberation of victims of racism. It gave $85,000 to the Patriotic Front Guerrilla Group of Zimbabwe, only a matter of a few weeks after two teachers were killed on June 7th 1978 at The Salvation Army's Usher Institute in Zimbabwe, by guerrillas loyal to Patrick Nkomo's Zimbabwe People's Liberation Army. Commissioner Williams' report, following the Nairobi conference, had already highlighted the apolitical instincts of the international Salvation Army, in contrast to the growing political activity of the WCC on the world stage:

21. Nissiotis and Vischer, "Letter to Commissioner Williams."

In the last seven years the World Council of Churches has been the subject of keen controversy not only in the World Press but at many Church assemblies. Rumbles of discontent, even associated with cries for secession, have been widespread in our ranks ... The burden of criticism has been doctrinal in terms of "liberal" theology; sociological or political in terms of capitalist systems at times so strong as to call forth suspicion of a communist orientation; and, finally, activist programmes which appear to countenance violence.[22]

The Army's apolitical stance was challenged as being naïve, by a WCC delegation which met Salvation Army Commissioners.[23] Furthermore, the PCR special fund was aimed to support the humanitarian programs of liberation movements, largely in Southern Africa, from voluntary church contributions, rather than from general money from member churches. Nevertheless, whilst General Brown denied that there was a link between the Usher Institute's deaths and the Army's protest,[24] Commissioner Norman Marshall, National Commander in the USA, summed up the growing consensus of discomfort in North America with the Army's WCC membership. He suggested to the Army's Chief of Staff, Commissioner Cottrill that "perhaps it is a fortuitous moment for The Salvation Army generally to reconsider its continuing relationship with the WCC."[25] During the process of consultation with Dr. Philip Potter, General Secretary of the WCC, and the Central Committee, the Army's eleventh General, Arnold Brown, a Canadian, clarified the Army's position and priorities, including its non-sacramental concerns.

22. Williams, "The W. C. C.," 61.

23. "Notes of the Meeting of the Advisory Council to the General of The Salvation Army and a delegation from the World Council of Churches held on 12 December 1978." The notes record that, "Archbishop Sundby [Primate of the Church of Sweden, President of the WCC] asked whether The Salvation Army could really 'challenge social evils' in the extraordinary situation in Southern Africa without taking a political stance."

24. Brown, "Letter to Lt. Colonel L. Taylor." Brown concedes that "Black Salvationists have suffered in far greater measure than white Salvationists at the hands of the Terrorists."

25. Marshall, "Letter to Commissioner S. Cottrill."

The priorities for which our worldwide movement is known:

(1)Evangelism

(2)Concern for the poor and oppressed without distinction of race or creed which is not partisan in terms of support for any specific political party

(3)A history of support for socio-political changes which eschew violence

(4)A branch of the Church which does not practise the rites of baptism and the eucharist, and commissions women equally with men admitting them to all offices.[26]

Brown contemplated changing the Army's status from full active membership to a World Confessional Body; an observer member of future discussion without voting rights. Technically The Salvation Army's membership was peculiar in that membership was open to national churches, whereas The Salvation Army had grown into an international movement. In this it was not alone, as comparatively seen in the United Methodist Church. The Executive gave no suggestion that the Army should review its membership. Dr. Potter conveyed to General Brown

> our firm conviction that nothing in our constitution and manner of relating to our member churches prevents the Salvation Army from remaining a member church as it has been since 1948. It is also our firm resolve that everything should be done to find ways of relating to the Salvation Army which recognize its special character and of facilitating its full contribution towards realizing the prayer of our Lord that we may all be one that the world may believe.[27]

Whilst political concerns persisted, Salvationist leaders were fundamentally concerned that their "distinctive witness" with regard to the sacraments might be undermined. Dr. Potter, therefore, offered General Brown further encouragement to remain fully engaged in ecumenical discussion:

> We are aware, from our conversation with you, that the World Council's search for "full Eucharistic fellowship" poses problems for you as a non-sacramental movement. We can only re-iterate

26. Brown, "Letter to Dr. Philip Potter, 3 October 1979."
27. Potter, "Letter to General Brown, 18 May 1981."

the assurances we have given you that this phrase is not a part
of the basis for membership and therefore does not exclude you
from our fellowship.[28]

His appeal was unsuccessful and in 1981 The Salvation Army opted for
the new status of World Confessional Body, stepped out of the active
process of dialogue and decision making, and to date has not reversed
this decision.

On the other hand, under the leadership of the newly installed
General, Jarl Wahlström (1981–86) the opportunity to engage with the
Faith and Order Paper No. 111, *Baptism, Eucharist and Ministry*, published by the WCC in 1982, was embraced. Discussion groups were gathered throughout The Salvation Army. A draft document was discussed
at their 1984 International Conference of Leaders in Berlin, where it
was made clear that this was an opportunity "to participate in a major
Christian Church debate on equal terms with other denominations as an
important opportunity to offer our almost unique witness and to state
clearly our claim to theological soundness and our rightful place in the
church universal."[29] Privately, an internal leaflet sent to leaders expressed
the concern that, "a disconcerting new emphasis on 'visible unity' apparently to be achieved in 'eucharistic fellowship' has appeared to narrow
this interpretation of unity . . . and . . . to dictate the form of worship the
churches should adopt."[30]

Nevertheless, the official reply to *BEM* indicated a willingness to
respond "despite the fact that the Army's traditional approach to the
subjects dealt with differs significantly from the hypothesis on which the
present study rests." It expressed "regret and concern that the sincerely
held views of non-sacramentalist Christians are ignored in this document," requiring that the Army respond, "not in a spirit of confrontation
or denial, but of witness born out of our experience of the work of grace
in our midst for more than one hundred years."[31] It lodged concern that
the WCC document has reduced "the original recognition of the church
as the body of Christ, united in him irrespective of worship practices,
to a group of baptized people who observe the sacrament of the Lord's

28. Potter, "Letter to General Brown from Dr. Philip 24 August 1981."

29. Gauntlett, "Letter to: All Delegates Berlin Conference, 2 April 1984."

30. The Salvation Army, *The Salvation Army Statement on "Baptism, Eucharist and Ministry,"* 1.

31. Thurian, *Churches Respond to BEM*, 230.

Supper" and that this lack of recognition of "the continued existence of The Salvation Army and the Society of Friends renders such a definition invalid."[32]

The World Evangelical Fellowship equally regretted a statement that "apparently writes off all non-sacramentalist Christians, who do not tie together water baptism and Holy Spirit baptism as efficacious cause and effect, to say nothing of those who do not practice any baptism," and asserted that "in short, evangelicals will regret the persistently sacramentalist thrust of the entire document."[33] The Army response called it "a 'high church' pronouncement which comes close to advocating a 'baptismal regeneration' and a 'eucharistic sanctification,' with sacramental language seeming to take precedence over biblical terminology." [34] In this respect it complained that the biblical terms, "the body of Christ" and "the fellowship of believers" have been translated in the text into the terms "eucharistic community" worshipping in "eucharistic fellowship," with the sacramental overtones associated with such terms.

BEM did positively prompt Salvationists to give more thought to their identity and to the nature, form and mission of the Church. In this respect it officially confirmed that "we are convinced that The Salvation Army has all the essential characteristics of the body of Christ, his church"[35] In particular, Philip Needham was asked to present a fuller account of Salvationist ecclesiological reflection, and in 1987 *Community in Mission* was published as the first (and disappointingly only) extensive Salvationist treatment of this subject.[36] Such limited ecumenical engagement has not however prevented the Army from making a steady flow of pronouncements.

In 1996 General Paul Rader appointed an International Spiritual Life Commission "to review the ways in which The Salvation Army cultivates and sustains the spiritual life of its people." He impressed upon the members of the Commission that, "in recent years, and for a variety of reasons, we have begun to come more to terms with our churchly identity—that is, the accepted and publicly-acknowledged fact that we

32. Ibid., 231.

33. Schrotenboer, *The Text of the Lima Report Baptism*, 7. See also Barth, *Rediscovering the Lord's Supper*, 112f.

34. Thurian, *Churches Respond to BEM*, 234.

35. Ibid., 256.

36. Needham, *Community in Mission*.

are the church home for something upwards of two million people in the world."[37] Following the Commission's report in 1997, a full revision of the Salvationist *Handbook of Doctrine* was published in 1998, which included a chapter on the doctrine of the Church and affirmed The Salvation Army as a Christian church. Two successive International Theology and Ethics Symposia focused on Salvationist ecclesiology and a further ecclesiological statement was published in 2008.[38] Most recently, in 2010, the Army sent an as yet unpublished response to the WCC discussion paper *The Nature and Mission of the Church.*[39]

The rise of ecumenism in the twentieth century has therefore been the context in which The Salvation Army has developed its third ecclesial strand, which for the purpose of this study is called "church." There are, however, questions that must be asked about the depth at which The Salvation Army is engaged in this ecumenical journey. Its response to *The Nature and Mission of the Church* largely relies on Needham's account written twenty-five years previously, and makes no mention of WCC discussion since *BEM*. Equally its 2008 ecclesiological statement *The Salvation Army in the Body of Christ* represents in large part a reproduction of material first published in 1986 as *Reflections,*[40] a part of the inter-church process in Britain, "Not Strangers But Pilgrims." Whilst the Army's continued "observation" of the WCC process may in part explain this relatively superficial ecumenical engagement, it has at the same time become more assertive in articulating its conviction that it authentically counts as not just "part" of the church but itself *a* church. This in itself raises the question of whether it is seriously engaging in discussion, or merely "fighting its own corner." The Salvation Army's contemporary convictions must therefore be assessed in greater detail.

37. Street, *Called to Be God's People*, vii.

38. International Theology and Ethics Symposia were held in Winnipeg, Canada, 2001 and Johannesburg, South Africa, 2006. The Salvation Army, *The Salvation Army In The Body Of Christ.*

39. World Council of Churches, *The Nature and Mission of the Church*, hereafter known as *NMC*.

40. British Council of Churches, *Reflections*.

Salvationist Reflection on the Nature, Form, and Mission of the Church

The Salvation Army's International Mission Statement suggests that it is "an evangelical part of the universal Christian Church."[41] The same publication suggests it is "a worldwide evangelical Christian church with its own distinctive governance and practice."[42] Its 2008 ecclesiological statement, *The Salvation Army in the Body of Christ*, suggests it "is an expression of . . . the Church universal,"[43] and that it comprises local churches or congregations "in a relatively confined geographical location."[44] In essence the Army is grappling with an understanding of the Church that has been at the heart of ecumenical relations throughout the twentieth century, in which Christian denominations continue to multiply, and the search for an understanding of unity—the one, holy, catholic and apostolic Church—is ongoing. In this respect the Army suggests that "believers stand in a spiritual relationship to one another, which is not dependent upon any particular church structure," and in this respect "denominational diversity is not self-evidently contrary to God's will for his people."[45]

> We do not believe that an adequate definition of the Body of Christ on earth, the Church universal, can be confined in terms of ecclesiastical structure, but must rather be stated in terms of a spiritual relationship of grace that must find expression in all ecclesiastical structures. Members of the Body are those who are incorporate in Christ Jesus (Ephesians 1:1) and therefore reconciled to God through his Son. All such are in a spiritual relationship one with the other, which begins and continues regardless of externals, according to the prayer of Jesus that those who are his may be one (John 17:23) . . . This oneness is spiritual, not organizational.[46]

The Salvationist focus is therefore given primarily to the invisible church, in which it continues to celebrate the Booths' pragmatic conviction that

41. The Salvation Army, *The Salvation Army Year Book, 2011*, i.

42. Ibid., 11.

43. The Salvation Army, *The Salvation Army in the Body of Christ*, 1.

44. Ibid., 9.

45. Ibid., 1.

46. Ibid., 4. See also Coutts, *The Salvation Army In Relation To The Church*, 9; Needham, *Community in Mission*, 7.

the Army is free to order, structure and visibly express the church's spiritual reality in any way considered appropriate from human decision.

In contrast to this, the ecumenical journey which has much of its focus within the WCC, has been conducted on a different basis where the churches are called "to the goal of visible unity in one faith and one Eucharistic fellowship, expressed in worship and in common life in Christ, in order that the world may believe."[47] From this perspective, "the need to interpret, live, confess and celebrate the one faith in many contexts and accordingly in diverse forms of expression is not to be regarded as a threat to unity, but as the necessary consequence of the incarnational character of the Christian faith."[48] Furthermore, "it is also a task of the ecumenical community to engage in a process of theological dialogue in order to discern together whether certain understandings and uses of diversity threaten koinonia."[49] In this respect "the catholicity of the Church requires a communion of all local churches to be held together by faith, baptism, eucharist, ministry, and also by common bonds or structures."[50] Whilst it is recognized that not all churches "believe that common structures are necessary for visible unity, restrictive experience ought not lead us to believe that all structures stifle evangelical freedom."[51] Therefore the work of the WCC Faith and Order movement should "focus on right structures serving a conciliar communion of churches under the guidance of the Holy Spirit (John 16:13) and an authentic exercise of authority."[52] Attention is drawn to the *Canberra Statement*, which states that "full communion will be expressed on the local and the universal level through conciliar forms of life and action."[53]

By far the most extensive treatment of Salvationist ecclesiology is Needham's 1987 *Community in Mission*, in which he explains that "a peculiarly Salvationist ecclesiology" reflects a "prejudice toward the Church's missionary calling." He nevertheless betrays an ongoing individualistic approach to ecclesiology when he suggests that "it could

47. Best , *Faith and Order at the Crossroads*, 450.

48. Best, *On the Way To Fuller Koinonia*, 280.

49. Ibid.

50. Ibid., 281.

51. Ibid.

52. Ibid.

53. Ibid. See World Council of Churches, "The Canberra Statement," 2.1, 2. See also: World Council of Churches, "The Church: Local and Universal," 862–75.

never be seen as an ecclesiology for the whole Church, for no other reason than the fact that Salvationist history and experience have created a selection of emphases and priorities which would not be shared by all Christian fellowships."[54] Two comments are appropriate at this point before a more detailed presentation of Needham's Salvationist ecclesiology is offered. The first is in relation to the underlying Salvationist assumption that not all churches are equally as concerned for mission. It is fair to say, with Lesslie Newbigin, that mission must be seen as the *esse* and not merely the *bene esse* of the nature and purpose of the church.[55] In this respect *The Nature and Mission of the Church* explains that the name of the discussion document has been changed from *The Nature and Purpose of the Church* in response to the "frequent suggestions" to "strengthen the text's emphasis on mission,"[56] a decision that The Salvation Army unsurprisingly fully supports.[57]

Nevertheless, neither Needham, nor other Salvationist contributions to ecclesiology, give due recognition to a point made clear in The Evangelical-Roman Catholic Dialogue on Mission held from 1977–1984, several years before publication of Needham's account. The dialogue concludes that "both Roman Catholics and evangelicals agree that the church as the body of Christ is part of the gospel,"[58] and in that respect it is a disservice to the gospel to remain satisfied with the spectacle of visible Christian disunity. The report acknowledges that "the good news includes God's purpose to create for himself through Christ a new, redeemed, united and international people of his own."[59] The report also concedes that "evangelicals have sometimes preached an excessively individualistic gospel" emphasizing "personal salvation almost to the point of losing sight of the central place of the church."[60] This same tendency has been demonstrated in the history of The Salvation Army, and undermines its insistence that it primarily stands for the missionary declaration of the gospel's good news of reconciliation in Christ.

54. Needham, *Community in Mission*, 4.

55. Newbigin, *The Household of God*, 143.

56. *NMC*, 11.

57. The Salvation Army, "The Salvation Army Response," 2.

58. World Council of Churches, "The Evangelical-Roman Catholic Dialogue on Mission," 425.

59. Ibid.

60. Ibid. See also, Hunsberger, "Evangelical Conversion," 124f.

The second comment relates to Needham's remarks, that a Salvationist could not produce an ecclesiology for the whole church. The 1991 *Canberra Statement*, which admittedly postdates Needham's account, though not subsequent Salvation Army statements on the Army's identity as "part" of the universal church, says that "the goal of the search for full communion is realized when all the churches are able to recognize in one another the one, holy, catholic and apostolic church in its fullness."[61] David Thompson rightly suggests that this statement "implies that the one, holy, catholic and apostolic church in its fullness can be recognized in a single church (i.e., it is not something which by its nature is always above and beyond any particular church), and also that it can be recognized in several churches simultaneously."[62] This perspective is especially highlighted in the "Final Report of the Special Commission on Orthodox Participation in the WCC," which notes the "existence of two basic ecclesiological self understandings, namely of those churches (such as the Orthodox) which *identify* themselves with the One, Holy, Catholic and Apostolic Church, and those which see themselves as *parts* of the One, Holy, Catholic and Apostolic Church."[63]

Reflecting on this report, Heinz Joachim Held calls the "churches of the Reformation" to "critical evaluation of our own position" in the light of these two differing ecclesiological starting points, for "this difference goes to the very roots, like the mathematical sign in an equation that determines the whole of the expression in brackets, conditioning our Christian consciousness, our entire theological thinking and our ecumenical ideas."[64] His plea is supported by the 2006 ninth Assembly of the WCC in Porto Alegre, Brazil, which adopted the report *Called to be One Church*, and suggests that "each church is the Church catholic and not simply a part of it."[65] It is clear from ongoing Salvationist articulation of what is perceived in ecumenical discussion as an individualistic conviction that it is an "expression" of, or "part" of the Church, has not yet been acknowledged or addressed within Salvationist ecclesiology.

In *Community in Mission*, Needham chooses two predominant metaphors to explain The Salvation Army's self-understanding of the

61. World Council of Churches, "The Canberra Statement," 2.1, 2.
62. Thompson, "A United-Reformed Perspective," 28.
63. "Final Report of the Special Commission," 7.
64. Held, "A Remarkable Document," 61.
65. World Council of Churches, "Called to Be One Church," 257.

nature of the Church—a Pilgrim People and an Army. Whilst each metaphor in its own way highlights both Needham's emphases of "community" and "mission," he predominantly uses the metaphor of pilgrimage to emphasize "community" and of an army to emphasize "mission." Indeed the Army's recent official response to *The Nature and Mission of the Church* promotes these as the two metaphors that The Salvation Army would wish to add to the four images of People of God, Body of Christ, Temple of the Holy Spirit and Koinonia, to which the report gives a particular focus.[66] Both are chosen for their dynamic sense of mobility, and to reflect Needham's suggestion of a Salvationist "prejudice toward the Church's missionary calling."[67] In this respect he does not separate the three categories of the nature, form and mission of the Church. This study proposes to take Needham's two predominant metaphors of pilgrim people and army, and to judge the extent to which he incorporates the four biblical metaphors referred to in *The Nature and Mission of the Church*, and includes an understanding of the nature, form and mission of the Church.

The Church as a Pilgrim People of God

Needham explains that "the Church is a band of pilgrims called to separate themselves from the oppressive patterns of the present world order and to keep moving toward the possibilities which the new Kingdom in Christ offers."[68] To his mind the pilgrim journey involves "three key aspects of the Church's life in the world:" it "defines the Church as a people on the move," it "articulates the tentativeness of the Church's relationship to the social structures and behavioral patterns of contemporary society" and "it suggests a Church which is moving toward the future."[69] Needham does not wish to deny the key principle that the Church is called to be incarnational in the world, but he does wish to emphasize that it is "not tied to the structures and *status quos* of the society," that it values "flexibility," tends not to invest in "structures that stifle spiritual creativity" and is not "tied to blind dogma, perfunctory ritual, and in-

66. The Salvation Army, "The Salvation Army Response," 2, referring to *NMC*, 18–24.

67. Needham, *Community in Mission*, 4.

68. Ibid., 35.

69. Ibid.

stitutional self-preservation."[70] He develops the pilgrimage metaphor by presenting three further pictures of a "caravan in motion, the people in pilgrimage and the army on duty" as images that "best describe the New Testament understanding of the Church, as in the world but not of it."[71]

The metaphor of the Pilgrim People is undoubtedly a key concept contained within the overall biblical picture of the People of God, which Küng describes as "the oldest and most fundamental concept underlying the self-interpretation of the ekklesia."[72] Küng, like Needham, draws out the pilgrimage aspect of this people when he suggests that "a Church which pitches its tents without looking out constantly for new horizons, which does not continually strike camp, is being untrue to its calling" as "the pilgrim people of God."[73] Needham, unlike Küng, does not consider the ecumenical dimension of this metaphor. His interest is specifically focused on the Army's supposed lack of emphasis upon any particularly required visible form, in which he offers a limited amount of self-criticism on what has become the very visible and specific form of an army. Küng uses the metaphor to develop, in particular, the provisional nature of the community, "always a people of sinners, constantly in need of forgiveness," in essence "*ecclesia semper reformanda*."[74] He believes this image guards against an "idealizing misconception of the Church, by which it would become an unreal, distant ideal surrounded by a false halo, rather than a real historical Church."[75]

Pilgrimage is equally a familiar concept within WCC discussion. Reviewing Faith and Order reflection on the church since the first conference at Lausanne in 1927, Alan Falconer, sometime Director of the Faith and Order Commission (1995–2004), comments on the first phase of the ecumenical movement as being "comparative" in which churches sought to move beyond competition towards "acceptance of each other's existence and co-existence."[76] Falconer suggests that such methodology, helpful though it was, remained a monologue rather than a dialogue, "could not effect real relationship" and served ultimately "to affirm the

70. Ibid., 36.

71. Ibid., 38.

72. Küng, *The Church*, 119.

73. Ibid., 130–31.

74. Ibid., 131.

75. Ibid.

76. Falconer, "Introduction," 3.

status quo."[77] Therefore the third world conference on Faith and Order at Lund in 1952 adopted a different methodology of attempting to reach consensus, in which members were asked to see the church as "the pilgrim people of God—a community which learns from each other on the journey and seeks to discern truth."[78] Falconer recalls the conference statement of the church as pilgrim people:

> Those who are ever looking backward and have accumulated much previous ecclesiastical baggage will perhaps be shown that pilgrims must travel light and that, if we are to share at last in the great supper, we must let go of much that we treasure . . . It is easy for us in our several churches to think of what our separated brethren need to learn. Christ's love will make us more ready to learn what He can teach us through them.[79]

Needham, whilst keen to "travel light," falls into the trap outlined above, of giving greater focus to the example of Salvationist practice, than to what baggage the Army has acquired, or has to learn from other churches. This is not an uncommon Salvationist trait, as is especially evident in its 2008 ecclesiological statement. Whilst it confesses that "we do not believe that narrowness or exclusiveness are consistent with God's will for his people, or that God has nothing to teach us by our sharing and co-operating with his people in other denominations," and that "in humility we learn from others,"[80] the statement gives no indication of what has been learnt. It appears to focus, rather, on the conviction that "we come to the ecumenical table ready to share whatever God in his wisdom has graciously bestowed upon the Army."[81]

Equally, Salvationist ecclesiological reflection from its London Headquarters makes no mention that the metaphor of "pilgrim people" is used by Churches Together, from the launch of the inter-church process *Not Strangers But Pilgrims*, by the British Council of Churches on 8 November 1985 in St. Peter's Church, Eaton Square, London. Thirty-two participating Churches, including The Salvation Army, lit candles 'symbolising the undertaking given by those Churches to work side by

77. Ibid., 4.

78. Ibid., 5.

79. Ibid., 4. Falconer cites Tomkins, *The Third World Conference on Faith and Order*, 20f.

80. The Salvation Army, *The Salvation Army in the Body of Christ*, 12.

81. Ibid.

side in prayer, study and discussion."[82] The Army's contribution to this process, published in *Reflections*, and then revised for publication as *The Salvation Army in the Body of Christ*, continues to see the Church as "a spiritual relationship one with the other, which begins and continues regardless of externals."[83] In this respect from a Salvationist perspective ecumenical relationships are positively embraced, though without the need for a search for visible unity, unreflectively implying a lack of the need for human agency, since unity is only invisible and from God.

In truth the metaphor of the pilgrim people of God suits Salvationists for the way in which it gives focus supposedly to a "lightweight" ecclesiology shaped by the aggressive Christianity of holiness revivalism, which gives permission for the movement to be unfettered by such ecclesiastical tradition as is perceived to be burdensome in its mission. Salvationists identify such burdensome traditions as an historical line of apostolic succession, any specific biblical pattern of governance that must be adhered to and the necessity of particular sacramental observance. It is unsurprising that it found *BEM* disturbing, and has remained on the sidelines of the WCC's search for "visible unity."

In his 1978 centenary essay, Coutts defends the Army's freedom as pilgrims in matters of church order and governance.[84] With regard to an apostolic succession, he refutes from biblical evidence "any single set procedure laid down for the appointment of the Church's leaders," pointing out that "nowhere in the Acts of the Apostles do the Twelve ordain their successors," for "the New Testament provides no one pattern to be followed universally and in perpetuity" and "the picture given is one of freedom in the Spirit."[85] He suggests that it is difficult to discern any clear and uniform episcopal ordering of the Church within the New Testament record, is clear that "order and structure were fluid" within a community that declared "it seemed good to the Holy Ghost and to us . . . ,"[86] and is convinced that people "were used of God to communicate the apostolic message because they possessed the apostolic spirit."[87] His conclusion is that God's people are united, not by any form of organiza-

82. British Council of Churches, *Reflections*, v.

83. The Salvation Army, *The Salvation Army in the Body Of Christ*, 4.

84. Coutts, *The Salvation Army in Relation to the Church*, 8.

85. Ibid., 11.

86. Ibid., 14.

87. Ibid., 12.

tion "however venerable" or "authoritative," but by "the grace of the one God and father of all, the presence of the only Saviour, and the outworking of the one Spirit in the life of each believer."[88] The question of order and ministry will be revisited shortly in an examination of the Church as an army, in which The Salvation Army has created a definite visible form.

Salvationists, as a people in pilgrimage with a "spiritual" understanding of the Church, remain committed to defending their non-sacramental position. Yet there is considerable equivocation about visible forms, as seen in comparison with the Society of Friends, who equally do not have baptism and the Lord's Supper. The Friends United Meeting confirms that it is "not identifiable as a eucharistic Fellowship employing rites which use material signs," but does have "a sacramental life through the living Presence of Christ which is shared in common with Christian bodies who are identifiable as eucharistic Fellowships."[89] Nevertheless their response to *BEM* is straightforward. They can accept the use of "material signs" as "significant expressions of oneness in Christ."[90] Salvationists, on the other hand, who have recognized the value of visible signs and substituted their own, remain uncomfortable with the Church's traditional material signs being used in any expression of unity. The reason for this reluctance is a continuing Salvationist pre-occupation with the question of whether or not these signs are "means of grace."[91] Salvationists continue to believe unequivocally that they are not. Little consideration continues to be given as to whether, as in Zwingli's understanding, for example, they are constitutive of the church.[92]

In regard to the sacraments, *The Nature and Mission of the Church* acknowledges that there remains disagreement over whether they are "the means of, or simply witnesses to, the activity of the Spirit through the divine Word, which comes about in an immediate internal action

88. Ibid., 9.

89. Thurian , *Ecumenical Perspectives on Baptism*, 161.

90. Ibid.

91. See, Booth, "Sacraments," reprinted in Booth, *Echoes and Memories*; The Salvation Army, *Salvationists and the Sacraments*; idem., *The Sacraments*; Metcalf, *The Salvationist and the Sacraments*; Kew, *Closer Communion*.

92. See Zwingli, "An Account of the Faith," 48.

upon the hearts of the believers."[93] Salvationists view them simply as cultural accretions that can be discarded. Needham is particularly insistent that the Army abandoned the sacraments because of the way in which the poor had become excluded from what he describes as "a private celebration of cultural Christianity."[94] Nevertheless he illustrates his pre-occupation with them as "means of grace" in his insistence that "it is a disservice to the gospel to insist that grace must be received through the mediation of a particular ritual or procedure, and there is no evidence in the New Testament from which a case can be argued for such a view."[95] For Needham the logic of this conviction is that "each Christian fellowship is therefore free to develop those symbolic acts which best nurture and celebrate a response to the gospel which is attentive to the social, cultural and historical context of its life and mission."[96] Needham gives little theological indication of what he means by the term "symbol." Clearly, however, he more has in mind a Zwinglian sense of "signification" than Karl Rahner's theology of symbols as "the self-realization of a being in the other, which is constitutive of its essence,"[97] and in which "the symbol renders present what is revealed."[98]

Needham's view appears to allow Salvation Army congregations the freedom in their pilgrimage to be flexible and adaptable to changing terrain, to abandon the symbols of water, bread and wine, and to adopt new symbols such as the mercy seat, the love feast, the flag and Salvation Army uniform, not as "prescribed rituals" or "the requisite means of experiencing that grace," but simply as symbols which "celebrate the immediacy of grace."[99] In effect The Salvation Army claims to affirm all the theological significance of both baptism and the Lord's Supper, without requiring the rites.[100] Needham advises that baptism "is not the only public witness to this spiritual reality" for "the Salvationist fellowship has its own rites of public witness to conversion."[101] In this

93. *NMC*, 15.

94. Needham, *Community in Mission*, 25.

95. Ibid., 8.

96. Ibid.

97. Rahner, *Theological Investigations*, 4:225.

98. Ibid., 239.

99. Ibid., 8–9.

100. See Robinson, "A Salvation Army Perspective on Baptism," 173–80.

101. Needham, *Community in Mission*, 10.

respect "kneeling at the mercy seat points to the true humility of those who see the inadequacy and shame of their life outside discipleship, and the longing to be converted to true discipleship through spiritual death and resurrection."[102] He is quick to point out that this symbol is not essential to conversion, nor is it a guarantee of conversion. Similarly, in regard to the Lord's Supper he suggests that "a Salvationist ecclesiology . . . sees the love feast as a more apt celebration of the pilgrim life of God's people," for "as a more spontaneous and less institutionalised rite, it is better suited to the journey."[103] There are "no *prescribed* elements" and "love feasts which are conducted in the corps setting are really symbolic of what all meals are for those who invite the Christ to preside at every table."[104] It should be noted that Needham's proposal for Salvationists to hold love feasts does not reflect common practice, but rather the call for a re-instatement of an early Salvationist practice, from Methodist and Moravian example. It has largely fallen into disuse.[105] The more familiar practice for Salvationists has been to have no direct symbol for the sustaining presence of God in everyday life, other than the witness of the individual, whose energetic Christian life is an everyday living sacrifice upon God's altar.

Needham makes his proposal for the renewal of "love feasts" because he recognizes "that man has a need to nurture and celebrate profound spiritual realities through symbolic acts" and that "a Gnostic disparagement of palpable symbols and rituals which communicate through the senses is, or borders on, Christian heresy."[106] He views the love feast for Salvationists as "a less ritualized version of the early Christian common meal" and "an invitation to affirm the reconciliation of life in Christ by opening themselves to one another and accepting the responsibility of nurturing unity in Christ and service to one another."[107] Yet when he explains how a love feast would work in practice in a congregational setting, it is difficult to imagine why he would wish to differentiate it as a ceremony, from the way in which many churches celebrate the Lord's

---

102. Ibid.

103. Ibid., 46.

104. Ibid., 29–30.

105. A small booklet was published in the USA, following Needham's suggestion. See Thomson, *The Love Feast*.

106. Ibid., 8.

107. Ibid., 29.

Supper, in a congregational and liturgical setting.[108] Ultimately it is not clear what additional benefits there are in Needham's substituted symbols, and questions remain as to whether they contain all the theological depth of those symbols that the Church has used since Christ.

Needham's account of the Church is more prominently focused upon the presence of the Holy Spirit (the concept of the "Temple of the Holy Spirit" is not directly mentioned,)[109] than it is upon the concept of the "Body of Christ."[110] This metaphor is only referred to briefly in relation to the subject of "spiritual gifts and to the equipping of the saints."[111] It is not discussed in relation to the visible presence of God's people as Christ's body on earth, in which symbols of bread, wine and water might come to prominence. This must be seen as a significant weakness, and one that will be further addressed in the second part of this study, in dialogue with Karl Barth.

Equally, whilst Needham speaks repeatedly about the fellowship of God's pilgrim people, there is little mention of the NT concept of *koinonia,* being the word that most acutely describes the nature and quality of that fellowship. In fairness, much of the current ecumenical focus upon the church as *koinonia* postdates Needham's account, yet it is significant that current Salvationist ecclesiology which largely rests on Needham's study, is not engaged in this discussion, and the place which baptism and the Lord's Supper have within it.[112] Salvationists, in contrast, place a growing emphasis upon "the sacramental life," which to some extent seeks to explain what they mean by Christian fellowship, without using the concept of *koinonia*. It is therefore proposed to explore the development of this theme within The Salvation Army before comparing it to the ecumenical discussion that has focused upon the church as *koinonia*.

108. See ibid., 29–30.

109. See *NMC,* 21.

110. Ibid., 20–21.

111. See Needham, *Community in Mission,* 86–88. Needham discusses briefly the subject of "equipping" in reference to Ephesians 4:11, 12.

112. World Council of Churches, "The Canberra Statement," was adopted in 1991, several years after Needham's *Community in Mission*. See in particular the literature previously referred to: Best, *On The way To Fuller Koinonia*; Grdzelidze, *One, Holy, Catholic and Apostolic*; Gros, *Growth In Agreement II*; Gassmann, *The Unity of the Church as Koinonia*; World Council of Churches, "Perspectives on Koinonia," 735–52.

The Sacramental Life of the Pilgrim People of God

The sacramental life is for Needham the spirituality that exists at the heart of the pilgrim people of God. His theology of the sacramental life is built upon the Booths' holiness revivalism; their emphasis on the pragmatic adaptation of methods for effective mission, and their subjective emphasis on the conditional immediacy of God's entirely sanctifying grace. Needham believes, therefore, that sacraments cannot be seen as means of grace, and can be adapted to changing cultural circumstances. He offers little recognition of their role in establishing fellowship.

John Coutts summed up the unifying factor in all Salvationist accounts, when he suggested in 1965, during the movement's centennial year, that it had made two distinctive theological contributions to the wider church; the first concerning the ministry of women, and the second the immediacy of grace as found in the Army's stand on the sacraments, explaining that "both arise from the same conviction; that the Holy Spirit is personal, sovereign, and immediate in the heart of the believer."[113] In relation to the immediacy of grace he claims that the heart of the Salvationist position lies in a true understanding of the doctrine of grace, for "the majority of Christians, both in East and West, belong to churches whose doctrine of grace does not, we think, satisfactorily explain how God, as Personal Spirit, succours and sustains His children," describing the view of grace that Salvationists are rejecting as one "which sees God's help as a quasi impersonal 'force,' inherent in rites, hierarchy and ritual."[114] He sweepingly complains of the "exclusiveness" of this idea in which, "if the right words are not recited, if the right hands are not laid on the right people, if the libation is poured in the wrong way—then all is uncertainty and the blessing is lost,"[115] and promotes the Army's position as a positive contribution to the churches:

> It may distress Eastern Christians to encounter Christian worship led by a woman. It may confuse high churchmen to find believers unbaptised with water. We may be deplored, but we cannot in the ecumenical context be ignored. Our witness is a positive one, provided we show forth also in our lives that lost

113. Coutts, "The Army's Contribution to the Churches," 600.

114. Ibid., 601.

115. Ibid.

men and women can, through our testimony, be brought into immediate fellowship with the living God.[116]

If "immediacy of grace" is a catch-phrase that has captured the Salvationist defense of its position, it has been accompanied by, at Catherine Booth's insistence, the suggestion that "the over-riding concern of Salvationists will be personally to experience that inward spiritual grace to which the sacraments testify."[117] In this sense the "Salvationist believes in the Real Presence as earnestly as any churchman."[118]

Needham draws "the immediacy of grace" back to The Salvation Army's understanding of the new covenant initiated by Jesus, and to the doctrine of the Holy Spirit. In this he reminds the movement of its roots in holiness revivalism, declaring that the major theological rationale for Salvationist discontinuance is, "the growing emphasis upon the call to holiness as the imperative for Christian character and lifestyle."[119] In this he follows the response that Salvationists made to *Baptism, Eucharist and Ministry*, when in answer to the question of what "guidance . . . The Salvation Army can take from this text for its worship, educational, ethical and spiritual life and witness," it replied that "we have been challenged to a reaffirmation and intensification of our teaching of the scriptural doctrine of holiness—that 'full salvation' which, as our name implies, is our central theme," for "it is our belief that sanctification by the Holy Spirit is intended by our Lord to replace dependence on outward forms and ceremonies."[120] The latest ecclesiological statement affirms that God's calling is for Salvationists "to witness to a life of sanctity without formal sacraments," but personally "to experience that inward spiritual grace to which an external observance testifies," since "we can meet with God and receive his grace anywhere at any time through faith."[121] For the Salvationist, therefore, the holy life is simply lived sacrificially for God, and in this faithfulness open to the empowering and sustaining presence of God, the Holy Spirit, as the essential and far more crucial focus than the symbol.

116. Ibid.
117. Coutts, *The Salvation Army in Relation to the Church*, 15.
118. Ibid., 17.
119. Needham, *Community in Mission*, 26.
120. Thurian, *Churches Respond to BEM*, 256.
121. The Salvation Army, *The Salvation Army in the Body of Christ*, 13.

The poetic words of Albert Orsborn have been at the heart of the growing Salvationist emphasis upon the sacramental life. During an Easter visit to Salvationists in war-damaged Berlin in 1947, Orsborn explained that he was struggling to find adequate words for the occasion, when "God revealed to me that not only that day, but always, we have no hope of being a blessing to other souls unless our lives become a part of the Saviour's sacramental consecration."[122] As his car drove from Berlin towards Holland, he wrote the words:

> My life must be Christ's broken bread, my love his outpoured wine,
> A cup o'erfilled, a table spread, beneath his name and sign.
> That other souls, refreshed and fed, may share His life through mine.[123]

Orsborn had primarily in mind the nature of Christ's sacramental life and death and the participation of Salvationists as "living sacrifices." Encouraged by the popularity of these words, Harry Dean concluded in 1960: "Thus the Salvationist's attitude to the sacraments aims to make the whole of life sacramental."[124] The idea, articulated in Orsborn's song, is increasingly popular, yet continues to be confusingly maintained from a position of non-sacramental observance. In 1980, referring to Booth's 1883 address, Kew simply adds, "Each meal should be sacramental—in fact the whole of life should be," and cites the words of William Temple in *Christus Veritas*: "It is possible to make a 'spiritual communion' which is in every way as real as a sacramental communion . . . Everywhere and always we can have communion with Him."[125]

Equally Needham maintains the Army's non-sacramental observance by declaring that "the holy life is the sacramental life," and that "sanctification is God's work of grace by which all of life becomes sacred and therefore every moment is a potential sacrament."[126] Since the sacramental life is lived in the power of the Spirit, Needham explains that "those who 'walk by the Spirit' look for the sacredness of every moment, the presence of God in every encounter, the divine possibility in every human soul, the sacrament in every experience," and contends that "the

---

122. Avery, *Companion to the Song Book*, 150; Taylor, *Companion to the Song Book*, 118.

123. The Salvation Army, *The Song Book of The Salvation Army*, No. 512.

124. The Salvation Army, *The Sacraments*, 78.

125. Cited in Kew, *Closer Communion*, 48.

126. Needham, *Community in Mission*, 26.

sacramental life is a repossession, through Christ and in the power of the Holy Spirit, of God's original and enduring intention for human existence."[127] Therefore, sacramental rites can be seen in "a very different light," not "as prescribed occasions which have been designated as essential means by which God's grace in Christ must be experienced, but rather as celebrations of a far greater grace—the grace which is given to the whole of life and which consequently makes living a continuing sacrament."[128] Needham objects to sacramental ritual as an unnecessary separation of sacred and secular, and declares that "the sacramental life is lived on the premise that all such 'dividing walls' have been broken down in the cross, that all of life is now sacred and should be celebrated as such, that holiness is the freedom to live every moment in God's presence."[129]

Most significantly for this study, however, Needham adds that it is "doubtful that the Salvationist movement would have discontinued the Lord's Supper had this interpretation been that of the Victorian churches."[130] Yet, at no point is consideration given to the reality that objective symbols of water, bread and wine may be used by Salvationists to underline the sacramental life. In 1996 the Army's *Spiritual Life Commission*, of which Needham was a member, was called to review the way in which spiritual life was sustained in the movement. It affirmed the idea that life can be sacramental. It reviewed the Salvationist position on the sacraments at some length, and finally recommended to the General that the sacraments should not be re-introduced, pointing to "the continual need to explain the Army's perceived 'sacramental' but not 'sacramentalist' position."[131] The commission puts it this way: "Christ is the one true sacrament, and sacramental living—Christ living in us and through us—is at the heart of Christian holiness and discipleship."[132] Whilst the NT concept of *koinonia* is never used in a Salvationist description of the sacramental life of the pilgrim people of God, it is clear that Salvationists are attempting to describe the sustaining life of the Trinity, God's generous gift to individuals who receive the Holy Spirit

127. Ibid., 19.
128. Ibid., 27.
129. Ibid., 19.
130. Ibid., 27.
131. Street, *Called to be God's People*, 87.
132. Ibid., 89.

into their lives. What this account of the sacramental life lacks, however, is the explicit understanding that it is lived in community, which the concept of *koinonia* unmistakably adds. This weakness is particularly apparent in the continuing individualistic emphasis upon the immediacy of God's grace, without reference to the relationship of God's grace to the community. It is not that Salvationists are unaware of the communal dimension of a commitment to sacrificial living, but that they don't take advantage of the full theological possibilities available when this concept is enunciated. Donna Geernaert is right to suggest that "although 'koinonia' is never equated with 'church' in the New Testament, it is the term that most aptly expresses the mystery underlying the various New Testament images of the church."[133]

Salvationists might wish to continue to speak of God's action as an immediate relationship of grace, but if they fail to hold clearly the concept of *koinonia* they are in danger of missing the context of that action, which is within the community of God's people and their witness in the world, and not simply in a personal and individual relationship. Furthermore, John Zizioulas suggests that the understanding of the church as *koinonia* has important implications for the effectiveness of its mission in the world. "If communion is made a key idea in ecclesiology, mission is better understood and served not by placing the gospel over against the world, but by inculturating it in it."[134] When Salvationists view the Lord's Supper as no more than a cultural accretion that may be discarded, it appears that they have given little reflection to the Apostle Paul's reference to the bread and the cup as *koinonia*, or as *TNIV* has it, "participation" in the body and blood of Christ (1 Cor 10:16), a participation that inspires and guides the mission of the community to pray that this communion will ultimately unite the whole of creation.

Effectively, holiness revivalism has taught Salvationists, who abandon baptism and the Lord's Supper, to move beyond the dominical signs in substituting their own symbols and signs. In this respect they will continue to find difficulty with the language of "the church as sacrament" that stems from the discussion of the "church as *koinonia*." Karl Rahner suggests that "the Church is the abiding presence of that primal sacramental word of definitive grace, which Christ is in the world," and therefore "the Church is the 'fundamental sacrament,' the well-spring

133. Geernaert, "Church as Koinonia," 63.
134. Zizioulas, "The Church as Communion," 103.

of the sacraments in the strict sense."[135] Timothy George notes in this respect, that the Vatican's statement on the church, *Lumen Gentium*, suggests that "the Church is a kind of sacrament" and in the footnotes that this is by "analogy with the seven sacraments properly so called."[136] George suggests that Baptists and evangelicals "are likely to find the 'sign' and 'instrument' more congenial terms for describing the reality and mission of the church than the more historically freighted word 'sacrament.'"[137] Nevertheless he believes that the "qualified expression *veluti sacramentum*"[138] holds promise for further ecumenical discussion.

It is clear that Salvationists, in their explanation of the sacramental life, without reference to the biblical concept of *koinonia*, and in maintaining the non-sacramental absence of baptism and the Lord's Supper, discard key visible testimonies to God's grace that should properly stand alongside the sacramental life as its visible symbol and sign, identifying its communal nature. These elements are not as culturally limited as Salvationists suppose. In their relation to the life and ministry of Christ, they may be inculturated into every age and culture, regardless of any particular theological significance given to them as "means of grace." This is a matter that must be picked up in the second part of this study. There is an equal challenge, however, to those churches that may, in practice, use baptism and the Lord's Supper as highly individualistic rites, in which the emphasis is placed upon a personal spiritual relationship to the detriment of the community.

The Church as Army of God

Needham's second key metaphor is understandably the Church as an army, a form chosen by the Booths to express the priority of mission, in "word and deed," an emphasis that the contemporary Salvation Army maintains.[139] The attraction of the military metaphor for mission is in Needham's estimation its mobility. He views the two metaphors of Pilgrim People and Army as "inseparable" for "a Church on the move is

135. Rahner, *The Church and the Sacraments*, 18.

136. Abbott, *The Documents of Vatican II*, 15 n. 3.

137. George, "The Sacramentality of the Church," 28.

138. Ibid., 36.

139. See for example in Britain where the Salvation Army began: The Salvation Army, *In Darkest England Now*; Gauntlett, *Today in Darkest Britain*.

a Church at war,"[140] or alternatively, "the fellowship and the mission of the Church are two parts of one whole."[141] Needham explains that "the Church as an army derives from the reason for which it exists in the world" and he is clear that this "reason is *mission*."[142] In particular he recognizes that this mission has a particular focus upon the poor, in which the challenge for its founders in nineteenth-century Victorian Britain was to shed the ecclesiastical baggage that inhibited mission. He states:

> Static ecclesiastical symbols, for example, were replaced by mobile symbols, symbols of mediation were replaced by symbols of mission. The Army adopted language, practices and customs which represented departures from the established churches and made the Christian faith more available to the working man. The clear intent was to remove the gospel from the prejudice and confinement of sanctuaries, which were foreign to his culture.[143]

Such is Needham's estimation of the challenge which faces the pilgrim people of God in their determination to travel light and to be effective and flexible in their mission across changing terrain. To his credit Needham remains alert to some of the tensions that exist between these two metaphors; in particular the reality that improvisation of the Church's form for the sake of mission, can over time become institutionalized, develop new ecclesiastical baggage, and therefore become a barrier to effective mission. He does not, however, attend to the tension that is created between the Church as a sociological and a theological reality, in which its visible form requires careful theological reflection. Whilst the Church may assume a variety of sociological shapes within a diversity of time, geographical location and culture, Needham never considers the idea that the Church's "spiritual" or invisible nature must have adequate theological expression in its human and visible sociological form.

In what follows, firstly, Needham's positive recommendation of three particular aspects of the Church as army; its mission, its order and its membership, will be examined. Secondly, Needham's awareness of the danger of institutionalization that may develop in each of these three aspects will be acknowledged. Thirdly, and most critically, each of these

140. Needham, *Community in Mission,* 52.

141. Ibid., 75.

142. Ibid.

143. Ibid., 67.

three aspects of the Church as army will be critiqued for the adequacy of theological reflection that has been afforded them.

The Mission of an Army

At the heart of the combination of the two metaphors of pilgrim people and army, is the tension created by pilgrims traveling light in order to enhance their ability to be flexible and adaptable in meeting the demands of their mission, and yet at the same time adopting a bold new military metaphor with all its accompanying visible accoutrements. Needham is confident that the military metaphor is more suited to the Church's primary task of mission, in view of the mobility and disciplined focus that it brings to the task. Unconcerned that the image of warfare might undermine the gospel of peace, he suggests the Church is "a peace-keeping force in a world that opposes the peace and that consequently attacks the keepers of the peace; and it is a movement dedicated to inviting enemies to abandon enmity and accept peace."[144]

He recommends the figure of the Church as an army for what he sees as the way in which it "cannot automatically identify itself with the world or with any particular culture or society" for it is free to keep "a critical distance" from such potential entanglements.[145] He views the members of an army as disciplined soldiers, disciples who are not "passive" in their membership, but active.[146] He welcomes the mobility and flexibility that an army has in adapting to changing "battlefields," rather than the "preservation of its own historical structures and methods for the sake of institutional survival."[147] He applauds the amount of time that the Church as an army is called to invest in training, equipping and preparing its troops for battle, and he notes the character of the soldier who must ultimately "be prepared to lay his life on the line."[148]

Needham is not totally unaware of the idealistic nature of these sentiments and keeps alert to three potential threats to the mobility of an army. The first, is the reality that the army which is flexible must continue to maintain that flexibility and adaptability in order to be able to

---

144. Ibid., 54.
145. Ibid., 55.
146. Ibid.
147. Ibid.
148. Ibid. Needham refers to 2 Tim 2:3.

pursue its mission effectively. In this respect he admits that "the use of a military pattern and form of organization, and the symbolic use of military language, do not necessarily mean that worthwhile missionary battles are being joined," for "rituals of a tradition" may be "perpetuated" and an army "become immobile and inflexible, and incapable of meeting new battle challenges."[149] Presumably in this respect, an army is no different from any other church denomination, yet somewhat unconvincingly, he stands by this metaphor as the most appropriate in relation to the Church's mission, in which undoubtedly significant mission has been consistently maintained.

Secondly, Needham admits that "uniformity of procedure and method needs to be evaluated in the light of an increasingly pluralistic milieu," in which "greater social and cultural pluralism within the Army expands the movement's capacity to minister in a highly pluralistic terrain."[150] This is an astute observation, though one wonders whether Needham has gone far enough in recognizing that to identify the Church so completely with one particular bold metaphor, when there are so many others, is to compound the issue of uniformity. Furthermore, Needham is reluctant to engage fully with the problem of uniformity enforced by an autocratic hierarchy.

Thirdly, he concedes that "the Army's predilection for action as opposed to reflection needs reassessment," since whilst it is able "to respond quickly to missionary challenges," it has been "scarce on theological tools with which critically to evaluate its responses." Needham pleads for "the development of an ongoing theology of mission informed both by Scriptures and tradition and by the contemporary situation."[151] In this regard it is hoped and intended that this particular study can be one such response, and in this respect these three potential difficulties with the military metaphor, as raised by Needham, will be returned to in the second part of this study.

There are three further difficulties that Needham does not raise. Firstly, whilst he recognizes that early Salvationist expressions of mission were individualistic, no reflection is offered on the possibility that the metaphor itself reflects that individualism. Salvationists see an army as a legitimate expression of community, and it certainly has potential to

149. Ibid., 73.
150. Ibid.
151. Ibid., 74.

inspire in its members a level of camaraderie and self-sacrifice for each other and for a hurting world. On the other hand, less consideration is given to the sectarian trait that an army may equally shoot the deserter. In this respect Salvationists should reflect more fully upon those aspects of the life of an army which characterize it more as a collection or aggregation of individuals traveling in the same direction, intent on fulfilling a task, rather than a community that simply exists as God's people. Some of these aspects will be discussed in the next two sections, with regard to the kind of relationships that an army engenders, in which there is autocracy, hierarchy, submission and unquestioning obedience to orders, in which the group is focused so completely upon the task, and the preparation for the task, that the enjoyment of the community for its own sake is undermined. In particular, an army does not instinctively focus upon the reality that its own community life is an integral part of its mission; that the church is part of the gospel.

In this respect Salvationists would do well to give consideration to Paul Fiddes' reflection upon the nature of the covenant relationship that exists between God and the community, as well as within the community, in which the people of God are "walking together" with God and each other.[152] In this reflection, Fiddes explains his concern at what he perceives in some minds as the "secularizing of the church covenant as a voluntary society," in which the concept of covenant can "be simply *replaced* by voluntarism."[153] Fiddes sees the influence of John Locke's writings in this development, in which he refers to Locke's notion that "a church as voluntary society has the freedom to make its own rules and prescribe its own membership qualifications."[154] He refers to John Briggs' study of the Baptists in the nineteenth century and Briggs' comments on the decline of the theology of covenanting in an age when churches and mission agencies were working together in "associations" and "alliances."[155] This is the same context in which The Salvation Army was born as a mission agency, drawing the voluntary response of individuals to engage in a shared task. Fiddes wishes to resist, however, "any reduction of a covenant bond to a mere 'strategic alliance,' a union

152. Fiddes, *Tracks and Traces*, 21–47.

153. Ibid., 43.

154. Ibid., 42. Fiddes cites Locke, *A Letter Concerning Toleration*, 9.

155. Ibid., 43. Fiddes refers to Briggs, *The English Baptists of the Nineteenth Century*, 15–20.

only for the sake of performing certain tasks, or making economies, or providing resources," in which he draws attention "to the 'ontological' element in covenant, that is the dimension of sheer being which under-lies any doing."[156]

Fiddes questions the individualistic traits of the local Baptist church as a "voluntary society" and its assertion of its local ecclesias-tical authority over against the wider Church, for the way in which it competes against an understanding of the unity of the one, holy, catholic and apostolic Church. In this respect he suggests that the freedom of the local church is "not based in Enlightenment concepts of the freedom of the individual, or in the self regulation of a voluntary society, but in the lordship of Christ."[157] He demonstrates how this same concept may be extended to allow a national union of local churches to see themselves in covenant relationship, and in turn how denominations may equally embrace a covenant relationship in their "walking together" as pilgrims.[158] The point is that there is a deeper theological concept of the ontological nature of covenant from the lordship of Christ, than simply a collec-tion of free individuals who choose to form an alliance to perform a specific task, as might be implied by the nature of an army. Clearly, in the Army's autocratic governance, local Salvation Army congregations are not in danger of the kind of autonomy that Fiddes fears. Nevertheless, this denominational autocracy on a wider ecumenical level breeds an in-dividualistic autonomy, as apparent in the Army's superficial ecumeni-cal engagement with ecclesiological concerns. The concept that Fiddes enunciates should encourage Salvationists to seek a deeper theological understanding of the universal Church, than the voluntary choosing of its own rules, regulations and practices, and within this circumference to call itself "church" or a "part expression" of the Church.

Secondly, little reflection has been given to the reality that a fierce expression of the doctrine of hell was at the root of that aggressive Christianity which inspired the development of the military metaphor, an expression that has lost much of its appeal. Richard Harries notes

156. Ibid., 37.

157. Ibid., 44. See also Volf, *After Our Likeness*, 3, who suggests that "voluntarism and egalitarianism are goods that must be preserved, but they must be redeemed from their own dark shadows—from the false autonomy of self-enclosed individuals whose relationships are at bottom contractual."

158. Ibid., 45. Fiddes refers here to the inter-church process *Not Strangers but Pilgrims*.

that the tragedy of the First World War encouraged a shift in belief from fearful judgment to "entrance into a world that was kinder than the ravaged violent earth,"[159] precipitating a change in focus from the next world to this one.[160] In that respect Gustaf Aulén, whilst he wished to resurrect the "classic idea" of the atonement as *Christus Victor*, to "keep steadily in view the reality of the evil in the world, and go to meet the evil with a battle-song of triumph,"[161] was clear that "the crude and realistic images which are to be found in the Fathers and in Luther," images that understandably "provoke disgust," miss the point, for "the images are but popular helps for understanding of the idea," where, "the idea itself is primary."[162] He is clear that in maintaining the idea, "it is not likely that it will revert to precisely the same forms of expression that it has used in the past; its revival will not consist in putting back of the clock,"[163] as seen in the Army's contemporary shift of focus from war against the devil to fighting social evils, in which the military metaphor is less dramatic and potent.

In contrast to its first edition, the Army's *Handbook of Doctrine* discussion of last things does not even mention either Satan or the Devil as the enemy.[164] The focus is the positive hope of God's kingdom, in which good will triumph over evil, and death will be defeated. Whilst hell is maintained as an eternal reality, biblical images are acknowledged as pictures, in which there is no clear distinction drawn between a view of eternal punishment and eternal annihilation. Indeed the Evangelical Alliance Commission on Unity and Truth Among Evangelicals (ACUTE), clearly documents in its report, the ongoing tension within its ranks of these two conflicting views.[165] As a result the military metaphor no longer clarifies the spiritual battle with equal appeal, in which Salvationists tend to practically project themselves less as soldiers rescuing captives from Satan and more as charity workers seeking to relieve the distress of human suffering and isolation in the world.

159. Harries, *Questioning Belief*, 33.

160. Ibid., 35.

161. Aulén, *Christus Victor*, 159.

162. Ibid., 158.

163. Ibid.

164. The Salvation Army, *The Salvation Army Handbook of Doctrine*, 223–46.

165. Evangelical Alliance, *The Nature of Hell*, 96–110.

Thirdly, in spite of this subtle changing of identity, Salvationist leaders are reluctant to face the possibility that the need for flexibility and adaptability to changing terrain might actually require the Army to divest itself completely of all its military vestments in its ongoing pilgrimage. When Needham suggests that an army does not identify itself "with any particular culture or society,"[166] he has neglected the reality that The Salvation Army and its metaphor is the specific product of an imperial age, as demonstrated in the first two chapters, and now lives in a post-imperial world. Salvationists might suggest that its growth into an international movement belies that fact. Nevertheless, anyone who broadly glances at the statistical analysis produced in The Salvation Army's annual *Year Book*, can see that its numerical strength has declined in nations with an established democracy and a growing egalitarian philosophy, in comparison to its growth in nations with a fragile democracy or none at all, where there is a more prevalent hierarchical society.[167]

Whilst such an observation requires a more detailed examination of its contributing causes, such as the rise of secularism and a postmodern aversion to so-called overarching authoritarian and manipulative metanarratives,[168] the general point may be made that the idea of the Church as an army is not cultureless. It has to be seriously contemplated that the metaphor could be totally inappropriate in a particular culture or society, with the resulting identity crisis that this might precipitate. Salvationists therefore need to reflect more deeply upon the uniformity that the metaphor of an army engenders, and its appropriateness as a visible expression of God's Church. It is in this respect that the cords of mission, army and church have become tangled. This will be developed more fully in the next two sections.

The Order of an Army

The discussion of the Church as a pilgrim people has already established that The Salvation Army points to the diversity of church order in the

166. Needham, *Community in Mission*, 55.

167. A comparison of the 1995 and 2011 yearbooks for example show the UK membership (Soldiers and Adherents) falling from 58,687 to 40,371 and the Zimbabwe membership (Soldiers and Adherents) rising from 69,353 to 129,765.

168. See Thiselton, *Interpreting God and the Postmodern Self*, 11–17.

NT, together with what it suggests is the essential "spiritual nature" of the church, in allowing it freedom to organize its life and ministry in the manner deemed to be most appropriate to its mission, and that this has resulted in a military form. Needham is confident that the decisive departure from a conciliar style governance by committee, and the adoption of an autocratic style of governance, of which Dr. Randall Davidson was so critical in early negotiations with the Church of England, is one of The Salvation Army's strengths, for "many situations on the missionary battlefield require a powerful leader who can act decisively" and many of the Army's "missionary advances would not have been possible without a strong central government."[169]

The Office of the General continues to be a defining and closely guarded characteristic of Salvation Army order, intent as it is to maintain a unified international denomination from central rule and command.[170] In this respect, whilst he or she chairs an International Management Council that "sees to the efficiency and effectiveness of the Army's international administration in general" and chairs the General's Consultative Council, which "advises the General on broad matters relating to the Army's mission, strategy and policy,"[171] the General remains in sole command. The model is both military and monarchical, with an extraordinary level of power and influence given to what is presumed as one functional role within the "priesthood of all believers." The General may value and most often welcome advice yet is not obliged to follow it. Separate nations or "territories" as they are known by Salvationists, (there are four territories in the U.S.A. for example), are afforded some relatively small degree of local autonomous decision making, but remain ultimately under the command of the General, whose prerogative it is to appoint the national Salvationist leader or move them as he or she thinks most appropriate.

Needham offers no theological reflection on what is essentially a sociological or organizational model of leadership, beyond his purely pragmatic comments as to its effectiveness in getting the task completed effectively.[172] The Office of the General sets up an hierarchical chain of

169. Needham, *Community in Mission*, 70.

170. See The Salvation Army, *Salvation Army Act 1980*, chapter XXX, 4–6.

171. The Salvation Army, *The Salvation Army Year Book, 2011*, 39.

172. Jewett, "An Examination of Ecclesiastical Authority," 49–65, is one critical reflection on Salvation Army governance, but not specifically from a theological point

command that descends to national level, from there to divisional or regional level, and from there to local level.[173] A burgeoning, bureaucratic, middle-management structure of advisory positions exists at all these levels to assist the chain of command in its leadership of the local level, which is broadly divided into what is known as "field" (evangelical mission in local corps congregations) and "social" (residential hostels, now known as "lifehouses" and care homes, together with other institutions such as hospitals and schools, depending upon the development of the Army's work in any particular country).

Even at local level, the congregational leader is a Corps Officer who is also known as the Commanding Officer. He or she leads the local congregation with an advisory council, to some of whom may be delegated the leadership of local aspects of the Army's mission and worship. These local leaders, who are Salvation Army Soldiers, are known as "local officers" and will be members of the congregation who usually find their everyday employment outside of the organization. Needham suggests that "Salvationist government is episcopal in substance—that is authority resides in a 'bishop' rather than in the local congregation or a judicatory."[174] In many respects this is a misleading analogy for a denomination that does not adhere to an apostolic succession. Furthermore, a regional leader, who might be viewed as a bishop, stands under the command of a Territorial Commander, who in turn stands under the command of the General. Needham himself admits that Booth "found more practical help from the regulations of the British Army than from the disciplines and methods of the churches."[175]

Little theological reflection has been given to this chain of command, in which all the relevant positions are filled by commissioned Salvation Army Officers following their residential training at a Salvation Army College for Officer Cadets. Considerable discussion has, however, developed about the nature of Officership in its relation to those local members of The Salvation Army known as Soldiers. Needham suggests that "the understanding of ordination which arises out of a Salvationist ecclesiology can be described in the word commissioning" in which

---

of view.

173. See Larsson, 1929, 310. Larsson relates how a motion to limit the powers of the General and make the General accountable to a council of Commissioners was lost.

174. Needham, *Community in Mission*, 68.

175. Ibid.

someone is "formally assigned to carry out a specific responsibility" in which "function . . . rather than ecclesiastical status, broadens the concept of ministry to include everyone in the fellowship."[176] Needham is insistent that "no Salvationist ecclesiology is adequate which does not affirm this inclusive calling to ministry because it is based on both scriptural imperative and Salvationist heritage."[177] He is, however, later forced to explain that whilst all members of the Church may be commissioned, and therefore supposedly ordained, the Army has introduced the language of ordination exclusively for Officers.[178]

This decision taken by General Arnold Brown in 1978, has encouraged some Salvationist reflection on the nature of Officership and Soldiership, and an intense discussion has ensued.[179] Much of this discussion has focused upon the term "ordination" which is foreign to Salvationist ears, in which concern is expressed that it creates, or to some minds exacerbates within the movement, the separation between the so called laity and clergy. In reality such discussion misses the point made by General Brown when he introduced an Ordination Ceremony for officers in 1978 that the commissioning ceremony "is in every way, and equals, an ordination."[180] In other words he was simply clarifying what was in actual practise already the case. This practise had already been intimated by General Orsborn in 1954, when in sharing his concerns about the WCC's search for visible unity, he commented that:

> We cannot allow the effective ordination (commissioning) of our officers, including the women, to be challenged. We should never agree to their re-ordination at the hands of anyone.[181]

Needham contends that the nature of this ordination remains functional and consists of a "commissioning to specific ministries within the con-

---

176. Ibid., 48.

177. Ibid., 49.

178. Ibid., 65.

179. Chapter 2 referenced: Hill, *Leadership in the Salvation Army*, which gives a detailed account of this discussion. On "ordination." See also: Brown, *The Gate and the Light*, 22; Thurian, *Churches Respond to BEM*, 4:256; The Salvation Army, *Servants Together*, 69–83.

180. Cited in Hill, *Leadership in The Salvation Army*, 155, from a letter in The Salvation Army International Headquarters Archives.

181. Orsborn, "The World Council of Churches," 77.

text of the Church's mission — ministries that require theological train-ing, specialized skills, pastoral leadership and a full time vocation."[182]

In reviewing the Army's governance, Needham accepts that "the autocratic form of government needs to be evaluated in relation to the contemporary mission field" for whilst invaluable in establishing the Army's presence around the world, "today, a complex and top-heavy bureaucracy encourages autocratic decision-making which is slow, cumbersome and insufficiently responsive to the needs of the field," and "needs to be mediated by grassroots participation in planning."[183] He also concedes that "there are 'status' overtones to the Army's military form of ecclesiastical government, and that some officers have mistak-enly viewed their calling as spiritually superior to that of the local officer [a member of the congregation with a delegated leadership function]."[184] This latter comment concurs with Hill's view that the combination of a military form of government and a process of institutionalization has effectively over time clericalized The Salvation Army's approach to ministry.[185]

In 1995 the International Conference of Leaders, meeting in Hong Kong, requested, "that the roles of officers and soldiers be defined and a theology of the 'priesthood of all believers' be developed to encour-age greater involvement in ministry."[186] General Paul Rader asked the International Doctrine Council to address this recommendation. The response focuses on the nature of "servant leadership" in which it affirms that in "not drawing rigid lines between officers and soldiers, it has been one of the distinctives of The Salvation Army to believe that . . . no es-sential ministry exercised by a Salvation Army officer . . . could not also be carried out by a soldier."[187] Nevertheless, the question is asked: "How does commissioning and ordination to Salvation Army officership differ from Christ's call to all Christians to be involved in Christian ministry?" The respondent struggles to pinpoint an answer, but suggests it has to do "with an authority of office in terms of the officer's relationship to the movement, the expectations of the movement towards the officer,

182. Ibid., 65.
183. Ibid., 73.
184. Ibid., 48.
185. Hill, *Leadership in the Salvation Army*, 73.
186. The Salvation Army, *Servants Together*, 127.
187. Ibid., 78.

decision-making powers related to finances, property, worship leadership and availability" in which "the officer has a particular function to be a focus for the mission and ministry of the Army,"[188] none of which are redolent of theological significance.

Regardless of efforts to oppose the process of clericalization, the autocratic structure and hierarchical nature of Salvation Army officer leadership has inexorably created a separation between the laity and the clergy that constantly threatens the exercise of ministry by all. Although reflection on what Hill calls the "Salvation Army's hierarchical institutional structure and the 'all lay' ethos which it inherited from its radical Protestant antecedents,"[189] or as this study maintains more specifically from its holiness revivalist origins, is vital, the issue will not be resolved without reform of The Salvation Army's structure.

In adopting a military metaphor, the debilitating nature of clericalization, in terms of its impact upon the mobilization of every member into ministry, has become ingrained in the very fabric of the movement. Salvationists who dislike this influence do not know how to deal with it, other than by dismantling the whole apparatus of a military command and rank structure, any suggestion of which is dismissed by those who support the *status quo* and who believe in strong central government.[190] Even if Needham's suggestion were maintained, that every member is essentially ordained in their commissioning to a specific ministry, Salvation Army autocracy and hierarchy would remain. Salvationists have not reflected deeply enough upon the fundamental issue, that a theology of ministry, however "spiritual" it may be in essence, requires an appropriate visible form. It is not appropriate to choose a sociological model of leadership and to assume that a theological rationale can be bolted on to this model after the event. In that respect Salvationists have continued to give little reflection to the nature of the Church, and in par-

---

188. Ibid.

189. Hill, *Leadership in the Salvation Army*, 274.

190. General Gowans (1999–2002) attempted to reduce and simplify the officer rank structure. General Clifton (2006–2011) overturned those reforms and re-introduced a senior rank (Lt. Colonel) that Gowans had eliminated. Harold Hill notes that the 2008 revised edition of *Servants Together* has taken out three recommendations from the first edition published in 2002, these being "develop non-career-orientated leadership models," "dismantle as many forms of officer elitism as possible," and "continue to find ways to expand participatory decision-making" (Hill, "The Language of Ordination," 14).

ticular to what has already been described as the "Church as *koinonia*," to which suggestions of hierarchy and a structure of military ranks are painfully at odds.

Ultimately Salvationists have not reflected upon the possibility that the desire for strong government and a command structure has stemmed from the highly individualistic expression of their early mission, in which autocratic leadership was required to efficiently marshal the early "voluntaristic" pioneers of the movement in the same direction, towards the execution of a task; such a pre-occupation offers little reflection upon the nature of the community from which the task ensues, in which *koinonia* cannot be forced obedience. There is widespread ecumenical rejection of this kind of dominating leadership. Joseph Ratzinger laments "an idea of ministry as the domination of a ruler on the model of the Enlightenment."[191] Paul Fiddes offers a theology of God's "suffering love" that "wins through without compulsion" and which "must undermine any view of a hierarchy of submission within the church." Such a "vision of God . . . shows us the central place of serving within authority."[192]

The Membership of an Army

The Salvationist expectation, above all odds, that Christian ministry should be expressed as a "priesthood of all believers," in which there is no ecclesiastical "status" but only diversity in the functions of ministry, has been sustained by the high expectations of what it means to be an active rather than a passive Soldier. Every soldier is called to live sacrificially in fulfilling God's mission. Needham is keen to equate the movement of grace in an individual's life from conversion to Salvation Army soldiership, with baptism. The mercy seat and the enrolment ceremony of a soldier are symbolic equivalents, a kind of "dry" baptism. Needham states that "the soldier enrolment makes clear that discipleship is the purpose of conversion, and it celebrates the convert's acceptance of this calling by utilizing the military metaphor of enlistment into a life of spiritual discipline and warfare (Eph 6:11–17; 1 Timothy 6:12; 2 Timothy 2:3, 4)."[193] He draws attention to the reality that the Church took the Roman military oath or *sacramentum,* and adopted it "to signify the decisive act of

191. Ratzinger, *Church, Ecumenism and Politics,* 129.

192. Fiddes, *Tracks and Traces,* 96.

193. Needham, *Community in Mission,* 11.

becoming a soldier of Christ" and that "baptism, and especially the vows taken at baptism, came to be called the *sacramentum*."[194] The life of the Christian disciple or soldier, is therefore one of obedience and "sworn allegiance to Jesus Christ as Commander-in-Chief" in which he or she "has been commissioned to do battle."[195] This commissioning unites all disciples of Christ, in which "the doctrine of the priesthood of all believers, therefore, has a profound affinity to the view of the Church as God's pilgrim people,"[196] not to mention God's army. Needham calls this "a *democratic* understanding of ministry" which "centres on the calling and contribution of each pilgrim," in a church that has "no time to create an ecclesiastical hierarchy."[197] In this sense everyone is a soldier, including the officers, who are simply functional servant leaders in the army, the "priesthood of all believers."

There is no doubt that this is the powerful metaphor that the Booths aimed to establish, and is the essential dynamic that lies at the heart of the movement's initial growth, under Booth's charismatic and visionary leadership. It has, however, been an impossible ideal to maintain within the terms of the military metaphor that became established and institutionalized, in which the dynamic autocracy of a visionary and charismatic founder, has given way to a more static and debilitating hierarchical structure.

On reflection, Needham is prepared to say that "outmoded traditions often survive past their time by becoming sacralised and institutionalized,"[198] and that "care needs to be taken to avoid an idolatrous pitfall: the spiritualization of the Army's regimented structure . . . which would obscure the sociological realities which underlie its life and structure and consequently cause organisational blindness."[199] This is another astute observation and warning, but does not acknowledge that the visible form of the Church, whilst expressed in human socio-

194. Ibid., 54. Needham's source for this information is: Weber, *Salty Christians*, 25. See Tertullian's use of *sacramentum*: "now that faith has been enlarged to include belief in his birth, passion, and resurrection, there is an enlargement added to the mystery [*sacramentum*], namely, the sealing of baptism," in Bettenson, *The Early Christian Fathers*, 144.

195. Needham, *Community in Mission*, 56.

196. Ibid., 42.

197. Ibid.

198. Ibid., 43.

199. Ibid., 74.

logical terms, must also be theologically credible. The metaphor of the soldier finds rich theological precedent in scripture, but can be pressed too far. The obvious correlation to the soldier is the officer or captain, who in scripture is presented as Christ, and not an elaborate human and hierarchical structure of military ranks, for which there is no theological justification offered.[200]

One further area that neither Needham nor Salvationists in general reflect deeply upon is the question of whether the enrolment of soldiers is indeed a kind of "dry" equivalent to baptism, in which the Salvationist position continues to maintain that true baptism is the baptism of the Holy Spirit, which does not require the use of water.[201] A summary of The Salvation Army's response to *BEM* suggests that the "Salvation Army cannot be termed completely 'non-sacramental' as its 'outward signs of inward grace' are sacred indeed . . . [including] . . . the scriptural discipline of a Soldier of Christ involved in the public declaration and enrolment ceremony for Salvation Army Soldiership (church member-ship plus)."[202] It is the phrase "church membership plus" which reveals that the requirements of soldiership are above and beyond the simple reception from God of a free gift of grace, and involve lifestyle choices that include the signing of *The Soldier's Covenant* (or *Articles of War* as it was formerly known). Promises are made to, amongst other things, total abstinence and absolute obedience to the command structure of The Salvation Army and its *Orders and Regulations for Soldiers*. When The Salvation Army suggests that it is *a* church, it has not reflected suf-ficiently on whether this highly disciplined expression of discipleship is the form that most clearly articulates what it means to enter into cov-enant with God and God's people in the one, holy catholic and apostolic Church, or whether it more accurately expresses the army as a special quasi-missionary religious order within that Church.

Soldiership is the only form of "full membership" in The Salvation Army. There is a secondary form of belonging as an adherent, signalled merely as "a step in the journey of faith," and an entry into "Salvation

200. For an explanation of how Joseph Ratzinger compares a "misunderstanding of hierarchy springing from the Enlightenment" with "hierarchical service and ministry" as "guarding an origin that is holy, and not making arbitrary dispositions and decisions," see Ratzinger, *Church, Ecumenism and Politics*, 128f.

201. See Street, *Called to Be God's People*, 94, 105.

202. Thurian , *Ecumenical Perspectives on Baptism*, 162. See also Street, *Called to Be God's People*, 94, 105.

Army fellowship," rather than an entry into "full commitment."[203] This distinction is seen in an altogether more revealing light when it is understood that in 2004, General Larsson upgraded the status of adherents to the new term of "adherent member," explaining that such a person is somebody "who, while not entering into the soldier's covenant, believes in the Lord Jesus Christ and seeks to follow and be like him; participates in the worship, fellowship, service and support of a local Salvation Army congregation; and identifies with the mission of The Salvation Army."[204]

Larsson explains the issue as "how best to recognise as part of The Salvation Army fellowship those persons who come to faith within the Army, or who are already believers when they come to the Army, but who do not wish to be—or for some reason cannot be—soldiers."[205] Most significantly, having considered various options as to the precise nature of the status of "adherent members" the General decided that the word "member" does not indicate that adherents are "full members of The Salvation Army in the way that soldiers are and do not make the same commitments" in which it is "possible to retain the lack of 'regulation' and the freedom that is such a valued part of the adherency system."[206] Such an expression leaves these "adherent members" in a strange state of limbo. Whilst they have made a profession of faith, they are not full members of The Salvation Army; they exist on a lower tier of membership, and in Salvation Army terms are not acknowledged as full members of God's Church and unable to enter into some aspects of ministry available to those soldiers who belong to the "priesthood of all believers."

Conclusion

This chapter represents the culmination of an analysis of the emerging ecclesiological practice and convictions of The Salvation Army, from its origins in nineteenth-century holiness revivalism, through three distinct phases of its life, as a young, non-denominational Christian Mission, as a newly named Salvation Army with a specific denominational identity and as a contemporary denomination seeking to explain the way in

203. The Salvation Army, *The Salvation Army in the Body of Christ*, 8

204. The Salvation Army, "Orders and Regulations of The Salvation Army," as recorded in *Salvationist*, March 6, 2004, 1.

205. Ibid.

206. Ibid.

which it belongs to and expresses the nature, form and mission of the one universal Church of Jesus Christ. All three phases are crucial to a full understanding of the complex influences that have been at work, in which it is maintained in this book that a cord with three identifiable ecclesial strands of mission, army and church has emerged. Rather than these three strands proving mutually beneficial and adding value to further ecumenical reflection upon the nature of the one Church, it has here been argued that in The Salvation Army's historical development and practise, these strands have become tangled and create unwelcome tension.

This chapter has in particular revealed a defensive lack of real engagement by Salvationists in ecumenical ecclesiology, and a reluctance to engage in a search for "visible unity" as its goal. This is partly illustrated by the way in which a Salvationist emphasis upon the pilgrim people of God, does not give any focus to that ecumenical journey. The resistance of Salvationists to this process may be explained by their emphasis upon the spiritual nature of the Church to the detriment of the theological adequacy of its visible expression. It is not that Salvationists betray a docetic lack of interest in the visible form of the Church. They are pre-occupied with a highly visible sociological form of their life together to the detriment of an adequate theological reflection upon that visible form.

This is most dramatically seen in the way that Salvationists discard baptism and the Lord's Supper as being of no importance, when they should be retained as the visible signs and symbols of the fellowship of the sacramental life that they seek to articulate. In this lack of focus on the sacraments, and the concept of *koinonia* that they embody, they support a visible sociological form inspired more by an individualistic expression of their mission, to save souls, than by one which might more clearly symbolise their life together, in the Trinitarian life of God, from which their mission can overflow. This in turn has been supported by a highly subjective focus upon the human conditions of salvation. Ironically, the Salvationist longing for diversity in the Church of God, has been supplanted by uniformity within its own life. This uniformity is entrenched by an autocratic and hierarchical governance structure that focuses more specifically upon the task in hand than the interdependent life of the community held in common together.

In this structure, in which the military metaphor is pressed too far, the positive metaphor of the soldier of Christ fully mobilized within the "priesthood of all believers" is overwhelmed by the clericalizing influence of a military command structure. The Salvationist lack of theological reflection upon this sociological form has ironically left it vulnerable to the sacralization of its human structure, in which it ultimately finds it almost impossible to contemplate that this form, adopted for its mobility and flexibility on the pilgrim journey, might prove obsolete at some point along the changing terrain of that journey. Overall in these three chapters it has been suggested that the Booths' conception of an aggressive Christianity, characterized by Orsborn as a "permanent mission to the unconverted," further conceived and institutionalized as a military army—a special, disciplined, emergency service or quasi-missionary religious order—creates real and unwelcome tension in its efforts to faithfully express what God has called and commissioned God's Church to be.

It is therefore of vital importance that the Army reflects theologically upon its practise, and in this connection the second part of this study will enter into dialogue with the ecclesiology of Karl Barth. The need for reflection is most graphically illustrated by a recent rallying call from the Army's leadership to those Salvationists who might be tempted to divest the military metaphor:

> I believe that the Army was raised up by God for a great purpose, and that he wants us to be what we were raised up to be, and to do what we were raised up to do. He wants us to be The Salvation Army—not a pale imitation of some other church. He wants us to be ourselves! God wants us to be The Salvation Army. Let's dare to be different.[207]

Nothing in this statement of separate identity attempts to enunciate for Salvationists how they faithfully express the nature, form and mission of the one, holy, catholic and apostolic Church of God.

---

207. Larsson, "Being True to Ourselves," 3.

Part Two

The Salvation Army
in Dialogue with Karl Barth

Introduction

Ecclesiology is an integral aspect of Karl Barth's theology. Speaking in 1957 on the subject of evangelical theology in the nineteenth century, he explains that a more fitting description of the Christian task than theology, defined by him literally as "the science and doctrine of God," requires

> the more complex term "The-anthropology." For an abstract doctrine of God has no place in the Christian realm, only a "doctrine of God and of man," a doctrine of the commerce and communion between God and man.[1]

John Webster is prepared to signal this concept of "the-anthropology" as the "larger purpose of the *Church Dogmatics* . . . an extended description of the history of the covenant between God Creator, Redeemer, and Reconciler, and the human creature and partner."[2] In his 1956 lecture "The Humanity of God" Barth outlines his mature understanding of this theological anthropology, that "who God is and what He is in His deity He proves and reveals not in a vacuum as a divine being-for-Himself, but precisely and authentically in the fact that He exists, speaks, and acts as the *partner* of man, though of course as the absolutely superior partner."[3] Central to this understanding is the Christological recognition that "it is precisely God's deity, which rightly understood, includes his humanity," for "in Jesus Christ . . . we encounter the history, the dialogue, in which God and man meet together and are together, the reality of the covenant mutually contracted, preserved, and fulfilled by them," and in which "Jesus Christ is in His one Person, as true *God, man's* loyal partner, and

---

1. Barth, *The Humanity Of God*, 11.
2. Webster, *Barth's Ethics of Reconciliation*, 118.
3. Barth, *The Humanity of God*, 45.

as *true man, God's.*"[4] Barth maintains that this understanding of the humanity of God has as one of its main consequences that "one must take seriously, affirm, and thankfully acknowledge *Christendom*, the *Church*. We must, each in his place, take part in its life and join in its service."[5]

Ecclesiology is, therefore, an integral aspect of Barth's "Theanthropology," but a complex study nonetheless, for it is already apparent that it must be understood in *Church Dogmatics* in relation to the doctrines of God, Revelation, Christology and Reconciliation. Kimlyn Bender assures us that this should come as no surprise, "for ecclesiology itself is a derived system, dependent upon other theological doctrines and their attendant propositions and principles to provide it with shape and substance,"[6] and further that it is also "a synthetic doctrine—it includes within it many aspects of theology."[7] Bender is convinced that only by understanding Barth's doctrine of the church in the wider context of the *Church Dogmatics* as a whole, and by appreciating the way in which he incorporates ethics into dogmatics, can "many missteps in the interpretation of Barth's ecclesiology"[8] be avoided.

This indicates the first reason why Barth is a helpful conversation partner. He offers a denomination like The Salvation Army, which has engaged in limited reflection upon the nature, form and mission of the Church, a coherent ecclesiology fully integrated within his theological anthropology.

Secondly Barth's is an ecclesiology fully integrated within his avowedly evangelical theology, and therefore readily accessible in assisting the avowedly Protestant evangelical Salvation Army to articulate its own confession. This does not negate the value in Salvationists reflecting upon other approaches, but recognizes Barth's own insistence that one can only begin to listen to God from within one's own church, and within an ecumenical context allow particular confessions to meet and challenge each other.[9]

Thirdly, Barth's re-working of Protestant theology is insightful for Salvationists whose doctrinal confessions are largely the product of a

4. Ibid., 46.

5. Ibid., 62.

6. Bender, *Karl Barth's Christological Ecclesiology*, 1.

7. Ibid.

8. Ibid., 2.

9. See Barth, *The Church and the Churches*, 49f.

practical theology worked out within a polemical argument between what might be called high Calvinists and Wesleyan Arminians. Barth attempts to chart a new way between these two approaches. In that Salvationists have, from this polemical argument, developed a highly individualistic and subjective focus in their soteriology, Barth, who as Daniel Migliore suggests, "opposed all forms of individualism and subjectivism in his theology,"[10] is a helpful dialogue partner, and his ecclesiology is of significance. This relates in particular to his doctrine of election and to his soteriology, in which his account of the scope of salvation and the holiness of the Church is pertinent to the Salvationist reflecting upon her holiness revivalist heritage.

Fourthly, in view of the first part of this study presenting The Salvation Army's ecclesiology as a tangled cord of mission, army and church, there is value for the Salvationist in reflecting upon what has often been termed Barth's "christological ecclesiology,"[11] for it positively offers to identify and untangle these strands towards a deeper understanding of the nature, form and mission of the Church.

Finally, this study suggests that Salvationists need to rehabilitate a positive understanding of baptism and the Lord's Supper in their life and witness, with a more objective appreciation of God's grace. Barth's account of the Holy Spirit's realization of God's self-determined and actualized covenant of grace in Christ, which controversially views these practises as human actions or testimonies in response to God's initiative, helps Salvationists to be clear on what kind of sacramentality they are advocating in their seemingly confused articulation of the sacramental life, and whether these practises should have an important place or not.

10. Migliore, "Reforming the Theology," 509.
11. See in particular Bender, *Karl Barth's Christological Ecclesiology*.

4

Electing the Christian Community

Barth is clear that the doctrine of election, in the way that it is bound up with the doctrine of God, is the essential foundation for an understanding of ecclesiology, for "if, in our later treatment of the doctrine of the Church, we are to stand on the firm ground which is none other than the Church's eternal divine election . . . then we must begin our consideration . . . in the doctrine of God Himself as the Lord and founder of the Church."[1] This is immediately difficult language for the Salvationist informed by a line of protest against Calvin's doctrine of election, from Jacob Arminius and the Dutch Remonstrants in the seventeenth century, to John Wesley and the Arminian Methodists of the eighteenth century and Charles Finney and the "arminianising" American New Divinity theology of the nineteenth century. Each in turn attempts to articulate, against Calvin's "absolute decree," that salvation and therefore the Church is potentially God's gracious gift for everyone.

Barth's Doctrine of Election as the Foundation of Ecclesiology

Salvationists should reflect upon Barth's account of election, as it charts a new way forward; one that he believes avoids the errors of both Calvin's *decretum absolutum* and an Arminian account of co-operating free will that focuses too heavily upon human decision, from a position of apparent freedom. Barth strikes a positive note:

1. Barth, *Church Dogmatics*, II. 2, 89; hereafter cited as *CD*. (In all page references to the Church Dogmatics, the bracketed page references are given which refer to the original English publication in 14 volumes, rather than the page references of the newly published version in 31 volumes.)

The doctrine of the election is the sum of the Gospel . . . that God elects man; that God is for man too the One who loves in freedom. It is grounded in the knowledge of Jesus Christ because He is both the electing God and elected man in One . . . Its function is to bear basic testimony to eternal, free and unchanging grace as the beginning of all the ways and works of God.[2]

Key elements of this statement require fuller explanation. Firstly, Barth is clear that theology "must begin with Jesus Christ, and not with general principles,"[3] since "Jesus Christ is indeed God in His movement towards man, or more exactly, in His movement towards the people represented in the one man Jesus of Nazareth, in His covenant with this people."[4]

Secondly, since God "is disclosed only in the name of Jesus Christ . . . then we cannot stop at this point, defining and expounding the Subject only in and for itself."[5] Rather, God's revelation of the Word of God and of Jesus Christ is the starting point for working back to an understanding of God in God's eternity, "without engaging in speculation,"[6] moving from the "particular to the general,"[7] for "in Him [Jesus Christ] God stands before man and man stands before God."[8] Therefore a Christian doctrine of God "makes the Subject known as One which in virtue of its innermost being, willing and nature does not stand outside all relationships, but stands in a definite relationship *ad extra* another."[9] In other words, to know God is to know the One who has self-determined to be for God's people in the God-human relation of God's Son Jesus Christ, for the "doctrine of God would be incomplete without . . . the decision in which God gives Himself to another, to man."[10] Barth does not mean that God's eternal self-determining differentiation as Father, Son and Spirit,

2. Ibid., 3.

3. Ibid., 2.

4. Ibid., 7.

5. Ibid., 5. For an explanation of Barth's understanding of an "abstract" proposal as opposed to a "concrete" proposal, see Hunsinger, *How to Read Karl Barth*, 32.

6. McCormack, "Grace and Being," 92. I am indebted to McCormack for his understanding of the moves which Barth makes in his doctrine of election, which McCormack himself esteems as Barth's "greatest contribution . . . to the development of church doctrine" (ibid.).

7. *CD* II.1, 602.

8. *CD* II.2, 94.

9. Ibid., 6.

10. Ibid., 52.

understood theologically as the immanent Trinity, is, as McCormack puts it, "collapsed into the historical act of incarnation."[11] Barth is explicit that the God-human relation "is a relation *ad extra*, undoubtedly; for both the man and the people represented in Him are creatures and not God," nevertheless, "it is a relation which is irrevocable, so that once God has willed to enter into it, and has in fact entered into it, He could not be God without it."[12] Barth suggests, therefore, that the immanent Trinity is identical in content with the economic Trinity,[13] and God's anticipation in eternity of what God will reveal of God's self in time, when the pre-temporal and "primal decision" is revealed in history.

Thirdly, this is not a necessary decision for man that would undermine God's freedom and therefore God's graciousness. God's determination is a free decision, for "God is the One who unconditionally precedes the creature."[14] As a decision that God makes in freedom, it is therefore a gracious and loving decision, "the self-determination of God as Lord and Shepherd of this people."[15] Barth affirms that "God has decided for this loftiest and most radical movement towards His creation, ordaining and constituting Himself its Friend and Benefactor."[16] He is clear that election "is the sum of the Gospel . . . the whole of the Gospel, the Gospel *in nuce*,"[17] and "the beginning of all the ways and works of God."[18]

Fourthly, Jesus Christ is, therefore, both the subject as well as the object of election, for "God is none other than the One who in His Son or Word elects Himself, and in and with Himself elects His people."[19] Barth refutes Reformation statements that abstractly begin "either with the concept of an electing God or with that of elected man," insisting that they "must begin concretely with the acknowledgement of Jesus Christ as both the electing God and elected man."[20] The "critical significance" of this assertion for Barth, over against the traditional doctrine, is that

11. McCormack, "Grace and Being," 100.

12. *CD* II.2, 7.

13. See *CD* I.1, 479.

14. *CD* II.2, 27.

15. Ibid., 53.

16. Ibid., 26.

17. Ibid., 13.

18. Ibid., 93.

19. Ibid., 76.

20. Ibid.

"it crowds out and replaces the idea of a *decretum absolutum*," which "speaks of a good-pleasure of God which in basis and direction is unknown to man and to all beings outside God Himself."[21] Barth defends his view that Jesus is the subject of election through his exegesis of the prologue to John's Gospel,[22] which makes it clear that Jesus Christ was in the beginning with God. On this basis Barth implores us to abandon any suggestion that there might be "a *decretum absolutum*" or "a secret and hidden will of God"[23] behind the revelation of Jesus Christ, for God "does not exist . . . without the covenant with man which was made and executed in this name."[24]

Jesus Christ is also elected man, with foundational implications for ecclesiology. Barth explains that Jesus of Nazareth is "not merely one of the elect, but *the* elect of God."[25]

> What singles Him out from the rest of the elect, and yet also, and for the first time, unites Him with them, is the fact that as elected man He is also the electing God, electing them in His own humanity. In that He (as God) wills Himself (as man), He also wills them. And so they are elect "in Him," in and with His own election.[26]

The covenantal relationship of grace established by God's eternal act of self-determination is first a relationship with the man Jesus, and only "in Him" a relationship with others. The humanity of Jesus, therefore, has real and representative significance for what it means to be truly human.

> God awakens man to existence before Him and summons him to His service. God in His Son is Himself the person of man . . . God creates Him for His own Word. God vouchsafes to grant Him a part in His own suffering for man's frailty and sin . . . God justifies Him, raises Him from the dead, gives Him a part in His own glory. All that man can and will do is to pray, to follow and obey.[27]

21. Ibid., 103.
22. Ibid., 95–99.
23. Ibid., 115.
24. Ibid., 509.
25. Ibid., 116.
26. Ibid., 117.
27. Ibid., 177.

Barth insists that this is not God's "autocratic self-seeking, but a love which directs itself outwards, a self giving to the creature" in which God is "willing and recognising the distinct reality of the creature, granting and conceding to it an individual and autonomous place side by side with Himself" even if "the individuality and autonomy are only of such a kind as His own goodness can concede and grant."[28] Crucially, it is not an individuality and autonomy that "should be possessed outside Him, let alone against Him, but for Him, and within His kingdom; not in rivalry with His sovereignty but for its confirming and glorifying," as "decision for Him."[29] This is the free human decision that Barth sees in the man Jesus, who

> Prays . . . speaks and acts . . . He thinks of Himself as the Messiah, the Son of God. He allows Himself to be called *Kyrios*, and in fact, conducts Himself as such. He speaks of His suffering, not as a necessity laid upon Him from without, but as something which He Himself wills.[30]

In Jesus Christ, therefore, God is for man in free and gracious, covenantal relationship, and man is for God in free and obedient human decision and faith.

Fifthly, Barth still sounds the note of judgement, a "double predestination" found in traditional presentations, but without what he describes as its "dualism," or its "equilibrium," for "the only knowledge which we have of man's foreordination to evil and death is in the form in which God of His great mercy accepted it as His own portion and burden, removing it from us and refusing to let it be our foreordination in any form."[31] This removal took place in Jesus Christ. Rather than equilibrium, Barth posits God's predominant "Yes" for the "life and blessedness" of man, with the subordinate "No" of man's reprobation. "The first is an authoritative Yes, the second a No which is determined only by the Yes, thus losing its authority from the very outset."[32] God, therefore,

28. Ibid., 178.

29. Ibid.

30. Ibid.

31. Ibid., 171f.

32. Ibid., 172, 13.

"takes upon Himself the rejection of man with all its consequences, and elects man to participation in His own glory."[33]

Barth's Doctrine of Election and The Salvation Army

The Salvation Army draws its understanding of salvation broadly from John Wesley, albeit mediated through holiness revivalism. Booth adopted *carte blanche* the doctrinal formulations of the Methodist New Connexion. He would have recognized in broad terms, and "in the perspective of Protestant history" Henry Rack's summary of Wesley's attempt "to reconcile the notion of a salvation that depends on a divine act of grace to save fallen men with a desire for a positive and progressive attitude towards a recreation of the personality by a progressive realization of the mind of Christ in which men can take an active part."[34] His attempt was shaped by his lifelong opposition to what he saw as Calvinistic determinism, predestination, unconditional election and limited atonement. A year before his death Wesley wrote, "I still witness the same confession . . . The sum of all is this; the God of love is willing to save all the souls that he has made."[35]

Wesley's attempt to reconcile divine initiative in grace and co-operative human response, has led many scholars to investigate sources in his Anglican High Church roots, and in Puritanism, where both his parents began their faith journey. Rack is unconvinced that analyzing sources is ultimately helpful due to the highly selective way in which Wesley used them, preferring to view Wesley as "a High Churchman led almost accidentally by his own quest for holiness into leadership of a semi-popular religious movement in areas subject to gradually accelerating social change."[36] Yet Herbert McGonigle finds Wesley's sources compelling evidence for distinguishing his "evangelical Arminianism" from both Dutch Remonstrant theology and the contemporary English Arminianism of his High Church Anglicanism. He argues that, "John Wesley was an Arminian, but he was a new-style Arminian; his Arminianism was unashamedly orthodox and, beyond even Arminius

33. Ibid., 94.

34. Rack, *Reasonable Enthusiast*, 409.

35. Wesley, *The Works of John Wesley,* Bicentennial edition, 4:148; Hereafter *Works* [BE].

36. Rack, *Reasonable Enthusiast*, 409.

himself, it had caught the fire of the Holy Spirit and burned with evangelical fervour."[37]

Surveying the wide field of current eighteenth-century theology,
McGonigle makes the case for a unique Arminian theology, distinguished
from Remonstrant, Jansenist, Latitudinarian or Socinian Arminianism,
for "so clearly and carefully did he sift from this Arminianism all lingering traces of Pelagianism, humanism, and rationalism, and thus
made it the vehicle of an impassioned and biblical evangel of grace, that
subsequently it may be accurately designated Wesleyan Arminianism."[38]
In this respect Wesley claims to come "within a hair's breadth"[39] of
Calvinism and Antinomianism, when in 1745, no doubt anxious to
minimize as far as possible divisions and disputes between the Wesleyan
and "Calvinistic" Methodists, he confirms:

> Wherein may we come to the very edge of Calvinism? . . .
> (1.) In ascribing all good to the free grace of God. (2.) In denying
> all natural free-will, and all power antecedent to grace. And, (3.)
> In excluding all merit from man; even for what he has or does
> by the grace of God . . . Wherein may we come to the edge of
> Antinomianism? . . . (1.) In exalting the merits and love of Christ.
> (2.) In rejoicing evermore.[40]

Wesley's acceptance of an Augustinian doctrine of original sin and
his commitment to the concept of total depravity is crucial. He makes
this clear in both his long 1756 treatise *The Doctrine of Original Sin:
According to Scripture, Reason and Experience*,[41] and in his shorter
1759 sermon *Original Sin*. In the latter he confirms that: "This then is
the foundation of the new birth—the entire corruption of our nature."[42]
Notably, however, Wesley asserts that the negative effects of original sin
are opposed by prevenient grace. Whilst

> all souls of men are dead in sin by nature, this excuses none, see-
> ing there is no man that is in a state of mere nature; there is no
> man, unless he has quenched the Spirit, that is wholly void of
> the grace of God. No man living is entirely destitute of what is

37. McGonigle, *Sufficient Saving Grace*, 8.

38. Ibid., 331. For a more critical assessment see Sell, *The Great Debate*, 61–76.

39. Wesley, *The Works of the Rev. John Wesley, A. M.*, 8:284; Hereafter *Works*.

40. Ibid., 285.

41. Wesley, *Works*, 9:191.

42. Wesley, *Works* [BE], 2:170.

vulgarly called "natural conscience." But this is not natural; it is more properly termed "preventing grace."[43]

Prevenient or "preventing grace" is for Wesley Christological in the way that he uses John 1:9 to describe the light of Christ that enlightens everyone born into the world,[44] and in his understanding of Romans 5:19 to mean: "Therefore no infant was or ever will be 'sent to hell for the guilt of Adam's sin,' seeing it is cancelled by the righteousness of Christ as soon as they are sent into the world."[45] Prevenient grace, in Wesley's explanation, is mediated by the Holy Spirit. There is no innate capacity by which a person can know God, but "being reconciled to man through the Son of his love, he [God] in some measure re-inscribed the law on the heart of his dark, sinful creature."[46] According to Albert Outler, Wesley's *ordo salutis* begins with prevenient grace, in which a relationship with God is progressively deepened through convincing (convicting), justifying, sanctifying and glorifying grace. Most importantly, against the espousal of unconditional election, prevenient grace is Wesley's explanation of how God restores a measure of free will in sinful human lives. Mankind does not possess an inherent power of choice for, "natural free-will, in the present state of mankind, I do not understand: I only assert, that there is a measure of free-will supernaturally restored to every man, together with that supernatural light which 'enlightens every man that cometh into the world.'"[47]

In this sense Wesley affirmed that the Spirit "which waiteth not for the call of men,"[48] brings irresistible prevenient grace, awakening people totally depraved, by "opening the eyes of our understanding and enlightening us."[49] Yet critically, this irresistible restoration of human faculties and senses can ultimately be resisted by the person who chooses to ignore or oppose such an awakening. Wesleyan scholars refute charges of Pelagianism against Wesley's view of human co-operation. Outler, in introducing Wesley's sermon "On Working Out Our Own Salvation," declares that "if there were ever a question as to Wesley's alleged

43. Wesley, *Works* [BE], 3:207.

44. Wesley, *Explanatory Notes upon the New Testament*, John 1:19, 303.

45. Wesley, *The Letters of the Rev. John Wesley*, vol. 6.

46. Wesley, *Works* [BE] 2:7.

47. Wesley, Works, 10:229–30.

48. Wesley, *Works* [BE] Vol.3, 207.

49. Ibid., 2:410.

Pelagianism, this sermon alone should suffice to dispose of it decisively."[50] McGonigle agrees that with "the doctrines of original sin and prevenient grace . . . as the twin theological foci of John Wesley's scheme of salvation . . . his doctrine of prevenient grace enabled him to assert human responsibility while totally rejecting all forms of Pelagianism."[51]

The Salvation Army's *Handbook of Doctrine* has only recently acknowledged Wesley's understanding of prevenient grace. In its subjective account of the conditional nature of God's salvation, the 1881 *Doctrines and Discipline of The Salvation Army* did not mention it, nor did subsequent revisions introduce it. Only in 1999 were Salvationists officially informed of "grace available before coming to Christ" in which "humans are enabled to choose good, and ultimately by faith to accept God's saving grace," so that "salvation by grace through faith begins then with preventing—prevenient or enabling—grace, grace which can be resisted by free will, but if accepted, becomes the beginning of the path to salvation."[52] It is an important renewal of understanding and objectivity in a Salvationist account of soteriology.

Dialogue with Barth, equally, affords Salvationists the opportunity to engage with what Eugene Rogers calls Barth's "marvelous reworking of the doctrine of election, in which Barth makes it safe to be a Calvinist again."[53] Central to his account, in a way that distinguishes it from Wesley, is Barth's objection to the possibility that a theological understanding of the word freedom might be conceived as an individual's free-will ability to choose evil. In this respect Barth's theological anthropology in election and subsequently in justification and sanctification, attempts a dialectical account of divine and human agency in precedence and subsequence, that Salvationists must ultimately weigh against Wesley's account of a "measure of free-will supernaturally restored," in which as Rack suggests, the individual "can take an active part."

Barth twice employs the term "prevenient grace." The first instance is in relation to his discussion of God's gift of time to humanity, where he suggests that "if we are to speak of prevenient grace it is difficult to see in what better form it may be perceived and grasped than in the simple fact

---

50. Ibid., 3:199.

51. McGonigle, *Sufficient Saving Grace*, 330f.

52. The Salvation Army, *The Salvation Army Handbook of Doctrine*, 124.

53. Rogers, "The Eclipse of the Spirit in Karl Barth," 175.

that time is given to us men."[54] The second relates to Barth's discussion of infant baptism, where, in spite of his disapproval of this practice, he affirms, with Wesley, "that infant baptism is so remarkably vivid a depiction of the free and omnipotent grace of God which is independent of all human thought and will, faith and unbelief."[55] In this respect "the grace of God which has appeared in Him, even before they can respond thereto with gratitude or ingratitude, has already embraced them with high objective reality as *gratia praeveniens*."[56] For Barth, prevenient grace is the free gift of God eternally self-determined in election and objectively actualized in the atoning death and resurrection of Christ, prior to its subjective realization by the Spirit in human lives. Against Wesley, Barth is concerned to highlight grace as God's free gift for the person's freedom to respond obediently to Christ, rather than free-will ability to accept or reject Christ. For Barth, this rejection is a contradiction of God's grace which he will not discount, but will equally not characterize as freedom.

It is a position that draws considerable criticism from those who, like Rowan Williams, consider that "an emphasis upon the compelling, irresistible character of revealed truth leaves almost no room for a conception of free, creative, and *distinctive* human response"[57], which we have already seen was Wesley's concern. Barth is sympathetic of attempts to overcome Calvin's *decretum absolutum*, but ultimately critical of the seventeenth-century Dutch Remonstrants. He views them as the very first Neo-Protestants in their basic decision "that in the understanding of God and His relationship with man, in the question of the formulation of Christian doctrine, the criterion or measure of all things must always be man, i.e., man's conception of that which is right, and rational, and worthy, therefore, of God and man."[58] Even though they attempted to make Christ the basis of election, in effect their attempt did not "contend for the dignity of Jesus Christ, but for the dignity of man standing over against Jesus Christ in an autonomous freedom of decision," in which "Christ is the essence of the divine order of salvation." Barth suggests that

---

54. *CD* III.2, 526.

55. *CD* IV.4, 189.

56. Ibid., 181.

57. Williams, *Wrestling with Angels*, 140.

58. *CD* II.2, 67f.

> It is by their belief or unbelief in Him that the decision is made—according to God's foreknowledge, but independently—whether the grace of God profits or does not profit them. The Remonstrants did not say that Christ is the electing God . . . there is no more than a divine foreknowledge of what individuals will become as measured by this order of salvation and on the basis of the use which they make of their creaturely freedom.[59]

Barth's charge against their best efforts, is "a fresh approximation to the doctrine of man elected *in abstracto*, or of man's electing of God."[60] He prefers that "when we utter the name of Jesus Christ we really do speak the first and final word not only about the electing of God but also about elected man."[61] Without wishing to deny a measure of human autonomy, in which "man can and actually does elect God," he maintains that this "simple but comprehensive autonomy of the creature . . . is constituted . . . by the act of eternal divine election . . . as the One who elects God has absolute precedence over the One who is elected."[62] Barth attempts to overcome an autonomous enlightenment view of man's freedom:

> The decisive point is whether freedom in the Christian sense is identical with the freedom of Hercules: choice between two ways at a crossroad. This is a heathen notion of freedom. Is it freedom to decide for the devil? The only freedom that means something is the freedom to be myself as I am created by God . . . Being a slave of Christ means being free.[63]

Barth has been criticized by those who believe he actually articulates universalism, either replacing the determinism of double election for a determinism in which all must be saved, or of allowing God's love to undermine human freedom.[64] Understandably he refutes this criticism believing on the one hand that "we have no theological right to set any sort of limits to the loving-kindness of God which has appeared

---

59. Ibid., 68.

60. Ibid., 76.

61. Ibid.

62. Ibid., 177.

63. Barth, *Table Talk*, 37.

64. See Berkouwer, *The Triumph of Grace*, 287–96; Brunner, *Dogmatics I*, 346–53. Berkouwer thinks Barth undermines God's free decision to elect or reject, whilst Brunner thinks Barth undermines human freedom.

in Jesus,"[65] and on the other, that we cannot affirm theologically something that is only known to God. "If we are certainly forbidden to count on this . . . as though it were not supremely the work of God to which man can have no possible claim, we are surely commanded the more definitely to hope and pray for it as we may do already on this side of this final possibility."[66] Integral to Barth's position is his understanding that a theological account of universalism actually limits the freedom of God's love. As Joseph Bettis puts it, "this limitation is not primarily in the assertion that *all* men must be saved but in the assertion that any man *must* be saved."[67] In other words, whilst God may be eternally self-determined in grace for God's creation, it is a free decision in which God's love and grace are complete even without this *ad extra* towards mankind, and is therefore not a necessary determination.

Against both a *decretum absolutum* and an Arminian account of free will, Barth advocates an analogical correspondence of human decision that is dependent upon divine decision. Of particular note for Salvationist reflection is the way in which Barth handles the objective and subjective realms of salvation. As Webster notes,

> the objective is not a complete realm, separate from the subjective and, therefore, standing in need of "translation" into the subjective. Rather, the objective includes the subjective within itself, and is efficacious without reliance on a quasi-independent realm of mediating created agencies.[68]

Whether or not Barth's account of election, and his theological anthropology in general, can ultimately be accepted, an issue that will be addressed in the final section on Barth's account of baptism, it is of particular note that he speaks directly into both a highly subjective Salvationist account of salvation and confusing Salvationist accounts of sacraments and a sacramental life. Whilst affirming that they follow Wesley's account of human co-operative free will, and wish to make the case for a sacramental life, they depart from Wesley in a non-sacramental understanding of human agency without baptism and the Lord's Supper. They appear to be caught between a Wesleyan and a Barthian

65. Barth, *The Humanity of God*, 62.

66. *CD* IV.3, 478.

67. Bettis, "Is Karl Barth a Universalist?," 429.

68. Webster, *Barth's Ethics of Reconciliation*, 128.

perspective, in which their account of human agency appears, in some respects, to be closer to Wesley, and in other respects to Barth. The suspicion is that Salvationist practise is more pragmatic than theological. This confusion must also be addressed more fully in the final section of this study, where a suggestion must ultimately be made as to how it may be resolved.

5

Reconciling the Christian Community

B arth places his account of the Church largely within the context of the doctrine of reconciliation where "the covenant fulfilled in the atonement is its centre."[1] Since this doctrine presents the fulfilment of God's self-determined and eternal covenant of grace, described in God's election by Barth as "the sum of the gospel," reconciliation is therefore "the heart of the subject-matter of the Christian faith."[2] It is also the context in which Barth fully utilizes both his "actualism" and his Christological ecclesiology.

Barth's Actualism

To understand Barth's account of the Christian community, its gathering, upbuilding and sending, it is essential to understand the actualism that he employs in his doctrine of election and develops in his doctrine of reconciliation. He can call predestination a "living act" or "event,"[3] in the same way that he calls reconciliation or the Church an "event." In his description of the various motif's that Barth uses in the *Church Dogmatics*, Hunsinger explains that these are not "systematic or philosophical principles" but "qualifications of the subject matter" which Barth thinks "help to illuminate certain peculiar modes of thought implicit in the witness of scripture."[4] In Barth's use of "actualistic"

1. *CD* IV.1, 3.

2. Ibid.

3. *CD* II.2, 180. For a discussion of Barth's use of the motif of "actualism," see Hunsinger, *How To Read Karl Barth*, 30–32.

4. Hunsinger, *How To Read Karl Barth*, 29.

language, such as event, act, happening, occurrence, history, and decision, he is more interested in thinking ontologically upon active relations than upon static metaphysical substance. God is known in the act of God's revelation, and so the essence of God is known in an event or happening. Barth can say that "this essence of God which is seen in His revealed name is His being and therefore His act as Father, Son and Holy Spirit."[5] God is therefore a being-in-act in eternity, complete in the active and loving relations of Father, Son and Spirit, and in time and history, in active relation with God's creatures. Barth explains: "We must remember that *praedestinatio*, like *creatio* and *reconciliato*, like *vocatio*, *iustificatio*, *sanctificatio* and *glorificatio*, describes a divine activity, and that there is no reason whatever why we should suddenly substitute for this concept a concept of isolated and static being."[6] All these events owe their existence to an act of God in which as Herbert Hartwell puts it, Barth "does not know of any 'es gibt' ('there is') nor of any 'having' or 'possessing' that is independent of God's giving, but only a constant 'giving' and 'receiving.'"[7]

Barth describes his activist understanding of election as "an eternal happening,"[8] which "depends wholly and utterly upon the identifying of it with the election of Jesus Christ."[9] He explains that this "dynamic and activist" ontological understanding of God in God's active relations, opposes "the assertion of the divinity of static being as the beginning of all things."[10] In the "activated history" which Barth posits, "there is no knowledge of predestination except in the movement from the electing God to elected man, and back again from elected man to the electing God."[11] This directly opposes the "thought of predestination as an isolated and given enactment which God had decreed from all eternity and which to some extent pledged and committed even God Himself in time."[12] McCormack asserts that "the collision between Calvin and Barth . . . is not simply a clash between two views of the *extent* of election," but

5. *CD* II.1, 273. See *CD* II. 1, 257–321.

6. *CD* II.2, 184.

7. Hartwell, *The Theology of Karl Barth*, 33.

8. *CD* II.2, 184.

9. Ibid., 187.

10. Ibid.

11. Ibid., 186.

12. Ibid.

"at the most fundamental level . . . a clash between a theologian working with what we might call an 'essentialist' ontology and a theologian working with an 'actualistic' ontology."[13]

Since for Barth God's being positively is in God's act and negatively, God's act is in God's being, in which God cannot be described apart from the act in which God lives, then election may only be known in Jesus Christ, and not in a hidden reality behind this revelation. Furthermore, because this election is an act of sovereign grace and freedom, it means negatively that human beings have no innate ahistorical capacity to enter into fellowship with God other than positively, in the historical terms of God's activity and sovereignty. Reconciliation and the Church are equally dynamic events, anticipated by God in God's eternal and free self-determination of grace, and actualized in time and history.

Barth's dynamic conception of the Church has been criticized by some for what is perceived as an occasionalistic event that lacks continuity, undermining the "continuing historical institution"[14] that is the Church. Such criticism fails to acknowledge that the continuity of these acts is maintained by God's constant, faithful giving. As Mangina puts it, "the point of event-language is not presence or absence along a time line, but the divine mystery of the church's existence at every moment of its life" for "God sets people free to be his community by the mysterious activity of the Holy Spirit."[15] Furthermore, Barth can say that because "the being of Jesus Christ . . . takes place in the event of the concrete existence of this man," then this event is not just "a being, but a being in a history."[16] The atonement is equally "truth actualised in history and revealed in this history as such—revealed, therefore, as history," and "when it is revealed and grasped and known, it is so in its priority, its precedence, its superiority to all other histories, to the existence of all the men who take part in it."[17] As Hunsinger puts it, the event of our active relationship with God is "a history of love and freedom; we are capable of it not because it stands at our disposal, but because we who stand at

---

13. McCormack, "Grace and Being," 98.

14. Newbigin, *The Household of God*, 50.

15. Mangina, *Karl Barth*, 154.

16. Ibid., 126.

17. Ibid., 157.

God's disposal are given it . . . It is not possessed once and for all, but is continually established anew by the ongoing activity of grace."[18]

Ingolf Dalferth interprets this as "the scandalous nature of his theology and the continuous challenge which it poses to most of our ways of doing theology,"[19] for it is "a sustained hermeneutical enterprise which does not deny the secularity of the world but reinterprets it theologically in the light of the presence of Christ and the world of meaning which it carries with it."[20] Dalferth calls this Barth's "eschatological realism" by which "the truth-claims of the Christian faith are the standards by which we are to judge what is real, not vice versa."[21] As Barth puts it, "all the required and necessary looking away from . . . ourselves to Him, can only be with a view to seeing in Him the real world, the real man, the real Church and real faith, our real selves."[22] In Barth's theological anthropology, general history is ultimately abstract if not understood from the concrete perspective of Christology. Indeed Barth maintains that "this abstraction itself, the concept of a history of man and men and mankind apart from the will and Word and work of God, is itself the product of the perverted and sinful thinking of man, one of the manifestations of human pride."[23]

Bender sees Barth's understanding of history as an example of the way he uses the Hegelian pattern of *Aufhebung*,[24] by which something is re-defined, or as Hunsinger describes it, through a process of "affirming, cancelling, and then reconstituting something on a higher plane."[25] In this way Christ is at the center of history, and world history finds its meaning in Christ. It has particular significance for Barth's ecclesiology, as Barth explains:

> The insignificant and petty history of Christians, as capacitated and actualised by the Holy Spirit, is not merely one history among others—however much this may appear to be the case from the external and historical standpoint—but a kind of cen-

18. Hunsinger, *How To Read Karl Barth*, 31.

19. Dalferth, "Karl Barth's Eschatological Realism," 14.

20. Ibid., 30.

21. Ibid., 22.

22. *CD* IV.3.1, 279.

23. *CD* IV.1, 505.

24. Bender, *Karl Barth's Christological Ecclesiology*, 142.

25. Hunsinger, *How To Read Karl Barth*, 85.

tral history among all others . . . And the Church must also mean and say this, not in order to advance an empty claim for itself, but in order to be conscious of the incomparable responsibility of its existence and mission and task.[26]

Barth's dynamic actualism enables Salvationists to reflect upon the way in which the ontological existence of the Christian community is successfully combined with its missionary task, within the active relations of God. As a dynamic event actualized in time and history, The Salvation Army as the Christian community is called by God to be the gospel that it preaches. It is called to visibly, faithfully and obediently demonstrate the community life of God's grace actively sustained in relation with the dynamic and active relations in God. In other words, it is not merely organized for a functional task, as its early origins and visible form suggests.

Barth's Christological Ecclesiology

Just as Barth's actualism is essential to understanding his concept of dynamic divine agency, initiative and precedence, in which the church is a dynamic event or happening, so Barth's Christological reasoning is equally an essential foundation for understanding his ecclesiology. Barth suggests that "Christology is the key to the whole,"[27] in that it focuses upon the God-man relation in Jesus Christ. Correspondingly, it provides Barth with a pattern for all divine-human relations, including the Christian community as a human creature. There are three specific elements of this Christological thinking that must be highlighted.

Firstly, Hunsinger identifies in Barth's account what he calls the "Chalcedonian pattern" and suggests that "it is probably safe to say that no one in the history of theology ever possessed a more deeply imbued Chalcedonian imagination."[28] The pattern is regulatory throughout *Church Dogmatics,* both explicitly and implicitly, for a conception of the divine and human natures in Jesus Christ, and by analogy is extended to include the relation of God and God's church. Barth pays rigorous attention to the three controlling elements of the two natures in Christ found

26. *CD* IV.2, 334.

27. *CD* IV.1, 138.

28. Hunsinger, *How To Read Karl Barth*, 85. See also 173–80, 185–87, 204f. Also Hunsinger, "Karl Barth's Christology," 131–47.

within this Chalcedonian formula; in unity, "without confusion, without change,"[29] in differentiation, "without division, without separation,"[30] and in asymmetry, "complete in deity and complete in humanity; the precedence of the divine and the subsequence of the human nature of Jesus Christ."[31] How this works in practice for Barth's ecclesiology will shortly be discussed.

Secondly, Barth adapts the post-Chalcedonian clarification of the asymmetrical nature of the divine-human relation in the union of Jesus Christ as the God-man, and in particular the subsistence of the human nature,[32] calling it the theologoumenon of *anhypostasis* and *enhypostasis*.[33] McCormack judges this to be a "watershed"[34] concept in the development of Barth's thought, taken initially from seventeenth century Reformed theologians, though deriving, Thomas F. Torrance suggests, from Cyril of Alexandria.[35] Literally the negative term *anhypostasis* means in relation to the union of natures, "without (human) hypostasis" and the positive term *enhypostasis* means "in (divine) hypostasis." It was employed principally to explain how two natures could subsist in one hypostasis rather than two, to avoid suggestions of adoptionism. Barth clarifies that the intention in using the couplet is to denote that "what the eternal Word made His own, giving it thereby His own existence, was not a man, but man's nature, man's being."[36] He is equally keen to refute the misunderstanding that this implies that the human nature of Christ has no personality, as seems to be implied in the Latin translation of *anhypostasis* by *impersonalitas*. Barth maintains that the Latin word for what we call personality was *individualitas* and that *personalitas* was the name for what we call existence or being. Therefore:

> Their negative position asserted that Christ's flesh in itself has no existence, and this was asserted in the interests of their positive position that Christ's flesh has its existence through the Word

29. See Bettenson, *Documents of the Christian Church*, 73.

30. See in particular the discussion in *CD* IV.2, 63–69.

31. See *CD* IV.2, 116.

32. For a discussion of the logic involved in this asymmetry see Hunsinger, *How To Read Karl Barth*, 286–87 n 1.

33. See *CD* I.2, 150, 163. Also *CD* IV.2, 49f, 91f.

34. McCormack, *Karl Barth's*, 366. See 358–67.

35. Ibid., 362. See also Torrance, *Karl Barth*, 200 n. 40, and 198–201.

36. *CD* 1.2, 163.

> and in the Word, who is God Himself acting as Revealer and
> Reconciler . . . It is in virtue of the eternal Word that Jesus Christ
> exists as a man of flesh and blood in our sphere, as a man like us,
> as a historical phenomenon. But it is only in virtue of the divine
> Word that He exists as such . . . Because of this positive aspect,
> it was well worth making the negation a dogma and giving it the
> very careful consideration which it received in early Christology.[37]

It is in this sense that Barth upholds the real human agency of Jesus.
Torrance suggests that Barth used the couplet as "a technically precise
way of speaking of the reality, wholeness and integrity of the human nature of Jesus Christ in the incarnation, without lapsing into adoptionism,
and of speaking of its perfect oneness with the divine nature of Christ
without lapsing into monophysitism,"[38] such as Barth considered was
a danger in Lutheran orthodoxy with its doctrine of *communicatio idi-
omatum.*[39] Barth first introduced the couplet in his *Göttingen Dogmatics.*
McCormack suggests the significance for Barth's development is that
the "anhypostatic-enhypostatic model . . . supplanted the time-eternity
dialectic as the central parable for expressing the *Realdialektik* of God's
veiling and unveiling,"[40] or, God's positive and immediate revelation or
unveiling in the Word, the transcendent hypostasis which is the eternal
Son, is at the same time veiled and mediated through the human flesh
of Jesus Christ.

Barth's use of this theologoumenon has been received critically,
and two objections in particular may be mentioned. Firstly, F. LeRon
Shults has challenged Barth's technical use of this formula.[41] Whilst he
concedes that Barth was legitimately trying to express the patristic thesis
that "the human nature of Jesus does not subsist except in its union with
the Logos in the one Person of Christ,"[42] the technical way he expresses
this formula is not found in patristic theology, and has mistakenly been
attributed as deriving, in Protestant Scholasticism, from Leontius of
Byzantium. However, U. M. Lang convincingly demonstrates that the
doctrine, if not the technical formula, does in actual fact derive, in

---

37. Ibid., 164–65.
38. Torrance, *Karl Barth*, 200.
39. See *CD* 1.2, 163–64.
40. McCormack, *Karl Barth's*, 367.
41. See Shults, "A Dubious Christological Formula," 431–46.
42. Ibid., 433, 446.

Protestant Scholasticism, from John of Damascus, and was therefore legitimately taken up by Barth.[43]

Secondly, Donald Baillie, acknowledges Barth's understanding of the doctrine behind this couplet, but questions his use of the term *anhypostasis*. He is critical of the dialectical use that Barth makes of it, leading to the life of Jesus being a concealment of God's revelation, in which Barth appears not to be interested in the historical Jesus. Baillie charges that "his theology has become so austerely a theology of the Word that . . . it is hardly a theology of the Word-made-flesh."[44] Trevor Hart reckons this to be an unnecessarily harsh judgement, but one borne more out of the nature of Chalcedonian two nature theology than of Barth's handling of it.[45] He is willing to acknowledge that Barth "fails to develop the model of divine self-communication as inherently relational," as "a relationality which in Jesus embraces humanity into the network of its own rich dynamics, and witnesses God not just as a human *speaker* of the Word, but also its *hearer* and *respondent* from the human side."[46] In this respect he judges that whilst Barth supplies the potential for an Antiochene emphasis, his "inclinations" are "finally in an Alexandrian direction."[47]

On the other hand, he is a sympathetic reader of Barth's attempt to communicate the transcendent nature of God's revelation in which "it is not . . . that the objective form in which revelation comes to us is unimportant but simply that it is not sufficient and is not in itself the object of our knowing of God, but merely its creaturely and phenomenal vehicle."[48] The importance of the humanity of Jesus is "not that it is a snapshot of God, and made-over to 'look like' God; but rather that it is the firstfruits of a new redeemed humanity in correspondence with God."[49] In this sense, Barth is clearly attempting to conceive of human personhood and agency that, following Jesus, may actively live in obedience to God in an appropriate autonomous reality.

---

43. Lang, "Anhypostatos-Enhypostatos," 630–57.

44. Baillie, *God Was In Christ*, 53.

45. Hart, *Regarding Karl Barth*, 18.

46. Ibid., 23. Hart acknowledges that this criticism is substantiated by Torrance. See Torrance, *Persons in Communion*, 100–19.

47. Hart, *Regarding Karl Barth*, 23.

48. Ibid., 21.

49. Ibid., 22.

The third element of Barth's Christological reasoning is, therefore, his extensive use of the analogical and referential language of correspondence to positively portray the character of human agency in relation to divine agency. Hunsinger describes Barth's use of the language of correspondence as indicative of his motif of "realism," in which "theological language, as represented by scripture (or based on it), is understood to refer to its subject matter by way of analogy, to address its subject matter to the whole person, to convey its subject matter with certainty, and to narrate its subject matter in the form of legendary witness."[50] He claims that this was Barth's hermeneutical alternative to the extremes of what Hunsinger calls "literalism" and "expressivism."[51] Correspondence principally describes the real and material character and integrity of Christ's whole human existence in the way that Barth can say "the man Jesus is the image and reflection of God Himself."[52] Barth can say that "the royal man of the New Testament tradition is created 'after God,'" which means that "as a man He exists analogously to the mode of existence of God," for "in what He thinks and wills and does, in His attitude, there is a correspondence, a parallel in the creaturely world, to the plan and purpose and work and attitude of God."[53] To be clear, "this is not a correspondence and similarity of being, an *analogia entis*:"[54]

> It is a question of the relationship within the being of God on the one side and between the being of God and that of man on the other. Between these two relationships as such—and it is in this sense that the second is the image of the first—there is correspondence and similarity. There is an *analogia relationis*.[55]

Just as the humanity of Jesus can be termed correspondingly a reflection or image of God, so there is a correspondence in activity that Barth outlines in his account of the "Divine accompanying."[56] For whilst "there is no identity of the divine and creaturely operation or *causare*, there is similarity, a correspondence, a comparableness, an analogy," which

50. Hunsinger, *How To Read Karl Barth*, 43. See also Hunsinger, *Disruptive Grace*, 210–25.

51. Hunsinger, *How To Read Karl Barth*, 43.

52. *CD* IV.2, 179.

53. *CD* IV.2, 166.

54. *CD* III.2, 220.

55. Ibid.

56. *CD* III.3, 90–154.

Barth this time calls, "an *analogia operationis*, just as elsewhere we can speak of an *analogia relationis*."[57] In terms of correspondence, Barth's maxim is always that "*charis calls* forth eucharistia."[58]

All three elements, Barth's use of correspondence, his regulative Chalcedonian pattern and the *anhypostasis/enhypostasis* formula comprise, as Bender puts it, "the Christological logic that shapes Barth's ecclesiology and provides its inherent principles of reasoning."[59] The divine and human natures in Christ are a paradigm for understanding all divine-human relations as analogous to the unique and definitive relation of the incarnation. In this respect Barth describes the Church as *anhypostasis* and *enhypostasis* in relation to Christ.[60]

Barth speaks of the church both constructively, in conceiving the nature, form and mission of the church and critically in highlighting errors that he constantly keeps in view to the left and right of his theological position, in what he calls Neo-Protestantism and Roman Catholicism.[61] In part one of his account of reconciliation he confides: "I have found myself in an intensive, although for the most part quiet, debate with Rudolf Bultmann."[62] Barth saw the work of Bultmann, with his existentialist and demythologizing programme, as "a new and vigorous Schleiermacher renaissance."[63] The "common denominator" for Barth was simply "the consciously and consistently executed anthropological starting point which is evident as the focus of their thought and utterances."[64]

---

57. Ibid., 102.

58. *CD* IV.1, 41. For a discussion of Barth's correspondence in relation to Christian ethics, see Biggar, *The Hastening That Waits*, 105–9; Webster, "The Christian in Revolt," 124–26.

59. Bender, *Karl Barth's Christological Ecclesiology*, 3. I am indebted to Bender for his clarification of this reasoning.

60. *CD* IV.2.59. Torrance asserts that he discussed with Barth, "that he might work out more fully the implications especially of *enhypostasia* for the doctrine of the Church as the Body of the risen and ascended Christ, pointing out to him that unlike Calvin he had not yet given corresponding attention to a realist understanding of the Church in its union with Christ" (Torrance, *Biblical and Evangelical Theologian*, 133). Barth equally considers the miraculous awakening to conversion of the individual Christian along these lines. See *CD* IV.2,557–63, IV.3.2, 542.

61. See in this respect Barth, *God in Action*, 20–22.

62. *CD* IV.1, ix.

63. Barth, "Concluding Unscientific Postscript," 77.

64. Ibid., 79.

In Barth's theological anthropology, with priority given to God's re-velatory incarnation in Christ, this was the wrong place to start. Equally, Barth regards his account of the "Exaltation of the Son of Man," "and its anthropological implications," as "an attempted Evangelical answer to the Marian dogma of Romanism—both old and new," by which "it is made superfluous."[65] Says Barth, "the fact that the man Jesus is the whole basis and power of guarantee of our exaltation means that there can be no place for any other in this function, not even for the mother of Jesus."[66] Just as Barth seeks to avoid Christological heresies in which Jesus Christ is anything but fully God and fully man, so he interprets ways in which the Church's own relation to God might be heretically misinterpreted, becoming invisible at the expense of its visibility (Docetic), visible at the expense of its invisibility (Ebionitic), or confused and synergistic in its expression (Eutychian). These insights are invaluable in highlighting the tangled Salvationist strands of mission, army and church, as will be demonstrated.

Some of Barth's critics point to this Christological logic as being at the heart of his ecclesiological deficiencies. Reinhard Hütter complains that: "Barth transfers the logic of Chalcedon to the entirety of theol-ogy. What doubtless constituted a meaningful regulative in a substance-ontological context does not in an action-determined context automati-cally apply."[67] His complaint focuses on Barth's dialectical theology in which he cites Barth's own conviction that:

> Only one who could say Jesus Christ, that is, could say God become flesh, God and man, in *one* word, and that word a true word, could pride himself on *not* being a "dialectical theologian." But the history of dogma teaches us and the christological dog-ma, especially that of Chalcedon, requires of us not to will what man cannot will in reason.[68]

Hütter objects to the "unstable 'center' of the always anew coming together of God's action and human witness in the Spirit" in which "the unequivocal referent, one already given in the christological context, is obviously missing in this kind of problematic action-determined nexus

65. *CD* IV.2, ix.

66. Ibid.

67. Hütter, *Suffering Divine Things*, 106

68. Barth, *Theology and Church*, 301.

of 'God and human being.'[69] Yet Hütter is citing from Barth's early writing and does not acknowledge Barth's development of correspondence to deal with these concerns, in which obedient human response is conceived more positively than a mere "unstable center." Nevertheless, in view of Hütter's opinion that "this model reduces the person and work of the Holy Spirit in a highly problematic fashion,"[70] his critique will be returned to in the final section of this study.

Shults objects to Barth taking the *anhypostasis-enhypostasis* formula out of its proper location in referring to the human nature of Christ, and using it as a paradigm that refers to the relation between God and the world. He maintains, contrary to McCormack's assertion, that the *anhypostasis-enhypostasis* formula cannot be the "central parable" that replaces the time-eternity dialectic in Romans, when it only properly refers to the human nature of Jesus.[71] Bender answers this objection, in maintaining that it is "an actualized Chalcedonian Christology wedded to a Protestant anhypostatic-enhypostatic doctrine that forms the 'central parable' which replaces the time-eternity dialectic of Romans."[72] As Bender suggests, Barth ultimately decides that whilst the hypostatic union in Christ is unique and without analogy, "precisely because this singular relation is God's self-elected means to establish a covenant with all of creation, the incarnation is the pattern on which all other divine-human relations are predicated, though they stand on a different plane and exist only in subservience to and as shadows of this unsubstitutable event."[73]

There are three relations that Barth brings to his ecclesiology from his Christological logic, which must be briefly examined before the reasoning can be applied to the evidence of tangled Salvation Army strands. Firstly, in his account of the Church's origin and nature Barth describes the relationship between the Spirit and the Church, as a twofold reality, in unity, differentiation and an irreversible and asymmetrical order of precedence and subsequence. Secondly, in his account of the Church's form and order he describes the relation between Christ and the Church in this same twofold reality. Thirdly, in his account of the Church's ordi-

---

69. Hütter, *Suffering Divine Things*, 106.

70. Ibid.

71. Shults, "A Dubious Christological Formula," 445.

72. Bender, *Karl Barth's Christological Ecclesiology*, 64 n. 12.

73. Ibid., 12.

nation and mission, he describes the relation between the Church and the world, in which there is a modification of the logic. Barth outlines a series of concentric circles in which Christ is the center, with the Church and the world as subsequent ripples, and in which Christ and the Church, the *totus Christus*, are at the center of the world. Barth develops these three relations across three main sections of his account of the Christian community, its gathering, upbuilding and sending by the Holy Spirit. These three relations form the basis of the next four sections of dialogue with Barth's friends and critics alike, and with The Salvation Army, on the nature, form and mission of the Church.

6

The Nature of the Christian Community

B arth's explanation of the relation of the Spirit and the Church, whilst keeping the relation of Christ and the Church very much in view,[1] establishes the divine origin and nature of the Church. Both relations represent a twofold reality in unity, differentiation and asymmetry, in which the true Church only exists in relation to the Spirit who makes Christ present. The same is apparent when Barth speaks predominantly of the relation of Christ and the Church; he keeps the relation of the Spirit and the Church in view, for it is the Spirit who enables Christ to be contemporary in every age. This is why he unusually places his account of the Christian community within this Christological section of his *Dogmatics*. Barth is clear that his theological anthropology demands a central focus on Christ, whilst keeping in view the work of the Holy Spirit, for "the one reality of the atonement has both an objective and subjective side . . . it is both divine act and offer and also an active human participation in it."[2] Barth explains what he means by this subjective realization and active human participation, when he explains that the Holy Spirit "is God intervening and acting for man, addressing Himself to him, in such a way that He says Yes to Himself and this makes possible and necessary man's human yes to him."[3] The initiative is entirely God's, for the Holy Spirit is "God in this particular address and gift, God in this awakening power, God as the Creator of this other man."[4]

---

1. *CD* IV.1, 643–739.
2. Ibid., 643.
3. Ibid., 646.
4. Ibid., 645.

This means that 'in everything that we have to say concerning the Christian community and Christian faith we can move only within the circle that they are founded by the Holy Spirit and therefore that they must be continually refounded by Him, but that the necessary refounding by the Holy Spirit can consist only in a renewal of the founding which He has already accomplished."[5] For Barth "the infallible sign of His presence"[6] is the expectation and desire of the Christian community to receive the Spirit, to cry in obedience and prayer "*Veni creator Spiritus*."[7] The Spirit cannot be controlled, directed or possessed by either the Christian community or the individual Christian. "He makes man free, but He Himself remains free in relation to him: the Spirit of the Lord."[8] The Spirit "is the power in which Jesus Christ attests Himself, attests Himself effectively, creating in man response and obedience."[9] The Spirit is sent by Jesus Christ. "He is the form of His action."[10] The Spirit therefore "is the power of Jesus Christ in which it takes place that there are men who can and must find and see that He is theirs and they are His, that their history is genuinely enclosed in His and His history is equally genuinely enclosed in theirs."[11] Barth will not speculate further on how this occurs, for "even the New Testament, although time and again it places the Holy Spirit between the event of Christ on the one hand and the Christian community and Christian faith on the other, does not really tell us anything about the How, the mode of His working."[12]

In Barth's actualistic understanding, the Church, grounded as it is in Christ through the awakening power of the Holy Spirit, is a dynamic event and history:

> To describe its being, we must abandon the usual distinctions between being and act, status and dynamic, essence and existence. Its act is its being, its status its dynamic, its essence its existence. The Church *is* when it takes place that God lets certain men live as His servants, His friends, His children, the witness of the rec-

5. Ibid., 647.

6. Ibid.

7. Ibid.

8. Ibid., 646.

9. Ibid., 648.

10. Ibid.

11. Ibid.

12. Ibid., 649.

onciliation of the world with Himself as it has taken place in Jesus Christ.[13]

Barth follows Luther in translating *ekklesia* as *Gemeinde*;[14] not "church," but a dynamic expression of the gathering of God's people as "community" or "congregation" through the presence and work of the Holy Spirit. It should be noted that Barth maintains a strict order in his presentation, speaking of the community before he speaks of the individual, in a conscious riposte to the individualistic assumptions of Enlightenment thought. It is a critique that equally challenges an early Salvationist assumption of an individualistic gospel. In his account of election he clarifies that "it is not men as private persons in the singular or plural" that God elects, but "these men as a fellowship elected by God in Jesus Christ and determined from all eternity for a peculiar service, to be made capable of this service and to discharge it."[15] As Barth further expresses it, "It is God's choice that for the sake of the Head whose name it bears He has created and established this particular body, this people, to be the sign of blessing and judgment, the instrument of His love and the sacrament of His movement towards men and each individual man."[16] Barth can therefore conclude that:

> The biblical witness to God is itself wholly characterised by the fact that this God has determined Himself the Lord of Israel and the Church, and as such Lord of the universe and man in general. It is for this reason and to this end that He wills the calling of Israel and the Church and the creation of the universe and man.[17]

Barth argues against what he sees as the "*cul de sac*" of "the individual experience of grace" and its impact upon the doctrine of the Church as demonstrated in Pietism including the "detour via Kierkegaard," and affirms that "our theme is the reconciliation of the world with God in Jesus Christ, and only in this greater context the reconciliation of the individual man" for "the city set on a hill, is the community of God and

---

13. Ibid., 650.

14. See Barth's comments in Barth, *Dogmatics in Outline*, 141; Barth, *Evangelical Theology*, 37.

15. *CD* II.2, 196.

16. Ibid., 54.

17. Ibid., 91.

not the individual Christian as such, although the latter has within it his assured place."[18]

As an event the community "is a phenomenon of world history which can be grasped in historical and psychological and sociological terms like any other,"[19] for "this involves—in varying degrees of strictness or looseness—an ecclesiastical organisation and constitution and order."[20] In this way the Church is at the same time both event and religious society, invisible and visible as a twofold reality. In that Christ is a real man, Barth's Chalcedonian pattern will not allow "christological Docetism" and in that the Church has a human history he will equally and correspondingly, not allow "ecclesiastical Docetism,"[21] for "the Christian community as such cannot exist as an ideal commune or universum, but ... only in the relationship of its individual members as they are fused together by the common action of the Word which they have heard into a definite human fellowship; in concrete form, therefore, and visible to everyone."[22]

Barth is determined to emphasize that this visibility can only be the true Church when it understands its reality negatively as *anhypostasis*, that it cannot exist without God, upon whom it is totally dependent. Rather than speak of an invisible and visible reality, Barth argues not simply for "a general but a very special visibility,"[23] in which in its total dependence on God, the Christian community can be visibly known in its reality as *enhypostasis*. For Barth, this means "a religious society within human society generally and side by side with other organisations,"[24] and equally, to be visibly and insightfully seen by Christian faith in "the third dimension of its existence,"[25] in the light of its awakening by the Holy Spirit. There can, therefore, be no heretical view of the Church that focuses on its visible and institutional character, to the detriment of its

18. *CD* IV.1, 150.
19. Ibid., 652.
20. Ibid.
21. Ibid., 653.
22. Ibid.
23. Ibid., 654.
24. Ibid., 655.
25. Ibid.

origin and essential third dimension in the awakening power of the Holy Spirit.[26]

Barth is critical of a church whether large or small, that fails to keep open the "special visibility" of this "third dimension," and "becomes un-serviceable to the will and act of God, to the extent that in its visible being it wants to be something more and better than the witness of its invisible being . . . taking itself and its doctrine and sacraments and sac-ramental observances and ordinances and spiritual authority and power . . . to be the meaning of its existence, its greatness, its true and final word, in place of the underlying and over-ruling power of Jesus Christ and His Spirit."[27] This is not to deny that the Church must take its visibil-ity seriously in the world, and create "forms which are indispensable to it as the human society . . . which are best adapted to its edification and the discharge of its mission."[28] These forms are, however, at best "pro-visional" in need of "constant reform," and can never allow the Church to be anything better than "an *église du desert* . . . a 'moving tent' like the biblical tabernacle" in which it "lives by the awakening power of the Holy Spirit."[29] Barth affirms that if the Church "lives also and primarily in its third dimension, it can and should act confidently on the level of its phenomenal being."[30]

The belief that The Salvation Army was an act of God, a living dem-onstration of the awakening power of the Holy Spirit, enabled Bramwell Booth to make confident claims about its phenomenal being. Of all the early Salvationist leaders, in the heat of the Army's ambiguous holiness revivalism, he made the most confident assertion that "of this, the Great Church of the Living God, we claim, and have ever claimed, that we of The Salvation Army are an integral part and element—a living fruit-bearing branch in the True Vine."[31] Timothy Bradshaw adopts a similar image in his Anglican evangelical ecclesiology, *The Olive Branch*,[32] where

---

26. See Barth, *Against the Stream*, 62–77, for his account of this "special visibility."

27. Ibid., 657.

28. Ibid., 660.

29. Ibid.

30. Ibid.

31. Booth, *Echoes and Memories*, 79.

32. Bradshaw, *The Olive Branch*.

he is clear that "the New Testament stress on the church's free adoption into the family of God unites the doctrines of salvation and church." [33]

Lesslie Newbigin suggests that in view of God's free, merciful and gracious gift of the Church, great care should be taken in assessing the respective merits of different versions of the Church, not to become judgmental and partisan. He is insistent that "the Church does not exist by virtue of something which it is in itself . . . It exists wherever God in His sovereign freedom calls it into being by calling His own into the fellowship of His Son."[34] He is clear that "when the Church claims to have the plenitude of grace in itself, it has abandoned the Spirit for the flesh."[35] He even sounds like a Salvationist when he declares, "It will be none other than the mercy-seat where alone Christ meets with us . . . nothing that the Church *is* can provide us with our basis of assurance,"[36] sentiments with which Barth would no doubt have wholeheartedly agreed. Newbigin believes we "should completely abandon . . . the idea that we can find some minimum of visible marks which will enable us to say: "This is a Church and God must recognise it as such,'" for "the Church exists, and does not depend for its existence upon our definition of it."[37] God is free,

> to break off unbelieving branches, to graft in wild slips, and to call "no people" His people. And if, at the end, those who have preserved through all the centuries the visible "marks" of the Church find themselves at the same board with some strange and uncouth late-comers on the ecclesiastical scene, may we not fancy that they will hear Him say—would it not be like Him to say—"It is my will to give unto this last even as unto thee?"[38]

In Barth's sense that the Church is an event, a happening, totally dependent upon God's call and commission, The Salvation Army can be affirmed as an authentic community of God's action in gathering God's Church, no matter how much of an "uncouth late-comer," to use Newbigin's phrase, it might to some appear to be. So Barth maintains that the true Church is in its essential third dimension, in the divine

33. Ibid., 134.
34. Newbigin, *The Household of God,* 132.
35. Ibid., 83.
36. Ibid., 134.
37. Ibid., 132f.
38. Ibid., 133.

action of electing, reconciling, gathering, upholding and sending the Church. On this inclusive basis it has been an integral participant in ecumenical life and work throughout the world. This is the source of the authentic "church" strand that runs through the tangled cord of mission, army and church. Barth is equally concerned, however, with the appropriate corresponding human form and action that must obediently follow. He therefore establishes the visible form of the Church in a dialectic of indestructible divine action and destructible human action. It is this appropriate corresponding visibility that Salvationists have not sufficiently reflected upon, and must be considered next.

7

The Form of the Christian Community

If the anhypostatic character of the Church is its total dependence upon divine agency—its actuality accomplished in Christ through the awakening power of the Spirit—then Barth is equally committed to describing the Church's enhypostatic character in which it may be visibly expressed and historically known through its existence in God's agency. This avoids a docetic misunderstanding of the Church, such as Barth ironically attributes to his friend Emil Brunner.[1] Similarly, in his Christological logic, he is anxious to avoid overcompensating towards an exclusively human understanding or a synergistic and confused understanding of divine and human agency. These concerns are carefully worked out in Barth's account of the form of the Church by introducing the major New Testament concept of the Church as the body of Christ, the "earthly-historical form of existence of Jesus Christ Himself."[2] Although continuing to acknowledge the first major relation of the Holy Spirit and the Church, since "the Church is His body, created and continually renewed by the awakening power of the Holy Spirit,"[3] there is nevertheless this second major relation of Christ and the Church to acknowledge and explore, where:

> He Himself lives in a special element of this history created and controlled by Him. He therefore lives in an earthly-historical form of existence within it. This particular element of human history . . . is the Christian community. He is the Head of this

1. See Brunner, *The Misunderstanding of the Church.* See also *CD* IV.2, 679–86.
2. *CD* IV.2, 661.
3. Ibid.

> body, the community . . . Because He is, it is; it is, because He is.
> That is its secret, its being in the third dimension, which is visible
> only to faith.[4]

Barth develops this concept at various stages of his second material account of reconciliation, as the upbuilding of the Church.[5] He introduces the concept of the body of Christ as a real existence, not just a metaphor, and is anxious not to be misunderstood as advocating a second incarnation of Christ. In an essay, in part delivered at the inaugural assembly of the World Council of Churches in Amsterdam in 1948, Barth calls this Church "the living congregation of the living Lord Jesus Christ."[6] In a discussion of the various analogies that may be drawn from the relationship between God and man as it has been revealed in Jesus Christ,[7] Barth is clear that "the incarnation of the Word is this fact, without precedence, parallel or repetition either in the divine sphere or (much less) in the human, natural and historical creaturely sphere," an event "to which theology can give only the assent that it has heard it and understood it as such."[8] This means that in any discussion of the Church "we cannot speak, then, of a repetition or extension of the incarnation taking place in it," and "there can be no question of a divinisation of the Church or the individual Christian."[9]

Barth is anxious to avoid any triumphalist expression, such as might be seen in Rahner's expression that "in its socially organized form the people of God as in fact redeemed by Christ, receives his permanent presence through history . . . as it were an incarnation, of the truth of Christ in the Church through Scripture, tradition and magisterium."[10] Hans Küng reinforces Barth's concern when he asserts, "it is extremely misleading to speak of the Church as the 'continuing life of Christ' or as a 'permanent incarnation,'" for fear that "the Church is identified with Christ so that Christ as its Lord and head takes second place to his Church, which pretends to be the Christ of the present in constantly

---

4. Ibid.
5. Ibid., 614–726.
6. Barth, *God Here and Now*, 75.
7. See *CD* IV.2, 50–69.
8. Ibid., 59.
9. Ibid., 60.
10. Rahner, *The Church and the Sacraments*, 19.

new incarnation."[11] For Küng, the Church finds its meaning more fully in Jesus' teaching of the Kingdom of God, for

> the Church does not reside in itself, in what it is, but in what it is moving towards. It is the reign of God which the Church hopes for, bears witness to, proclaims. It is not the bringer or the bearer of the reign of God which is to come and is at the same time already present, but its voice, its announcer, its herald.[12]

Any suggestion of a second incarnation is unacceptable to Barth, since "He Himself is the Subject present and active and operative in His community . . . His earthly-historical form of existence . . . as this form of His body."[13] Barth explains the two forms of Jesus Christ's existence:

> He has the one as the One, the Head, for Himself. And He has the other, again as the One, the Head, but in and with His body, His people, His community. The relationship between these two forms of His existence is not so much comparable as indirectly identical to the relationship between Himself as the eternal Son of God and His being as man.[14]

Barth agrees with Peter Lombard that there is a difference "between *gratia adoptionis* and *gratia unionis*."[15] What Barth, in the relation to the Christian community, there calls adoption, he now calls an indirect identity.

The suggestion that Jesus Christ as Head is able to be in both places at the same time, is realized and known subjectively "in faith by the awakening power of the Holy Spirit," so that "there arises and is, not a second Jesus Christ, a second Head, but the second form of His one existence, His people as the second form of His body."[16] Barth explains that whilst Christ, in his heavenly form of existence can in one sense be seen as "remote from earthly history,"[17] nevertheless, "He can be here as well as there, in the depth as well as in the height, near as well as remote,

11. Küng, *The Church*, 239.

12. Ibid., 96.

13. *CD* IV.2, 60.

14. Ibid., 59.

15. Ibid., II.1, 485.

16. Ibid., IV.2, 59. See Bender, *Karl Barth's Christological Ecclesiology*, 222f., for his concern that Barth is in danger here of a "static and pretemporal conception of election," such as he criticises in Calvin.

17. *CD* IV.2, 652.

and therefore immanent in the *communio sanctorum* on earth as well as transcendent to it."[18] This is possible because:

> The Holy Spirit, as the power which quickens the community, is the self-attestation of Jesus Christ . . . Where the man Jesus attests Himself in the power of the Spirit of God, He makes Himself present; and those whom He approaches in His self-attestation are able also to approach Him and to be near Him.[19]

Barth's Chalcedonian Christology is evident when he concludes that "Jesus Christ is the community," and since this "is a christological statement, and only as such an ecclesiological," then "the statement cannot be reversed . . . The community is not Jesus Christ."[20] The true Church's human visible form can therefore be clarified:

> It does not exist in independence of Him. It is not itself the Head, nor does it become such. It exists (*anhypostasis* and *enhypostasis*) in and in virtue of His existence. It lives because and as He lives, elected and awakened and called and gathered as a people by Him . . . Not for a single moment or in any respect can it be His body without Him, its Head.[21]

By the same logic, however, as the human body of Christ its Head, the Christian community in positive correspondence has a real human history. The Church's challenge is to understand how its corresponding responsible human action may be faithful and obedient to Christ, for in fulfilling this calling, the visible Church remains the true Church. In typical dialectical fashion, Barth conceives throughout his account of the Church, twin errors in its human response, in which it either does not take itself seriously enough, retreating into an invisibility that is careless of its visible form and action, or takes itself too seriously by over inflating its concrete visible form and action at the expense of its invisible nature. Barth variously characterizes these twin erroneous responses as "secularization" and "sacralization," or a church in "defect" and a church in "excess."[22] Describing the dangers to the left and right, Barth charts an obedient visible form of response and action for the Church.

18. Ibid., 653.
19. Ibid., 653f.
20. Ibid., 655.
21. Ibid., 59.
22. See Busch, *The Great Passion*, 251.

Barth's conception of the Christian community's faithful and obedient human form is a key insight in relation to what has been described as The Salvation Army's three tangled strands of mission, army and church. Each of the strands previously outlined, relate to different ecclesial conceptions of The Salvation Army's visible form. The "mission" strand relates to its individualistic and subjective roots in holiness revivalism, in which there was concern more for a "higher life" movement of aggressive spiritual passion and mission than a faithful visible form. The "army" strand relates to the institutionalization of this "aggressive Christianity" in which, in their pragmatism, the Booths did not fully reflect upon the faithful corresponding form of Christ's body. Finally, the "church" strand relates to an unreflective process in which, under the progress of twentieth century ecumenism, Salvationists all too readily assumed that the Church was like an army. It is proposed, therefore, in what remains, that these strands be placed under the scrutiny of Barth's Christological reasoning, firstly, through his account of the four "marks" of the one, holy, catholic and apostolic Church, and secondly through his account of the missionary calling of the Church, which Barth suggests is a fifth "mark" of the Church. It will be demonstrated that Barth's Christological reasoning is a valuable tool for Salvationist reflection on its visible form.

8

The Marks of the Christian Community

B arth's Christological reasoning lies at the heart of his discussion of the four classic "notes" or "marks" of the Church, in which its unity, holiness, catholicity and apostolicity, are specific aspects of the Church's "special visibility." They are a visible and definite historical human witness in the world, yet in the precedence and subsequence of divine and human agency they are a visibility given by God and therefore not under human control. In other words he wishes to emphasize the God-givenness of these marks of the Church which are only visible to faith, whilst equally recognizing the Church's calling to correspond in a visible obedience that takes seriously its unity, holiness, catholicity and apostolicity. Salvationist strands of mission, army and church may be scrutinized from Barth's perspective on the "special visibility" of the Christian community in terms of God's agency and corresponding human agency.

The Church Is One

Barth calls the Church, "a unity in the plurality of its members."[1] He reviews the different ways in which it could possibly be conceived otherwise, refuting each. "The visible and the invisible Church are not two Churches," for "the one is the form and the other the mystery of one and the self same Church."[2] Equally the Church militant and the Church triumphant are one, as are "the people of Israel in its whole history

1. *CD*, IV.1, 668.
2. Ibid., 669.

ante et post Christum and the Christian Church as it came into being on the day of Pentecost . . . two forms and aspects of the one inseparable community."[3] Finally, we can only speak in the plural of churches "with reference to the geographically separated and therefore different congregations," which though they appear to be separate and different both through geography and a whole range of genuine human factors such as language, environment, custom and tradition, "the community in one place can and must and will recognise itself in the community of another, and *vice versa*,"[4] for "the one Church exists in its totality in each of the individual communities."[5]

In this respect Barth fully affirms the Salvationist understanding that its congregations throughout the world represent the unity of the Church that God has gathered in each locality, even if Salvationists have given less thought to his conviction that this God-given unity bears a responsibility to demonstrate that unity in visible and not just "spiritual" form. Barth goes even further in his insistence that all manner of congregations, whether belonging to a denomination, or special communities of work, youth groups, mission societies, military congregations and such like, "should in no way evade the claim and the responsibility of being in fact congregations, whether large or small, conducting worship, thinking and acting in the service of God and therefore in their particular form, being also the one, holy, universal, and apostolic Church."[6] In particular, no denomination can separate itself and claim to be the one Church, for "it is an impossible situation that whole groups of Christian communities should exhibit a certain external and internal unity among themselves and yet stand in relation to other groups of equally Christian communities in an attitude more or less of exclusion."[7] In Barth's view undoubtedly the Church exists in Salvation Army congregations and "communities of work," which in this respect bear the responsibility for ensuring that they visibly constitute an obedient human form.

Barth, himself an active protagonist for Christian unity, against the "scandal" of disunity,[8] is sharp in his criticism of obstacles to unity that

3. Ibid.

4. Ibid., 672.

5. Ibid., 673.

6. Barth, *Here and Now*, 100.

7. *CD* IV.1, 676.

8. Ibid., 675, 677.

fail to recognise the Lord of unity and "obedience to His Spirit" as the appropriate human response to that Lordship.[9] "All human mediation" of whatever kind that "demands and maintains the oneness of the locally separated communities, is completely impossible," for it "can only be a free human service" and "is not an integral constituent of the essence of the Church."[10] Rather it is "the Lord who attests Himself in the prophetic and apostolic word, who is active by His Spirit, who as the Spirit has promised to be in the midst of every community gathered by Him and in His name," for "He rules the Church and therefore the Churches" and is "the basis and guarantee of their unity."[11] Barth has in view the rise of a plethora of denominations in which "it is possible to understand and explain historically the separation and opposition of such Churches,"[12] but is scathing of the kind of complacency, and acquiescent pleasure taken in these, and an attendant unwillingness to take personal responsibility for "obvious faults and errors of others."[13] He pungently declares that a person "may be a good and loyal confessor in the sense of his own particular denomination," but without regard for the *una ecclesia* "must not imagine that he is a good Christian."[14]

The persistent challenge which Christian denominations raise against the unity of the church is especially seen in The Salvation Army's strong command system and central controlling bureaucracy. Firstly, this bureaucracy has ultimate precedence over local congregational governance, and whilst it is not alone in this, few denominations can have the same level of precedence ascribed to an authority that stands outside the local congregation, as is found within this military command system. It stands in Barth's description as a "human mediation" between the reality of the one Church and the reality of the local congregation, which represents the one Church in each locality. In a congregational view of the church P. T. Forsyth, like Barth, draws together both the local and the universal in his New Testament understanding of the Church:

> The ecclesia was the gathering of a people . . . It was the assembly of all Christians with God and before God. The local gathering,

9. Ibid., 672.
10. Ibid.
11. Ibid., 674.
12. Ibid., 675.
13. Ibid., 676.
14. Ibid.

> therefore, was not *a* Church but *the* Church seen as God sees it
> . . . It means not the group there but the one community of faith
> everywhere which crops out there.[15]

The question is therefore raised as to whether and to what extent The Salvation Army as a denominational entity can claim to be *a* church, as it does in its ecclesiological statement, as opposed to simply upholding its congregations as full expressions of *the* church in each locality, as Forsyth and Barth suggest.

Kevin Giles, an Anglican theologian, recognizes that the NT understanding of the Church is essentially a congregational definition, in which the congregation is primary and precludes any notion of a denominational bureaucracy being *a* church, it being merely an organizational structure to link churches together of the same confession or origin. Nevertheless, on the evidence of both Paul and Luke's writings, Giles finds a third category which he calls "Christians in one location"[16] who may not actually assemble together but are in effect Christian communities by virtue of a geographical or associational connection. Beyond this Paul can use the word Church for groupings of Christian communities, who may only be linked ethnically, such as the "churches of the Gentiles" (Rom 16:4). Whilst this expression is admittedly plural, he makes the case for "Christians united together by a common heritage and confession as a distinct Christian community, a united entity—that is a church."[17] In that the modern denomination is a development unknown to the NT, he is prepared to accept them as churches on the basis that "Reformed theologians have generally allowed for an organic development in theology."[18] However he is careful to make the stipulation that such a theology of the Church is "a provisional ecclesiology," "a theology that neither completely denies the theological validity of the sociological form of the church, nor endorses it without any theological critique."[19] In this provisional sense, The Salvation Army's denominational form may somewhat tenuously in Giles' view, and with conscious theological critique, be given theological validation as *a* church, rather than merely a sociological form. Barth is surely right, however, that denominational

---

15. Forsyth, *The Church and the Sacraments*, 65. See also Sell, *Saints*.

16. Giles, *What on Earth is the Church?*, 205.

17. Ibid., 206.

18. Ibid., 207.

19. Ibid., 208.

bureaucracy must recognise its "free human service" to the congregations, rather than the reverse. The Salvation Army's military and hierarchical form of governance, which stems from an individualistic view of
authority, is deeply problematic in its visible expression of the Church.

The second issue Barth raises is the challenge faced by denominational confessors, in which their responsibility is first to genuinely
seek the unity of the Church, rather than the unity and priority of their
own confession. If the Church's unity is not a human possession, but
the gift of God, Salvationist leaders need constantly to heed Barth's call
for each to listen to God humbly and carefully as to the nature of the
Church's unity, without compromise, but equally without narrow and
blinkered denominational loyalty. In this respect Barth outlines two opposing temptations and errors for the Church. The first is "a movement
of escape up or on from the visibility of the divided Church to the unity
of an invisible Church" when either an individual retreats into a private
world of faith or when churches cease "to take themselves seriously" and
"exist in a kind of nondescript Christianity," when what is required is "a
healing of both its visible and invisible hurt."[20]

There is a suggestion of this kind of complacency in The Salvation
Army's ecclesiological statement, when it states: "Denominational diversity is not self-evidently contrary to God's will for his people."[21] This
may be so in some respects, in that as Barth rightly suggests there are
genuine human factors, such as geography, custom, language and tradition which are at work, but consider the following statement: "We do
not believe it is our task to comment negatively upon, or to undermine,
the traditions of other denominations, and certainly not in relation to
the sacraments," for "we seek to be careful not to belittle the doctrines
or practices of any other Christian group."[22] The Salvation Army's abandoning of baptism and the Lord's Supper has already been described,
and there might superficially appear to be genuine sensitivity in these
apparently non-judgmental sentiments. The issue though is surely not
a self-conscious concern about belittling others, but a God-conscious
concern to manifest God's unity, which can only affirm rather than belittle God's children. Barth would no doubt recognize this as an example
of not taking the unity of God's Church seriously. This matter must

20. Ibid., 678.

21. The Salvation Army, The Salvation Army in the Body of Christ, 1.

22. Ibid., 13.

be returned to under the discussion of the Church's catholicity. It has already been identified that The Salvation Army's emphasis upon the invisibility of the church detracts from the equally important emphasis upon its visibility.

Barth equally describes the opposite error of a turn to the visible Church, to an abstract external solution "the externally satisfying co-existence and co-operation of different religious societies,"[23] what Barth calls the "doctrine of toleration"[24] which he maintains "originates in political and philosophical principles which are not only alien but even opposed to the Gospel."[25] Whilst Barth's view is a sweeping dismissal of the virtue of toleration in the face of years of religious war and strife, he positively argues for "a Church which takes itself more seriously, and of a faith which is strong and certain and genuinely critical,"[26] but where the divided Churches "honestly and seriously try to hear and perhaps hear the voice of the Lord by them and for them, and then try to hear, and perhaps actually hear, the voice of the others."[27] In listening to the Lord the Church acknowledges that its unity is not its own possession but from Christ, and there is an identity and differentiation between the inner mystery of its unity in Christ and its visible form, that correspondingly it is called to reflect in this visible form.

The Church Is Holy

Barth simply means a holy body of holy members. He does not see a differentiation between individual and corporate holiness. "There is only one separation, that of the *communio sanctorum*: the awakening of the faith of individuals, the purpose of which is their gathering into the community—the gathering of the community in the form of the awakening of the faith of individuals."[28] This corporate account of holiness, like Barth's understanding of the priority of the community in reconciliation, is a positive corrective to what has been argued was the largely individualistic and subjective concerns that developed in holiness reviv-

23. *CD* IV.1, 678.

24. Ibid., 675.

25. Barth, *The Church and the Churches*, 35.

26. *CD* IV.1, 679.

27. Ibid., 684.

28. Ibid., 688.

alist evangelism. Salvationists increasingly recognise the weakness of an early preoccupation with individual sanctity, and increasingly seek to articulate the holy life as a gift of grace within the context of Christian community. Needham is clear that "if holiness is, as we Salvationists have claimed, perfect love, then it is meaningless outside a community in which the love of God can be experienced, expressed and learned."[29] Barth continues to challenge Salvationists to make the vital connection between holiness and the Christian community, in which love seeks to serve rather than to control. This theme will be taken up at several points in what follows.

The Holiness of the Community

Barth views the holiness of the community in three events. Firstly, in election the holiness of the Church is predestined, secondly, in reconciliation the holiness of the Church is historically actualized in Jesus Christ, and thirdly, reconciliation takes place in the work of the Holy Spirit as a provisional sanctification. Barth constantly keeps an eschatological perspective on the historical actualization of God's sanctification of the Church in Christ, and the provisional nature of this work as subjectively realized by the Holy Spirit, in a Church that is both *communio sanctorum* and *communio peccatorum*.

Firstly, Barth affirms that from the objective point of view the Church's holiness is historically and preveniently actualized in Christ. He "is always the Subject, the Lord, the Giver of the holiness of its action" in contrast to which the action of the community "can only be a seeking, an asking after holiness, a prayer for it."[30] Like unity, holiness is not the possession of the community. Its form and action are in the manner of Barth's correspondence not directly identified but in analogical relation to its inner holiness from Christ, in which this form and action can only reflect that holiness. Barth is determined to maintain his understanding that divine and human agency can never be conceived as synergistic, and this critically relates to an account of sanctification.

In 1929 Barth delivered a lecture in which he set out the dangers of a synergistic description of divine and human agency, evident he believed

---

29. Needham, "Integrating Holiness and Community" 14.

30. *CD* IV.1, 694.

in the writings of Augustine, in spite of his opposition to Pelagianism.[31] Barth sees the subtlety of this "sweet poison" as more dangerous than Pelagianism in the way that it places "man's work—the whole of work-righteousness in its inner and outer features (such as morality and mysticism, all human strivings after holiness and merit)—under the prefix of predestination and of grace and of the loftiest humility."[32] This synergism is the legacy that he believes has found its way into both his protagonists to left and right, for "no psalm-singing to the glory of God and no lowly knee-bending can alter the fact that when God's grace and man's doing are looked upon as two sides of an affair, where one can turn it round and say, instead of the words 'Holy Ghost,' with just as good emphasis, 'religious fervour,' 'moral earnestness,' or even 'man's creative activity'—then it is a simple fact that man has been handed over and left to his sins."[33]

The problem Barth sees is the failure to take sin seriously enough, and the creature's total reliance upon God's free grace in the Holy Spirit's attesting of Christ's atoning work. Speaking of holiness is not an occasion "to turn our back on the action of God in Jesus Christ by the Holy Spirit and to occupy ourselves in *abstracto* with a being and work of men as its result."[34] Rather, holiness is principally and objectively God's free gift. Because the community is holy as Christ is holy, so its holiness is "indestructible."[35] This does not deny Barth's constant theme "*ecclesia semper reformanda.*" It affirms that despite occasions of individual and corporate unfaithfulness, it is an article of faith that "because it is from Jesus Christ, because it is His body, it cannot cease to be this, it cannot become something else," for "it has not taken upon itself to be holy, and it cannot set aside its calling."[36]

From the subjective point of view, holiness becomes active in the Holy Spirit's work of upbuilding God's earthly historical form as "a provisional representation of the sanctification of all humanity and human life as it has taken place in Him."[37] The sanctification is provisional be-

---

31. Barth, *The Holy Ghost and the Christian Life*. See 11–18, 28–39.
32. Ibid., 35.
33. Ibid.
34. *CD* IV.2, 615.
35. Ibid., IV.1, 689.
36. Ibid.
37. Ibid., IV.2, 614.

cause its members are always at the same time saints and sinners. Using the Latin *communio* and the Greek *koinonia*, Barth works from the basis that "communion is an action in which on the basis of an existing union (*unio*) many men are engaged in a common movement towards the same union . . . in the power and operation of the Holy Spirit, and the corresponding action of those who are assembled and quickened by Him."[38] The existing *unio* is Jesus Christ, and the corresponding fellowship is the *communio sanctorum*, the fellowship of Christians united with the Holy Spirit "in the knowledge and confession of their faith."[39] This fellowship of God's saints with Jesus Christ in the Holy Spirit, is at the same time and always until the day of completion, *communio peccatorum*, "members of the race of Adam, participant in the transgression and fall and misery of all men."[40]

This contrast stands alongside Barth's understanding of the Church as invisible and visible, of God's indestructible work and human work which is destructible. Holiness is never something to be corporately possessed. It is an event, received moment to moment in faith as a gift, and acted upon as an "active participation"[41] in holiness which is always eschatological and provisional. The prevenient "objective participation" in holiness which Christ imputes *extra nos* becomes in the work of the Holy Spirit an imparted realization and imperative *in nobis*. It represents therefore a being and a becoming. In that holiness is a present reality in Christ, yet provisional and not fully realized, there is the need for growth. As Barth says, "the fact that saints become, that they are conceived and born and then live and act in the *communio* of all these *sancta* and therefore in mutual *communio*, is something which from first to last is primarily and properly a growth."[42]

The difference in this account to a Salvationist understanding is immediately apparent. John Wesley perceived that an account of sanctification which emphasized Christ's imputed righteousness, without an account of how the believer grew in grace and obedient, active love,

38. Ibid., 641.

39. Ibid., 643.

40. Ibid., 642.

41. I am indebted to George Hunsinger for his use of the terms "objective participation," and "active participation," in describing Barth's actualism in sanctification. See Hunsinger, "A Tale of Two Simultaneities," 78.

42. *CD* IV.2, 644.

invited the charge of antinomianism, a fear that was at the heart of his dispute with Calvinistic Methodists,[43] as McGonigle confirms:

> A study of John Wesley's reaction to Calvinism must come to one incontrovertible conclusion; he had a life-long fear of antinomianism in every shape and disguise. While he knew, and admitted, that many Calvinists lived exemplary lives, he never rid himself of the suspicion that Calvinism as a theological system lent itself too easily to antinomian tendencies.[44]

The first chapter demonstrated that Wesley's *via salutis* combined an account of Christ's imputed righteousness in justification, which initiated a process of growth in sanctification, towards a later crisis experience of entire sanctification. In contrast, the Booths considered partial sanctification a poor relation compared to the higher life of entire sanctification. Whilst entire sanctification was appropriated in faith, the "definite" teaching of an eradication of sin for victorious Christian living had a subjective concentration on the human conditions and behaviour necessary for claiming and receiving an entirely sanctified relationship with Christ through the baptism of the Holy Spirit. This squeezed out an objective appreciation of Christ's imputed righteousness, as a gift of sovereign grace in the life of a sinner. Ultimately both Wesley's and the Booths' accounts of entire sanctification were in practice impossible to maintain. Wesley's doctrine has continued within Methodism to be the subject of ongoing acrimonious dispute in which, as Jason Vickers suggests, "these divisions have often been so painful that many Wesleyan and Methodist communions have all but ceased talking about the doctrine that Wesley claimed was the reason that God raised up the people called Methodists in the first place."[45]

In The Salvation Army the doctrine has become confused, in which the latest *Handbook Of Doctrine* equivocates on whether there may or may not be a crisis experience that may or may not be dramatic or at conversion, and may or may not, in the growth of Christ-likeness, be entire. In order to explain entire sanctification, both Wesley and the Booths

43. Whilst this may have been true of some of his Calvinistic contemporaries, Hunsinger is clear that this tendency stemmed from Luther's doctrine of justification, rather than from Calvin, who had an account of gradual growth in sanctification. See Hunsinger, "A Tale of Two Simultaneities," 68.

44. McGonigle, *Sufficient Saving Grace*, 317.

45. Vickers, *Wesley*, 102.

had to formulate a less than satisfactory and ultimately unworkable understanding of sin. R. Newton Flew, who sympathetically reviewed Wesley's doctrine of Christian perfection with all its strengths and weaknesses, concluded that the problems "spring from an inadequate analysis of the nature of sin,"[46] in which Wesley, and for that matter the Booths were unable to take advantage of later advances in psychology, and an understanding of the subconscious mind and its interrelated human behaviour. More positively, they dramatically raised the ceiling of expectation, in which there could be no underestimation of God's grace in supporting an obedient life of love.

Chick Yuill has attempted to restate the doctrine of holiness for Salvationists. He suggests, firstly, that Salvationist accounts of holiness that begin in an anthropological focus on the believer's surrender and crisis, start in the wrong place, for "the place to begin is with Jesus Christ and his perfect adequacy."[47] In his estimation this turns the Salvationist's "crisis" away from "the need to find something extra" or "a second instalment of God's power,"[48] towards the simple reception of the fullness of the Holy Spirit in a person's life, as a relationship that leads to Christian discipleship and obedience. Yuill asserts that "such discipleship is nothing other than the holy life in action."[49] His contribution, like Barth's, is to put the focus back on God's prevenient sanctification in which God's creatures objectively stand complete, and subjectively in the power of the Holy Spirit are becoming free "to be what, in Christ, we are; not fretting for something which lies beyond our present reach."[50] Yuill does not refer to Barth, but his characterization of holiness as "being" and "becoming," suggests the importance of Salvationists reflecting upon Barth's distinctive approach in the important task of breathing new life and vitality into their doctrine of holiness.

Three important considerations for Salvationist's thinking about their ecclesiology arise in this discussion of the Booths' entire sanctification and Barth's account of the holiness of the Church. Firstly, it highlights the difference between the conception of a "pure" and a "mixed" economy within the Church. Following Augustine, Calvin maintained

46. Flew, *The Idea of Perfection in Christian Theology*, 332.
47. Yuill, *We Need Saints*, 143.
48. Ibid., 144.
49. Ibid., 148.
50. Ibid., 144.

a concept of the invisible Church of all the elect and the visible Church of those baptised throughout the earth in which are "mingled many hypocrites."[51] In relation to the invisible and visible church, Calvin instructed that, "just as we must believe, therefore, that former church, invisible to us, is visible to the eyes of God alone, so we are commanded to revere and keep communion with the latter, which is called 'church' in respect of men."[52] His instruction directly challenged those Anabaptists whom Calvin perceived, like the "Cathari of old," possessed "a false conviction of their own perfect sanctity"[53] in escaping to a supposedly pure Church; to which error he cited Jesus' parables of the net (Matt 13:47–58) and the weeds (Matt 13:24–30).[54]

Hans Küng takes the matter further when he suggests that "all of us are sinful, the Church is a dismal *communio peccatorum* which every day must ask God anew: 'forgive us our trespasses.'"[55] Küng is clear, like Barth, that "we do not simply believe *in* the holy Church, but believe in God who makes the Church holy," a reality that "does not stem from moral and religious behaviour," but "by being called by God in Christ to be the communion of the faithful . . . by being separated from the world and at the same time embraced and supported by his grace."[56]

Barth provides his own distinctive dialectical account of the invisibility or "special visibility" of the church, of which the visible church is a witness, but "at best" only "an equivocal witness."[57] Essentially, whilst affirming the objective actualization of the Church's holiness in Jesus Christ, he acknowledges the provisional nature of the Holy Spirit's realization of the Church's sanctification in believers who are at the same time saints and sinners. Therefore from the subjective point of view, the Church can only be a "mixed" Church in that it does not possess God's holiness. It can only pray for it. In contrast the Booths, whilst they followed Wesley in denying sinless perfection, through holiness revivalism they implicitly raised the spectacle of a "pure" Church of the entirely

51. Calvin, *Institutes of the Christian Religion*, 2:1021.

52. Ibid., 2:1022.

53. Ibid., 2:1027. The editor notes that "Calvin evidently refers to the Novatianists (ca.250)," fn. 24.

54. Ibid., 2:1028.

55. Küng, *The Church*, 322.

56. Ibid., 324–25.

57. *CD* IV.2, 617.

sanctified as an urgent and immediate subjective realization of God's holiness in human agency. It created schism in their day, and continues to be at the root of a subjectivism and individualism that hinders Salvationists from fully appreciating the one, holy, catholic and apostolic Church.

Secondly, the subjective emphasis upon "practical holiness" which the Booths bequeathed to Salvationists, relies ultimately on obedience to the discipline of a catalogue of rules and regulations along the lines of a military army. Whilst some might argue that obedience to these rules and regulations, does not earn, but is an appropriate thankful expression of God's grace and of what it means in practice to be holy, it is clear that the Booths laid legalistic human expectations on their followers that went beyond what Barth calls the "superior law of Jesus Christ."[58] It is still for example a regulation that a soldier's sanctity must be maintained through total abstinence. This will be addressed more fully under Barth's account of both the upholding and the order and law of the community.

Thirdly, the early Salvationist emphasis upon individual purity and sanctity failed, as Needham has already suggested, to adequately address the nature and shape of that perfect love within the community of God's people. As already demonstrated, the metaphor of an army shaped the life of the community through a military command system that was more functionally and materially concerned with the task of saving souls, than it was the quality of relationality within the community. Barth is clear, however, that the divine life of "co-existence, co-inherence and reciprocity" is a triunity where "He is Himself the One who loves eternally, the One who is eternally loved, and eternal love."[59] As Jason Springs comments: "This perfect and eternal love reciprocally shared in God's triunity is the *primary analogate* of the relational attitudes that people can, and ought to, take up one to another—individually and collectively—insofar as the relationship of mutual recognition and reciprocal accountability finds realization."[60] In contrast to this, a military form, with its hierarchical command structure, is unable to adequately facilitate such an expression of mutuality. This will be taken up further in a discussion of what apostolicity means in the Christian community.

58. Ibid., 681.

59. Ibid. III.2, 218–19.

60. Springs, "Gender, Equality and Freedom."

The Growth of the Community

Barth's second account of the Holy Spirit's provisional sanctification examines the growth of the community. Hunsinger examines the reasons why many, he cites Hans Urs von Balthasar in particular,[61] do not think that Barth's actualism allows the Christian to grow or progress, despite Barth's insistence otherwise. He perceptively notes that the criticism, in some sense true though not altogether accurate, stems from the way Barth combines both Calvin's *simul*, in which justification and sanctification as two distinct events are given to faith simultaneously, with Luther's doctrine of *simul iustus et peccator*. When Barth puts these two together, just as in Luther's doctrine the believer who is both justified and sinner turns repeatedly to Christ for righteousness and forgiveness, so also sanctification takes place in Christ objectively once for all outside the believer, but is received existentially not in a gradual but in a repeated manner. In this perpetual operation of grace, sin's dominion is overcome. In this sense Barth sides not with an excessive eradicationist doctrine detected in both Wesley and Booth, but in the rival softer doctrine expounded at Keswick, and more recently suggested in the Army's *Handbook of Doctrine*. Barth's emphasis on repetition, however, makes the gradual growth of the believer more difficult, though not impossible, to conceptualize. Barth combines repetition with a sense of moving forward when he says:

> [I]n the upbuilding of the Christian community—although it takes place in a succession of events in time, and there is a progressive building upon that which is already built—it is remarkable that there is no such thing as a finished task. Every step forward includes a repetition of those already taken and those which have still to follow.[62]

---

61. Hunsinger, "A Tale of Two Simultaneities," 68. See also 68–89.
62. *CD* IV.2, 631.

He can also say more explicitly:

> [S]anctification in conversion is not the affair of these individual moments; it is the affair of the totality of the whole life-movement of man. To live a holy life is to be raised and driven with increasing definiteness from the centre of this revealed truth, and therefore to live in conversion with growing sincerity, depth and precision.[63]

Barth can therefore introduce the concept of the Church's growth dialectically, as intensive and extensive, vertical and horizontal, spiritual and numerical. The goal is not numerical growth, but rather "the proclamation of the kingdom of God."[64] Barth is clear that the priority always rests with intensive growth over extensive,[65] in which the numerical growth that inevitably follows is always concerned for quality before quantity, for "nothing is more astonishing than the true, intensive, spiritual growth of the communion of saints on earth."[66] The Church's sanctification and growth therefore remains dialectically indestructible and destructible in a corresponding relation of precedence and subsequence that is patterned on the Word and flesh of Christ. Barth's comments are instructive for all congregations with an evangelistic eye to numerical growth, in an individualistic concern for the deployment of the right modern techniques and methods, as demonstrated by The Salvation Army's adherence to Finney's concept of new measures and means. Ultimately these techniques must remain subordinate to the relationality of intensive spiritual growth in the community judged ultimately not by numerical strength, but by the quality of its life and love together.

In fairness to holiness revivalism, The Salvation Army's astonishing growth represented a powerful combination of both spiritual intensity and imaginative human agency. Nevertheless, the ongoing temptation to dwell upon human techniques in the salvation of individual souls remains an ongoing tension in what Barth posits as the vertical and horizontal dialectic, in which it remains vital that a healthy wisdom of priority and subordination is exercised, in what can all too easily for churches embracing new techniques become equally competing demands.

63. Ibid., 566.
64. Ibid., 647.
65. Ibid., 648.
66. Ibid., 650.

The Upholding of the Community

Barth highlights several temptations that the Church faces in its provisional sanctification as a community of both saints and sinners. Firstly, it will be tempted on the one hand to overemphasize its visibility, and on the other to retreat into its invisibility. Barth explains that it overemphasizes its visibility when it understands its holiness automatically in relation to people joining it through baptism. Barth is famously critical of the practice of infant baptism in this respect.[67] As Barth is critical of a sacramental *opus operatum*, he is equally critical of a "religious and moral *opus operantis*" in which the attention is placed on "a certain style or habit of Christian life."[68] As this relates to The Salvation Army, it is clear that there is in Salvationist practice, as in Barth, no understanding of a sacramental *opus operatum*. Salvationists view holiness as a graced relationship in Christ, a gift appropriated through faith. Barth's comments on a "religious and moral *opus operantis*," however, are worthy of further Salvationist reflection.

The development of what became known in Salvationist jargon as "practical holiness" was the very precise detailing of behavior that was acceptable and unacceptable in living the holy life. Whilst much of the overly zealous regulation associated with the Booths has been revised, there remains at the heart of Salvationist practical holiness a "Soldier's Covenant,"[69] beautiful in many respects, but regulative of lifestyle and exclusive nonetheless. In particular, the holy life of a soldier, the only form of full membership of The Salvation Army, is still to be lived in total abstinence from alcohol

In his *Essentials of Christian Experience*, Coutts lists those "divine insights" given to Booth which "have been transmitted to our care," the abandoning of which "would be to commit spiritual suicide without cause."[70] Amongst them Coutts lists two: firstly, that "holiness . . . is seen in Christlikeness of character" and secondly, "certain patterns of daily living are required of those who acknowledge Jesus as Saviour and Lord, that my good can never by my neighbour's hurt, and that love is the fulfilling—not the abrogating—of the law."[71] Coutts has in mind here,

---

67. Ibid. IV.1, 696.

68. Ibid.

69. The Salvation Army, *The Salvation Army Handbook of Doctrine*, 2010, 319–22.

70. Coutts, *Essentials of Christian Experience*, 74.

71. Ibid., 75.

amongst other things, the Army's insistence on total abstinence, and in particular Paul's epistle to the Romans in which he asks them "not to put any stumbling-block or obstacle in the way of a brother or sister."[72] For Salvationist mission and ministry amongst those marginalized and down trodden by the abuse and abusers of alcohol, this passage, written by someone who himself took a Nazirite vow of abstinence,[73] is considered important. Whilst few Salvationists would in theory see abstinence as a universal requirement for all Christian disciples, in practice the issue is more confused. General John Larsson's keynote address to international Salvation Army leaders declares:

> We do not intend to soften our stand on abstention from alcohol.
> We intend to maintain the position that you cannot be a soldier
> of The Salvation Army and drink alcohol. Our challenge in this
> regard will continue to be one of teaching and of pastoral care for
> those who are tempted to depart from this norm.[74]

The "Soldier's Covenant" implicitly declares that generations of Salvationists may only be formally welcomed into God's Church as expressed through Salvation Army soldiership, if they are totally abstinent. Whilst such a loving and sacrificial response in honour of another's weakness should not be diminished, if it is a free response, it cannot be a lifestyle requirement for a member of God's Church. Barth had a deep respect for his school friend Ernst von May[75] who became a Salvation Army officer: "Confronted with this man I was really ashamed of my bit of inner activity . . . Here was this natural and simple life in the love of God, in which everything was so organic and not at all contrived."[76]

Nevertheless Barth, should he have wished it, would have been excluded from becoming a full member of this version of God's Church, without changing his habits. He recalls meeting "a very pleasant Salvation Army officer from France" and Busch adds, "to whom Barth defended his cherished lifelong habit of pipe-smoking."[77] In effect, for Salvationists, the holy life corresponds to, as Barth puts it, "a certain style

72. Rom 14:13 (TNIV).

73. For Paul's personal Nazirite vow see Acts 18:18, and his sponsorship of four others Acts 21:23ff. See also Douglas, "Nazirite," 819f.

74. Larsson, "Being True to Ourselves," 3.

75. Busch, *Karl Barth*, 29.

76. Ibid., 87.

77. Ibid., 469.

or habit of Christian life," rather than expressing a purely free gift of grace. This is one aspect, amongst others, that characterizes this community as a quasi-religious order, in which vows are voluntarily taken in disciplined Christian living. This habit or lifestyle requirement as a rule is highly problematic for an understanding of membership of God's Church, expressed as it must be both locally and universally.

If, in Barth's estimation, a religious and moral *opus operantis* such as the example of teetotalism, is an over inflation of visible human work in the Church then, secondly, he equally contrasts the internal dangers of the dialectical relation of "alienation (secularisation) or self-glorification (sacralisation)."[78] Alienation has its roots in the Church listening to the voice of a stranger. It is "a question of the translation of the Christian into the secular at the command of love; or conversely of a translation of the secular into the Christian, of a kind of baptism of non-Christian ideas and customs and enterprises by new Christian interpretations and the giving of a new Christian content, or of a minting of Christian gold on behalf of poor non-Christians."[79] On the other hand "sacralisation means the transmutation of the lordship of Jesus Christ into the vanity of a Christianity which vaunts itself in His name but in reality is enamoured only of itself and its traditions, confessions and institutions."[80] How then is the church upheld? Barth continues to hold dialectically the indestructible divine work of God alongside destructible human work, in view of which the community, whilst it "is destructible, it cannot and will not actually be destroyed."[81] The community gathers around the Bible, in which the Word of God is heard. In the work of the Holy Spirit, "He verifies Scripture simply by the fact that He is its content; that as it is read and heard He Himself is present to speak and act as the living Lord of the Church."[82]

The internal threat to the Church of either secularization or sacralization, of alienation or self-glorification has a vital place in The Salvation Army's reflection, in which Barth notes that "the one form usually involves the other," and "it is not difficult to see the face of the one in the

78. *CD* IV.2, 667.
79. Ibid., 668.
80. Ibid., 670.
81. Ibid., 672.
82. Ibid., 675.

other."[83] This is best illustrated by The Salvation Army's "baptism" of the secular idea or custom of wearing military uniform. It is representative of a number of non-Christian ideas that have been given Christian content through its military form. The spontaneous manner in which it was adopted as an aggressive form of witness, proved remarkably successful in Victorian Britain, but communicates far less effectively in the culture of a society that sees it more negatively, as overtly authoritarian, disciplinarian and regimented. Whilst bearing open witness may be construed very positively, challenging questions must be faced. The most obvious is whether the concept of uniformity can be judged to be a biblically based value, alongside the strong biblical appeal to diversity, whose corollary is not uniformity but unity. In reality, "uniform wearing" is the kind of baptized non-Christian idea that if not used thoughtfully, sensitively and guardedly, could ultimately represent a secularizing influence. Writing about the nature of the Church's diversity and multiplicity in ministry, Barth raises the problem of the concept of uniformity:

> The Holy Spirit does not enforce a flat uniformity. Hence the Christian community, quite apart from the natural individuality of its members and the consequent dangers, cannot be a barracks, nor can its members be the uniformed inhabitants, nor can their activity be the execution of a well-drilled manoeuvre. Their divine calling and endowment are as such manifold. They are always new and different.[84]

Equally, in a discussion of the Holy Spirit's distribution of spiritual gifts, Barth suggests that the image of regimentation and uniformity is unhelpful, in which baptism with the Holy Spirit "does not consist in . . . donning a uniform and clapping on a helmet and as a member of the community, as one specimen among many others, being subjected to the same regimented spiritual and ethical drill," for "the Holy Spirit, being the Spirit of the one, but eternally rich God, is no compactly uniform mass."[85] Whilst the wearing of Salvationist uniform has never been compulsory for all, non-uniformed members are barred in the exercising of their spiritual gifts within certain ministries.

The issue becomes more complex when looked at from the reverse face of sacralization. William Booth's grand-daughter, Catherine Booth,

83. Ibid., 667.

84. *CD* IV.3.2, 855.

85. Ibid. IV.4, 37f.

in a letter to young officers entitled "Why Wear Uniform?," suggests that "it would be interesting could we discover how much adherence to such distinction in dress has had to do with maintaining the definite characteristics of various religious bodies, and how far a persistence in the use of this outward sign of separation would have delayed the decline of spiritual vigour and activity in some societies."[86] She intimates that the wearing of Salvation Army uniform, adopted originally as a pragmatically aggressive measure of witness, is an outward sign and means of invisible grace, which is unexpected in a movement that does not find baptism and the Lord's Supper to be necessary means of grace. Luke Bretherton observes:

> In the Salvation Army there is, at present, an ardent but to an outsider baffling debate about whether wearing uniforms is a requirement for full membership of the Salvation Army. This debate is a good illustration of what happens when renewal movements abandon the given practices and theological coordinates of the Christian tradition—in the case of the Salvation Army it is the abandonment of the sacraments of baptism and Eucharist. The result is that they end up sacralising the non-essential. This can be seen again and again in modern holiness and revival movements.[87]

Barth's concern with the church's tendency towards a sacralizing of its human work is the self-glorification that results when divine and human agency are confused in a synergism of identification and cooperation. Salvationists believe in theory that grace is a gift of God; that no human work or merit counts in either justification or sanctification. Nevertheless in practice their subjectivity is more confused than this, and can in some instances lead to an identification of the human spirit and God's Spirit. Consider the Army's third general, Edward Higgins, writing to help and guide Salvation Army officers:

> *It has been proved to the world beyond all doubt that The Army plan is the best for dealing with the masses.* Non-conformist bodies of various kinds, Anglicans, Roman Catholics, and even Buddhists have shown their appreciation of this fact by imitating our methods and copying some parts of our organization. But perhaps they have failed to perceive that *The Army Spirit* is neces-

86. Bramwell-Booth, *Messages to the Messengers*, 126.
87. Bretherton, "Beyond the Emerging Church," 44.

sary to the successful use of Army methods. How many others have tried our methods without our *spirit*, and have therefore been frustrated in their endeavours![88]

Such triumphalist sentiments are less commonplace in a contemporary United Kingdom context, where numerically the Army is smaller than when Higgins' article was written. Nevertheless, its methods, inspired by Finney as pragmatic and dispensable tools, have in some instances taken on almost revelatory significance, in a community that can potentially confuse God's Holy Spirit with their own.

The Order and Law of the Community

Finally, in Barth's account of the third direction in which the upbuilding of the Church takes place as a provisional sanctification, and this intrinsically related to the other two directions of growth and preservation, is the form of the Church's order and law. If the community is the earthly-historical form of Christ's existence, with Christ as Head, then "in the Church, law is that which is right by the norm of this relationship,"[89] for "the christologico-ecclesiological concept of the community is such that by its very nature it speaks of law and order."[90] This is Barth's dialectical proposition that in the relation of precedence and subsequence, the Church exists in total dependence on Christ in which Christ Himself is the Church's order and law to whom the Church is called to obediently correspond. "In correspondence with this centre it is always a question of the ordering and commanding and controlling of the Holy One in whom all are sanctified and therefore of Jesus Christ, on the one side; and on the other side of the obedient attitude of the human communion of saints in subordination to Him."[91]

Barth's second point is, however, that on this "christologico-ecclesiological view of the community law and order are distinguished as Christian and ecclesiastical law and order from every other form, and are visible and effective in this distinctive form."[92] In contrast to other human societies, "community law is not a law to itself," but "He is the

---

88. Higgins, *Stewards of God*, 24. Higgins was General from 1929 to 1934.

89. *CD* IV.2, 679.

90. Ibid., 680.

91. Ibid.

92. Ibid., 681.

regulative law of their relationship to Him," and in this respect "all valid and projected Church law, if it is true Church law, will be clearly and sharply differentiated from every other kind of 'law,'"[93] more precisely, "the voice which has to be heard is that of Jesus Christ as attested in Holy Scripture,"[94] and in the following of whom the church avoids the twin dangers on either side of legalism and license.

On this basis Barth outlines four preliminary principles or "standpoints"[95] from which canon law can develop more detailed answers, which are the law of service, liturgical law, living law and exemplary law. Bearing in mind the previous discussion on sacralizing tendencies in the Church's work, it is Barth's discussion of living law that is particularly pertinent, in which Christ is the Head of the body, and the community is engaged in "listening, regard and respect," and therefore "a proper attentiveness, reverence and willingness in relation to its Head."[96] Living law "demands constant re-investigation by a community which is open for new direction (not from below but from above), and is therefore willing and ready for new answers."[97] In such living law, which Barth reminds is only human law and not divine, the Church takes itself seriously and avoids "ecclesiological Docetism."[98] Nevertheless the community will keep this law constantly open to reform, not viewing it as "an authority for all ages and to all eternity" and "will refuse to regard as necessary to salvation, or to invest with divine authority, the work of its obedience, and therefore the ecclesiastical propositions which it discovered and enforced yesterday."[99] The form of the community is not therefore unchanging divine revelation, and in this respect is "always open—as *ecclesia semper reformanda*—for the new ordering of its Lord, and is therefore ready for fresh obedience and prepared for the discovery and establishment of a new and better order on the basis of new and better instruction."[100] Barth steers a course between legalism and license when he affirms that as the community takes hold of,

93. Ibid., 682.
94. Ibid.
95. Ibid., 678.
96. Ibid., 711.
97. Ibid.
98. Ibid., 712.
99. Ibid., 714f.
100. Ibid., 717.

> this courage for living law, it will be protected against fatal indif-
> ference and negligence in respect of the question of order and
> therefore against disorder. But it will also be protected against
> the fatal overestimation of any particular answer to this ques-
> tion; against petrifaction in a particular tradition and against the
> legalism of sacrosanct institutions.[101]

The Salvation Army is not alone amongst churches in being prone to institutionalizing and traditionalizing tendencies that stem, in Barth's Christological conception, from a failure to maintain a proper differen-tiated unity and asymmetry between divine and human agency. Living law refers to Christ at the head of the Church, in which he is always able to ensure its renewal, reformation and vitality. The Salvation Army must face the challenge that in its "baptism" of a military command sys-tem, military terminology and practices such as uniformity and total abstinence, it has succumbed in its discipline to a legalism that exceeds that which is appropriate within God's Church. Whilst the Church re-quires law and order, Barth is right to affirm that the voice of Jesus Christ must always be heard, as attested in scripture. Whether the issue faced is membership criteria, uniform policy, habits of behavior and lifestyle, or structures of authority, its order and law cannot exceed the voice of Christ. The sociological form of a religious order cannot be the true and universal expression of God's Church, but only a distinct order, or an *ecclesiola in ecclesia*. In this respect, Barth's comments on the Church not investing with divine authority the work of its obedience, strike at the heart of his notion of the "church in excess" which is "the church exceed-ing the limit within which it alone can be the church of Jesus Christ."[102]

In conclusion, Barth's understanding of the holiness of the Church as a gift from God, reveals the extent to which The Salvation Army, from its holiness revivalist roots, has allowed a subjective emphasis upon the conditional nature of sanctification to overwhelm an objective under-standing of Christ's imputed holiness. As an ecclesial consequence, it has been tempted to over-inflate its human visible form and confuse the distinction between divine and human agency. When a Salvation Army General declares that "God wants us to be The Salvation Army,"[103] Salvationists must discern the extent to which this means the Church,

101. Ibid., 716.

102. Barth, *The Christian Life*, 136.

103. Larsson, "Being True to Ourselves," 3.

supported scripturally, that God calls it to be, visibly living in faithful, obedient, correspondence to Christ, and not simply the church that human endeavor has made it.

The Church Is Catholic.

Catholicity for Barth means "an identity, a continuity, a universality, which is maintained in all the differences."[104] He explores this catholicity in four dimensions concluding that the creed could be expanded to mean: "I believe that the Christian community is one and the same in essence in all places, in all ages, within all societies, and in relation to all its members."[105] In other words it has a geographical, historical, cultural and communal dimension, in which "it participates in the essence of the one Church, being faithful to it and knowing how to do it justice in its visible expression," which does not mean a continuity of form but "to maintain itself in forms which are always new," as "*ecclesia semper reformanda*."[106] Barth continues to view his protagonists to left and right in declaring that Catholic denotes not the oldest or most modern Church, but the true Church as opposed to the false or heretical Church, where "a true Church is humbly content to be thrown back entirely upon faith in respect of its truth, and confidently exist in this faith as the true community of Jesus Christ."[107] Just like the Church's unity and holiness, "its catholicity as its own actuality is grounded in Him as its Head,"[108] in which there is dialectically both unity and differentiation, an inner mystery and correspondingly an outer visibility of form that is "called to obedience and questioned concerning its obedience by Him."[109] The key question is how the Church may express visibly its essential identity and continuity, in forms that can constantly be new within the various dimensions of its existence.

There are two pertinently related issues here for The Salvation Army. Firstly, the manner in which it adopted a new, shocking, yet engaging form as a Christian community in Victorian society can on

104. *CD* IV.1, 701.
105. Ibid., 707.
106. Ibid., 704f.
107. Ibid., 708.
108. Ibid., 710.
109. Ibid.

these grounds in principle be affirmed, provided that it maintains the essential identity and continuity of God's Church. Questions continue to be raised, however, as to the depth of theological reflection given to the suitability of its dominant military form as a visible expression of God's Church. Whilst it did not initially set out to be this Church, its founders have left such a legacy for contemporary Salvationists to wrestle with; who seek to understand The Salvation Army in these terms.

Secondly, this single military form with its associated forms, has in its relatively short life spanned the dimensions of geography, history and society without necessarily asking whether this was the most appropriate form in each place, age and culture to denote the Christian community. Numerous examples of relatively minor adjustments in language and appearance have been made to suit changing places, times and cultures, and sadly the reality of warfare is a universal concept. None of this, however, can escape the overriding fact that The Salvation Army adopted its new dynamic form in a particular place, age and culture and within a limited understanding of community. The twin dangers of secularization and sacralization that arise in insisting that this form and its associated forms persist across the various human dimensions, has already been highlighted. Salvation Army practitioners in Britain, and more particularly London, are, for example, daily forced to ask questions about how its military form can visibly express God's Church, in the rapidly changing multi-cultural society that London has become, where hierarchy is an inadequate expression of community. A grassroots initiative in Britain called "Roots,"[110] recognized this challenge, and questioned what was essential in visible expression and what was mere changeable form, in a painful recognition that sociologically, institutionalization is an all too human reality left in isolation from the creative and renewing energy of the Holy Spirit, notwithstanding the late or post-modern debate with regard to detraditionalization.[111]

One such line of enquiry must surely ask whether The Salvation Army has in respect of baptism and the Lord's Supper mistakenly replaced the essential identity of the Church, the Church as *koinonia*, for its own newly adopted forms. The Salvation Army must re-visit its assumption that the sacraments were mere cultural accretions in a particular

110. This specific initiative has now concluded, even though its question is as urgent as ever it was.

111. See Heelas et al., *Detraditionalization*.

place and time and contemplate the theology with which these practices express the essential identity and continuity of the Church community, its catholicity, across all places, times and cultures. Salvationists should put to one side for the time being their pre-occupation with whether they are means of grace, listen again to Christ's words and reflect on those dominical signs and symbols of what it means to be the body of Christ. In following holiness revivalism's subjective and individualistic gospel, and Robert Barclay and the Quakers' scriptural arguments for their "spiritual" non-use, the Booths lost an objective and theological understanding of what it essentially means to be the Church in visible expression. In Barth's terms they pragmatically secularized and sacralized that form, in an otherwise commendable missionary attempt to reach the most poor and marginalized in society, in which the objective symbols of water, bread and wine were subjectively replaced by the individual's consecration upon God's altar.

Andrew Walker is confident that "there is a wind of change blowing through the evangelical world, carrying on its wings a new watchword, which is neither 'renewal' nor 'revival', but *'retrieval'*,"[112] in which there is a "regress to the *paradosis* of the church—that which in times past was believed to be the apostolic tradition of the New Testament, and which was handed on and jealously guarded by the community of faith: the church."[113] Speaking primarily to evangelicals Walker makes the plea for a renewed understanding of the "symbiotic" relation of scripture and tradition, in which "Scripture in a sense is affirmed, sustained and unfolded by tradition, but tradition is illuminated, judged and controlled by Scripture" for "together they are the content of faith: *paradosis*."[114] Salvationists should reflect on his assertion that one of the primary examples of the apostle Paul's use of the word *paradosis* is found in 1 Corinthians 11:23 where in explaining the Lord's Supper, he says, "For I received from the Lord what I also handed on [*paradidōmi*] to you . . ." where he uses the verb equivalent of the noun *paradosis*,[115] highlighting the importance of the information being conveyed.

The Salvation Army's 1997 *Spiritual Life Commission* deliberations focused on what it saw as the way in which the Lord's Supper as

112. Walker, *Remembering Our Future*, 59.

113. Ibid., 61.

114. Ibid., 72.

115. Ibid., 67.

a ceremony or ritual had become separated from the common fellow-ship meal shared by the Christian community. They recommended a renewal of Booth's suggestion that every meal be an opportunity to give thanks to God for his sacrificial gift of love and grace, and encouraged congregations to share *agape* meals or "love feasts." I. Howard Marshall's NT exegesis in *Last Supper and Lord's Supper* is clear, however, that "the early church met together for fellowship meals which included this rite, known as the Breaking of Bread," and "certainly by the time that 1 Corinthians was written we gain the impression that the Breaking of Bread was an integral part of the meal and that the meal was held on Sundays."[116] In summarizing the meal's significance he confesses that "there is such a rich catalogue of theological motifs in the Lord's Supper that it is far from easy to arrange them in a systematic manner."[117] He lists five theological emphases for reflection, "that it stands in continuity with acts of God in the Old Testament, that it brings out the saving significance of the Lord's death, that it is an occasion for communion with the risen Lord, that it is an anticipation of the heavenly banquet, and that it is an expression of fellowship within the body of Christ."[118]

It is regrettable that Salvationist attention is largely negatively focused upon defending the reasons not to have to use these ceremonies, rather than exploring their rich value. Published explanations tend to make use of the comments of biblical scholars that appear exegetically and theologically sympathetic, without paying attention to the full wisdom offered as to the importance of keeping baptism and the Lord's Supper a central focus. Two such examples may be given of this practice. The Army has used the words of Brunner when he affirms their position:

> Intimately as these two so-called sacraments are associated with the saving events in Christ, yet they are not identical with them—they are not therefore unconditionally necessary to salvation . . . the Reformers have therefore correctly understood the meaning of Scripture, in allowing to these sacraments only a *necessitas relativa*, not a *necessitas absoluta*.[119]

---

116. Marshall, *Last Supper and Lord's Supper*, 144.

117. Ibid., 146.

118. Ibid., 154.

119. Brunner, *The Misunderstanding of the Church*, 72.

On the other hand it has not chosen to include his equally positive affirmation that:

> Just as we cannot conceive of any act of worship in which all the necessary elements—the common act in fellowship, the foundation in saving history and the real union with Him and with each other—are so perfectly combined as in the Last Supper, so no form of initiation into the community is conceivable where the various moments—of confession, penance, and communion rooted in saving history—are so harmoniously expressed as in baptism.[120]

Equally, Bishop John Austin Baker was invited to address The Salvation Army's *Spiritual Life Commission* and affirmed "there can be no reason in Christian theology or Christian history why the Salvation Army should not retain in full vigour its insight that sacraments are not necessary, for a saving relationship with Christ can be had without them."[121] The Army is, however, not yet ready to hear his view that "if properly taught and explained, the sacraments can be 'of immense enrichment to believers.'"[122] In effect the Army's interest does not extend beyond the question of whether these ceremonies are essential for a saving relationship with Christ, remaining unwilling for the benefit of its members to explore how they might be enriching, and used in continuity with the church catholic. What began as a pragmatic decision has, over time, become an entrenched position, in which even non-sacramental accounts of baptism and the Lord's Supper are ignored.[123] In this respect, a dialogue with Barth reveals that whilst he supports an understanding of Christ as the one and only true sacrament, he positively affirms the merits of these actions in the church's mission:

> Baptism and the Lord's Supper are not empty signs. On the contrary, they are full of meaning and power. They are the simplest, and yet in their very simplicity the most eloquent elements in the witness which the community owes to the world, namely the witness of peace on earth among the men in whom God is well pleased.[124]

120. Ibid., 71.

121. Cited in Clifton, *Who are these Salvationists?*, 94.

122. Ibid.

123. See for example Eller, *In Place of Sacraments*; Barth, *Rediscovering the Lord's Supper*.

124. *CD* IV.3, 901.

The Church Is Apostolic

Barth introduces the fourth mark of the Church with the explanation that "in attempting to fill out the first three terms we could point only to Jesus Christ as the Head of the community which is His body, and therefore to the work of the Holy Spirit."[125] Apostolic, on the other hand, does not add anything new to these definitions, "but describes with remarkable precision the concrete spiritual criterion which enables us to answer the question whether and to what extent in this or that case we have or have not to do with the one holy catholic Church," for "the criterion is not sociological or juridical or psychological, but spiritual."[126] This means that Barth remains committed to highlighting the precedence of God's action and the subsequence of human response. In this case the corresponding human agency he has in mind is the exemplary and normative obedient witness and service of the apostles, for "the awakening power of His Holy Spirit has no other earthly-historical form than that of the power of their witness."[127]

On the other hand, it is an irreversible relation in which their human witness does not gain precedence over divine agency. Barth's theme is clear throughout this section when he states that "there can be no supposed human control over the Holy Spirit" as would be the case "if the relationship of the Church to its Lord were unformed because immediate, if it had control of His earthly-historical form."[128] Barth is clear that the relationship is irreversible, and therefore "it is not immediate but mediate,"[129] in which Barth understands its mediate role as witness.

When Barth speaks of the apostolic witness he has in mind the witness of scripture. He affirms that "what we have learned to know as apostolicity and therefore as the mark of the true Church is quite naturally identical in substance with the term . . . the 'Scripture principle.'"[130] The apostolic community is that which "hears the apostolic witness of the New Testament, which implies that of the Old, and recognises and puts

---

125. Ibid. IV.1, 713.

126. Ibid., 712.

127. Ibid., 719.

128. Ibid., 720.

129. Ibid.

130. Ibid., 721.

this witness into effect as the source and norm of its existence."[131] The Church does not control the Bible as "the book of the law of the Church's faith and order." Rather, the Bible is a servant and witness to Jesus Christ, for, "as Scripture stirs up and invites and summons and impels the Church to look in this same direction there takes place the work of the Spirit of Scripture who is the Holy Spirit."[132] Apostolic means, therefore, "in the discipleship, in the school, under the normative authority, instruction and direction of the apostles, in agreement with them, because listening to them and accepting their message."[133] Apostolicity is an event that can only be understood and recognized by "a living member," who knows "its basis in the apostles, himself standing in their discipleship,"[134] and therefore through scripture, the Holy Spirit and in faith.

Barth's theological anthropology based on the Christological principle of the relation between divine and human agency, between the Holy Spirit and the normative witness of the apostles in scripture, has implications for commonly held concepts of authority, ministry and order in ecclesiology, such as apostolic succession, threefold Episcopal ordering, ordination, clergy and laity. Barth radically re-conceptualizes them. He firstly rejects any notion of an apostolic succession as "a particular adornment[135] of certain denominations based on "historical and juridical grounds,"[136] for "it is obvious that neither the Holy Spirit nor faith is necessary for this purpose, but only an uncritical or critical archaeological knowledge of the lists."[137] Equally the "laying on of hands" by successive bishops "does not need either the Holy Spirit or faith but only a definite idea of law."[138] Barth contends that the apostles have a unique significance, but they are "not in any sense the lords of the community, nor do they play any autonomous role in relation to it," for "Jesus Christ makes use of them" and it is their "serving which in

131. Ibid., 722.
132. Ibid., 723.
133. Ibid., 714.
134. Ibid.
135. Ibid., 716.
136. Ibid., 715.
137. Ibid.
138. Ibid.

relation to the community gives them their exemplary, their normative significance, their greatness," and "their witness."[139]

He concludes that the legitimate apostolic succession is that, "the apostolic witness finds in a community discipleship, hearing, obedience, respect and observance," rather than "an institutional possession of and control over the high mystery of the free Holy Spirit, in the power to over-rule His work and gift, as though it were a matter of money or property or of the legal regulation of certain human demands and interests."[140] The apostles are in a school of service in which Jesus Christ "is the man who instructs and guides and corrects and qualifies them in this school" and the Church "will never regret it if it enters this apostolic succession," which is "the succession of service."[141]

Practically this means that there can be no hierarchy, when the only proper obedience and subjection is to Christ. An hierarchical view stems from the idea that some are exalted in ordination. Barth asks if there can be a rite of ordination "in fulfilment of which the Holy Spirit has to pass from one man to another, so that He can be controlled and His presence and action confined?"[142] The Holy Spirit is free to move where and when the Spirit decides, so "how can apostolic authority and power and mission, how can the Holy Spirit be transferred, when obviously apostolicity is His work and gift?—as though the Holy Spirit were a legal or technical or symbolic It, a property in the hands of one or many exalted members of the community . . . ?"[143] Barth makes it clear that ordination within the Christian community, "means helping another by making clear to him that he is ordained a witness of Jesus Christ."[144] Every member of the community is therefore ordained in ministry.

If all members of the body of Christ are ordained by Christ, then there is no division between the clergy and the laity. The community is ordered by "the character and intention of a law of service," and it "must always be law within an order of ministry."[145] In this Christ calls for obedient correspondence, for "He is the Lord as He is first the servant

139. Ibid., 718f.
140. Ibid., 719.
141. Ibid., 720.
142. Ibid., 717.
143. Ibid.
144. Ibid. IV.3.2, 886.
145. Ibid. IV.2, 690.

of God and all others."[146] The Church's service is firstly "unequivocal, non-dialectical and irreversible" in that there is no "accompanying law of rule."[147] Secondly it is total, in that there is no other sphere in which a different law operates, for "it must know only that it has always to serve with the totality of its being and action."[148] Thirdly it is universal, and though differentiated by many ways of serving, there are no exemptions. "Law and order in the community are never the particular priesthood of a few, but the universal priesthood of all believers," in which "all are office-bearers or none; and if all, then only as servants."[149]

Barth is himself unequivocal in his insistence that canon law must be "vigilant against practical clericalism; against every distinction between the active and the inactive (passive) Church; against every separation into the ruling and the ruled, the teaching and the hearing, the confessing and the established, the taxable and the enfranchised community."[150] For Barth, "the unity and universality of the Church's ministry will always be, not a beautiful ideal, but the absolute law of the community, and therefore that which must be maintained as the condition *sine qua non* of its life."[151] In the functioning of the community's ministry Barth maintains that: "In virtue of their origin in God, in Christ and in the Holy Spirit, it is made impossible that any one of them, i.e., of their particular representatives in the community should break loose and swallow the others, finally making itself out to be the one ministry or the one fellowship of ministry, and acting as such."[152]

In the ordination of its officers, The Salvation Army has not affirmed status but a particular function of leadership in which ministry is focused. Barth is not discounting human leadership within the community. He does, however, envisage a flexibility that discounts fixed orders and rigid hierarchy, allowing for "a leading worker or overseer again dropping back into the ranks and having an important contribution to make as a labourer; and a labourer or apprentice, without any long training or experience, having the opportunity to work at a higher

146. Ibid.
147. Ibid., 691.
148. Ibid., 692.
149. Ibid., 694.
150. Ibid.
151. Ibid., 695.
152. Ibid. IV.3.2, 858.

or even the very highest job."[153] Barth poses the awkward question for a Church that has presumed an hierarchical view of ministry, when he agrees that the Spirit is free "to give Himself from a higher minister of the Church to a lower," but asks provocatively, "why only or preferably from a higher? On what ground do we know or hold that His work and gift are preferably—and for the rest of the Church decisively—a matter for bishops and other clergy?'[154]

Hierarchy has dogged the Church and undermined the priesthood of all believers. Kevin Giles reviews the New Testament evidence and states:

> Nothing seen in the New Testament has endorsed the view that the ordering of the church was given from the start, or that the threefold order of bishops, priests, and deacons was known in the first century. This means that the church is not defined by its ministerial structures; it is defined by its communal existence given by God in Christ, and by the presence of the Spirit who provides the leaders needed.[155]

Whilst there is in all groups over time the sociological process of institutionalization and the development of structure, he discerns in the apostolic age the principle clearly laid down of "the freedom of the Holy Spirit to renew the church by raising up Spirit-filled leaders who will call the Christian community back to its roots."[156] James Dunn is more explicit in his account of the diversity recorded in the NT. The first century, and first generation of the early church, saw the "chaotic charismatic freedom of the Jerusalem church" settle into a more ordered pattern based on the synagogue, in contrast to the Pauline churches where "Paul vigorously advocated a much freer vision of charismatic community, where unity and maturity grew out of the living interplay of gifts and ministries without dependence on any office and hierarchy."[157] In the second generation, he suggests that the Pastoral letters represent a merging of Jewish Christianity and the Pauline churches, and a hardening "into the more rigid structures of future Catholicism" whilst in reaction to this there is in "John, Hebrews and Revelation protest against

153. Ibid. IV.2, 631.
154. Ibid. IV.1, 717.
155. Giles, *What on Earth is the Church?*, 187.
156. Ibid., 188.
157. Dunn, *Unity and Diversity in the New Testament*, 121.

the emergence of a church structured round office and intermediaries" and an insistence "on the immediacy of the individual believer's relation to God through Christ and on the corporate nature of priesthood and prophecy."[158]

In *The Priesthood of Some Believers,* Colin Bulley charts the rise of the special priesthood of the ordained over the first three centuries of the Church. Whilst he is clear that there is an expectation in the NT of people leading and being led, Bulley notes "the lack of a distinction between clergy and laity."[159] There is no clear evidence of the "succession of church leaders by ordination from the apostles and the high priesthood of Christ."[160] He expects that if the special priesthood of the ordained developed after the NT under the guidance and inspiration of the Holy Spirit, then it would in no way diminish but rather enhance the dignity and ministry of all Christians in virtue of their gifting by the Spirit. In reality he concludes,

> that both the understanding of the general priesthood and the active participation of the laity in the church's life, and above all in its public life, ministry and mediation of God's grace, were significantly limited, diminished and harmed by the rise in the clergy's specialized priesthood and the clergy's domination of the church's power and public ministry . . . [and that] . . . rather than enhancing the Spirit's ministry, they diminished it and restricted it increasingly to the ordained.[161]

His clear inference is that ordination, far from being the direct inspiration of the Holy Spirit, is a sociological sign of the institutionalization of the church.

Giles charts the development of an hierarchical view of the Church, and notes the profound implications that the sixteenth-century Reformation doctrine of justification by faith had for ecclesiology. However he states that:

> The Reformers' doctrine of the church was radical in its conception, but in actual practice it was not fully realized. They assumed the prevailing hierarchical view of society, where some were set by God over others. Each congregation was to be led by an or-

158. Ibid.
159. Bulley, *The Priesthood of Some Believers,* 7.
160. Ibid., 317.
161. Ibid., 319.

dained man who alone was to provide the teaching and administer the sacraments.[162]

Even though this ministry was considered in prophetic terms rather than priestly, he remarks that "a high view of the ordained ministry as a permanent office with special powers was therefore maintained."[163] Commenting further on the renewal of Trinitarian theology and its implications for a more egalitarian ecclesiology, he credits Barth's reformulation of the doctrine of the Trinity as the source of that fresh impetus.[164]

In his pastoral approach to the doctrine, Paul Fiddes acknowledges that a renewed understanding of perichoretic movements in the inner Trinitarian life of God, with its resistance to "ecclesiastical monarchianism"[165] or even "clerical monarchianism,"[166] offers language that can "draw us into participation in God, out of which human life can be transformed."[167] The challenge for the Christian pastor is therefore multiple: "The prophetic voice of protest must be raised against all domination and absolute power, but there is also the need to release people from the wish to be dominated by what seems to promise protection and security." In his discussion of authority in the Church and the role of pastoral overseers, Fiddes observes that "as we share in the self-giving movement of Father and Son in the power of the Spirit, we see that the only authority lies in being trusted" and that "authority cannot be imposed but only won through humble service," for "no other authority is of any worth."[168] It is clear that in this view of authority, which refers directly to the exemplary nature of Jesus as servant, Barth and Fiddes are united, and offer a direct challenge to the Salvationist idea that authority in God's Church is like a military command structure.

Furthermore, Fiddes goes beyond Barth in accepting "an 'order' of ministers . . . to which ordination points," as "a 'way of being' which is bound to carry authority with it, though it will be the authority of influence and persuasion . . . not of coercion."[169] In this respect he challenges

162. Giles, *What on Earth Is the Church?*, 216.

163. Ibid., 216.

164. Ibid., 282 n. 14.

165. Fiddes, *Participating in God*, 67.

166. Ibid., 99.

167. Ibid., 66.

168. Ibid., 100.

169. Fiddes, *Tracks and Traces*, 103.

a Salvationist view that ministry is purely functional. Having resisted a wrong view of status in ministry, in which authority is not domination and command, but influence and persuasion, Fiddes is rightly able to affirm that the minister's vocation may nonetheless be celebrated as a way of life. This clearly signals for Salvationists that whilst they should allow a potentially controlling military command structure to be reformed, the language of ordination, recently embraced, need not discount an ontological understanding of ministry. Fiddes is clear that ordination can signal a "way of being" without needing to imply an hierarchical view of ministry.

Sir Henry Lunn, when he was assistant editor of the *Methodist Times*, recalls writing a "savage review" of "a military manual for his officers" that William Booth had published, which Lunn called "a compound of Jesuitism and Pharisaism."[170] This criticism was hardly designed to endear himself to Booth, and he recalls being summoned to a meeting with him and told in no uncertain terms that:

> If you ever get to heaven, Lunn, you'll find a General there. There is a General in everything that God does. If John Wesley had had more courage and faith he would have left his powers to one man and not to a committee of a hundred.[171]

Booth's rejection of collegiate, committee style governance for autocratic leadership has already been documented. It set up a succession of unitary power from Booth as General, down through his officer command structure to the local commanding officer of a local corps (congregation), and eventually to the humble soldier. Whilst the image of a soldier is of a fully mobilized and dedicated participant, a member of the body of Christ, the priesthood of all believers, participating vigorously in ministry and exercising spiritual gifts, it is clear that the extension of such a metaphor to include a hierarchical military command system of officers, potentially undermines the servant nature of leadership, in an expectation of unquestioning loyalty and obedience to officers.

Harvey Cox, in his exploration of how the Church might operate if it were conceived as an army, from the Church's early adoption of the military oath or *sacramentum*, suggests on two counts that it cannot be adopted uncritically. Firstly, it cannot be allowed to set up an hierarchy

170. Lunn, *Chapters From My Life*, 188.
171. Ibid.

with officers who "tell the common Christians what to do" and secondly, rather than shedding someone else's blood, the soldier sheds his own: "He pours himself out as a sacrifice."[172] In Cox's vision of an army there is no clericalized church. Those who might ordinarily be conceived as clergy are rather the "kitchen troops of the army of the Lord" supplying the soldiers with their food and weapons, in which Christ is Lord, and the orders "arise from what Paul calls mutual submission."[173] Contrastingly, in The Salvation Army's tangled cord of mission, army and church, its view of authority is dominated by the military command structure, in which the officer hierarchy represents not so much the "kitchen troops" as those who must be obeyed.

Barth, for the most part, remains non-committal about an optimum form of visible Church polity in that the "rightness or wrongness of the constitution and order adopted will always depend upon whether the Word of God entrusted to them and ruling them is thereby honoured or dishonoured in a given time and situation," in which "its invisible essence must always be made visible in the fact that it is a confessing and missionary Church."[174] Perhaps his clearest indications come in his remarks to the 1948 WCC Amsterdam assembly, where he underlines the principle that runs throughout his account of ecclesiology in *Church Dogmatics*; namely *ecclesia semper reformanda*.

> The polity of the Church must in any case be so formed that it present the least possible resistance to the renewal of the Church by its living Lord, and guarantee humanly speaking the maximum degree of being open, free, and at the disposal of Him and the reformation which He accomplishes.[175]

In this respect, discounting all forms of hierarchy, domination and authoritarian control, he suggests that "an ecclesiastical polity which is not derived from observing the congregation and from the concept of congregation is not worthy of the name."[176] This emphasis on the local congregation does not discount the value of a variety of "organs of

---

172. Cox, *God's Revolution and Man's Responsibility*, 113.

173. Ibid., 116f.

174. *CD* IV.3.2, 741.

175. Barth, *God Here and Now*, 93.

176. Ibid., 95. See Sell, *Saints*, 91, for his comment that "no modern Congregationalist of note has declared that any one particular organizational shape of the Church is sacrosanct or incapable of modification."

their unity," "cross-connections"[177] that offer help, guidance, support, and most importantly a relational unity. His complaint "against the papal form, and also against the episcopal and presbyterian synodal forms of constitution . . . is this basic objection, that they not only do not serve the readiness, openness, and freedom of the congregation for the Word of God and therefore for the reformation of the Church; they actually hinder it."[178] The fundamental contradiction for Barth is that these forms of polity "entrust *too little* to men—namely, to the men gathered as Christians to be the living congregation of the Lord Jesus Christ—yet, on the other hand, they entrust too much to men—namely, to those particular office bearers and representatives within and without the congregation."[179] The irony is that "in one place these forms cannot be too careful to guard against human arbitrariness, in order in the other place to carelessly give it a free hand" and "where the former care and the latter carelessness are in effect, there can be no room for the renewal of the Church."[180]

Barth's comments are incisive observations for the Salvationist who finds herself in a military styled and hierarchical polity, with a large headquarters bureaucracy. Very quickly the local congregation becomes the servant or at best franchise[181] of a corporate entity, sanctioned at all times to maintain the corporate brand, dispense the products and advertise the special company offers, trusting the local congregation with a minimum of local initiative and creativity. The paternalism in this relationship competes against the vision that Barth holds of "the mature Christian and mature Christianity, it's thought, speech and action in responsibility to God, in living hope of Him, in service to the world, in free confession and in unceasing prayer."[182]

It is unrealistic to expect that Salvation Army governance and structure can easily change. Reformation can only gather pace from a Salvationist recognition that the visible expression of God's Army does not represent divine revelation, but only human work. In Barth's view human polity or "the Church's polity, no less than the preaching and

177. Barth, *God Here and Now*, 100.

178. Ibid., 102.

179. Ibid.

180. Ibid.

181. I am indebted to a colleague, David Robertson, for this analogy.

182. *CD* IV.4, x.

confession of the Church, must be shaped root and branch in correspondence to the Word of God."[183] He says, "why may not the constitution of the Church be at least based on the knowledge that the Church is wholly from God and must await *everything* from Him?"[184] Barth's concern is for a "living congregation," as an exemplary proclamation in the world, for "how can it have such a proclamation as long as the basis of its polity is contempt of the congregation and anxiety at the thought of its freedom?"[185] He cites Friedrich Loofs' prophetic words offered in 1901, when he asked, "whether it might not be the case one, day when the established Churches of the old world collapse, that the congregational form of the Church may yet have a future?"[186] The theologian or denominational church leader who scans the bookshelves of their local Christian bookshop will discover a burgeoning crop of popular titles relating to the emerging church movement, in which modern day Booths share stories of their flight from the overbearing nature of ecclesiastical control and the fear of change. Yet The Salvation Army's example suggests that without adequate reflection some might, over time, find themselves in a cycle in which like Booth they develop a polity of the kind from which they fled!

183. Barth, *God Here and Now*, 101.

184. Ibid., 102.

185. Ibid., 103.

186. Ibid., 104.

9

The Mission and Ministry
of the Christian Community

In its description of the analogous witness of the Christian community in obedience to Christ, Barth's Christological ecclesiology is, above all, a missionary ecclesiology, which he suggests should be a fifth essential mark of the Church. This in itself makes it a crucial account for Salvationists intent on prioritizing the Church's missionary task, as their response to *The Nature and Mission of the Church* makes clear. There are four particular aspects to Barth's account that help to highlight its significance. Firstly, it is placed under Barth's distinctive understanding of the prophetic office of Christ, secondly, it reveals his third relation of the Church and the world, thirdly, it describes the Church's function to exist for the world as witness and fourthly it outlines twelve specific ministry practices for the Church, in word and deed.

The Nature and Form of the Missionary Task

Firstly, Barth adds to the first two parts of his doctrine of reconciliation, under the priestly and kingly offices of Christ, a "third dimension"[1] in which reconciliation takes place. It does not add to the material content of the first two in which "the doctrine of reconciliation is in fact exhausted by what has to be thought and said from these two christologico-soteriological standpoints,"[2] and in this sense "is distinct from both

1. *CD* IV.3.1, 7.
2. Ibid., 6.

and must be considered separately."[3] Barth's third dimension is his distinctive account of God's self-attestation, through which he opposes, as Daniel Migliore suggests, "all forms of individualism and subjectivism."[4] It is in the prophetic office of Christ that the action of God as Reconciler of the world,

> expresses, discloses, mediates and reveals itself, not as a truth but as *the* truth, in which all truths, the truth of God particularly and the truth of man, are enclosed, not as truths in themselves, but as rays or facets of its truth. It declares itself as reality. It displays itself. It proclaims itself. It thus summons to conscious, intelligent, living, grateful, willing and active participation in its occurrence.[5]

Barth maintains that the third dimension is the "Christ-event" in which "revelation takes place as the revelation of reconciliation, as the How of this What, as the self-declaration of this history." Barth presents both the objective and subjective character of revelation as a divine work, the "self-attestation of Jesus Christ,"[6] as "the light of life,"[7] to avoid the "misunderstanding that can so easily creep in, as if the problem of knowledge, understanding and explanation of reconciliation . . . of the question how there can possibly be even the most rudimentary theology and proclamation of reconciliation, were really a problem of the theory of human knowledge and its spheres and limitations, its capacities and competencies, its possible or impossible approximation to this object."[8] In his description of the revelatory and prophetic office of Christ, Barth places his account of the Holy Spirit's work in ordaining and sending the Christian community out as witnesses to Christ in the world.[9] Barth is adamant that "the world needs the human historical fact of the declaration of the Gospel," but it cannot be the Church's role "to manifest it to the world in such sort that the world may believe and know it" for "this

---

3. Ibid., 7.

4. Migliore, "Reforming the Theology," 509.

5. *CD* IV.3.1, 8.

6. Ibid., 11.

7. See ibid., 38–165.

8. Ibid., 10f.

9. See Jüngel, *Karl Barth*, 48–49, for a helpful diagrammatic portrayal of this overall scheme in *Church Dogmatics* IV.

can only be the work of the prophecy of Jesus Christ Himself, of the Holy Spirit."[10]

Secondly, Barth adds to the relations of the Spirit and Church and Christ and Church, the third relation of the Church and the world. It is different from the first two in that it does not exist upon both the vertical and corresponding horizontal level of God and creature in the same way. Since the Church and the world are two creatures on the horizontal level, Barth's Christological logic requires some modification. Christ, the Church, and the world are viewed as concentric circles, where Christ is the center, and the Church and the world are each in turn peripheral ripples moving out from the center, but in which Christ, with the Church, is at the center of the world. Bender highlights the chain of correspondence envisaged in these circles when he acknowledges that "as the Word is to the flesh in Christ, so is Christ to the church, and so also is the Church with Christ, the *totus Christus*, to the world."[11] In relation to Christ Barth maintains a "strict irreversible super- and subordination," in which "the centre cannot become the circumference nor the circumference the centre."[12] However, the Church's relation to the world, whilst exemplary, is as servant and not ruler, allowing mutual and reciprocal influence rather than strict irreversibility.

Thirdly, Barth describes the Church's function, to exist for the world: "The community of Jesus Christ is the human creature whose existence as existence for God has the meaning and purpose of being, on behalf of God and in the service and discipleship of His existence, an existence for the world and men."[13] The Holy Spirit does not gather and build this community as an end in itself, but sends it out "beyond all that is promised to them personally."[14] Barth outlines three characteristics of this community.[15] Firstly, it is a community that understands clearly the nature of the world. Secondly, it is one that lives in solidarity though not conformity with the world, following its Lord's example in sitting at tables with sinners, "not tearing down bridges but building and traversing them, being with others and like them for all their singular-

---

10. *CD* IV.3.2, 844.

11. Bender, *Karl Barth's Christological Ecclesiology*, 151.

12. *CD* IV.3.1, 279.

13. Ibid. IV.3.2, 762.

14. Ibid., 764.

15. Ibid., 769, 773, 776.

ity, sharing and bearing as their own all the hopes and burdens in the existence, situation and constitution of others."[16] Thirdly, it understands that it is "under obligation to the world,"[17] and responsible for its future. It is these three characteristics of the Church's commitment to the world as a commitment to Christ, which Barth suggests should constitute a "*nota ecclesiae . . .* an external sign by which the true community of Jesus Christ may be infallibly known."[18] In his mind the Reformers failed to acknowledge this, in that in the Augsburg confession and subsequent creedal confessions there was a "yawning gap" in relation to the purpose of the Church, not by what was said, but by what was not said.[19] In contrast Barth marks out his ecclesiology for its missionary focus, in terms that a Salvationist would wholeheartedly support:

> The true Church may sometimes engage in tactical withdrawal, but never in strategic. It can never cease wholly or basically from activity in the world. It does not exist intermittently, nor does it ever exist only partially, as the sent community, but always and in all functions it is either leaping out or on the point of leaping out to those whom it is sent . . . It is always directed *extra muros* to those who are not, or not yet, within, and visibly perhaps never will be.[20]

The Church's missionary function is intrinsic to Barth's Christological reasoning, for "all ecclesiology is grounded, critically limited, but also positively determined by Christology; and this applies in respect of the particular statement which here concerns us, namely, that the Church exists for the world."[21] The Church's action is not to be confused with Christ's mission, for it is "summoned to give its own corresponding, and to that extent appropriate, and to that extent obedient answer to the Word of God."[22] In this sense however, "the Christian community can and should understand itself in the full New Testament sense of the term as a likeness," and as a "provisional representation of the divine-human reality distinct from itself," but "can only indicate, reflect and represent it

16. Ibid., 776.
17. Ibid.
18. Ibid., 772, 775, 779.
19. Ibid., 764–67.
20. Ibid., 780.
21. Ibid., 786.
22. Ibid.

subsequently and provisionally."[23] The community "is changed, not into an *alter Christus* but necessarily into an image of the unrepeatably one Christ."[24]

Significantly, Barth singles The Salvation Army out for its missionary enterprise of "leaping out" to those to whom it has been sent. He writes of the "English-inspired social and evangelistic movement of the later 19th and our own centuries," in which "on the left wing . . . stands the Salvation Army, which had its origins in Methodism, and the activities of which leave nothing to be desired from the standpoint of the extrovert."[25] Barth addresses the specific ministry of "evangelisation," and adds that "what is vital is that the evangelising community should say what it has to say to those around in a glad and spirited and peaceful way corresponding to its content, the Salvation Army setting a good example in this respect."[26]

Like Barth, Newbigin has a clear understanding that "missionary obedience" marks the authentic response to the gospel and therefore the essential nature of the Church. He says, "our doctrine of the Church will be distorted if it is not held in the perspective of a salvation which embraces the ends of the earth as well as the end of the age."[27] In this respect "each Christian congregation is the earnest and foretaste, the *arrabon* of the gathering together of all men of every tribe and tongue," and "is true to its own essential nature only when it takes this fact seriously and therefore treats the world-wide mission of the Church as something which belongs to the very core of its existence as a corporate body."[28] He comments further, "In all the discussions between Catholics and Protestants as to the *esse* and *bene esse* of the Church, I do not remember to have heard the fact seriously faced that a Church which has ceased to be a mission has certainly lost the *esse*, and not merely the *bene esse* of a Church."[29] Newbigin is quick to add that this missionary zeal cannot be divorced from the community as a foretaste of what is to come, and

---

23. Ibid., 792.
24. Ibid., 793.
25. Ibid., 569.
26. Ibid., 874.
27. Newbigin, *The Household of God*, 135.
28. Ibid., 143.
29. Ibid.

in this sense "an unchurchly mission is as much a monstrosity as an unmissionary church."[30]

The Salvation Army has sought to keep this missionary focus at the heart and center of its life, even if it has at times been tempted by a subjective focus upon its own mission rather than God's. Whilst there may be aspects of its visible expression that Barth might consider a retreat into invisibility or an inflation of its visibility, and Newbigin might consider "unchurchly," aspects that it needs to reflect more deeply upon, its human agency, its active witness in the world has made a large impact in relation to its relatively small size. The *Salvation Army Year Book*, reveals a growing international community and an expanding and diverse missionary activity in which "its mission is to preach the gospel of Jesus Christ and meet human needs in his name without discrimination."[31]

Fourthly, Barth distinctively maintains that the Church's missionary task in obedient response to the self-attestation of God, is one of witness in word and deed. He outlines twelve specific practices,[32] and explains that ministry "ordered in relation to that of Jesus Christ" is "a ministry to God and a ministry to man: a ministry to God in which it may serve man; and a ministry to man in which it may serve God."[33] In that The Salvation Army holds out the essential task of Christian witness and service in "word and deed," with "heart to God and hand to man," there is significant correlation with Barth's ecclesiology. Furthermore, Salvationists should reflect on what Barth outlines as the limitation of this ministry of witness, for it is "ministry to God and to man, no less, no more, no other."[34] He continues to maintain that divine and human action must be seen clearly in their unity, differentiation, and asymmetry, in which human ministry corresponds to divine. The Church,

> can neither carry through God's work to its goal nor lead men to the point of accepting it. It transgresses the limits of its mission and task, is guilty of culpable arrogance and engages in a futile undertaking if it makes this the goal and end of its activity, assuming responsibility both for the going out of the Word of God

30. Ibid., 148.

31. The Salvation Army, *The Salvation Army Year Book, 2011*, i.

32. For Barth's account of his twelve practices, six speech (word) and six action (deed) practices, see *CD* IV.3.2, 865–82 and 882–901.

33. Ibid., 831.

34. Ibid., 833.

and its coming to man. If this takes place at all, it does so in the power of the Holy Spirit over whom it has no power.[35]

Barth insists that the Christian community must explain the historical fact of the gospel in a way that allows it to "explain itself and make itself intelligible."[36] The community, "turning to the world in which it lives, has to introduce the analogy of the human historical fact of its witness."[37] This self-revealing fact, partnering with human witness, must be addressed and applied as an appeal delivered in word and deed. Says Barth, "what option has the community but to love, and to address in love, the men whom it knows to be loved by God?"[38]

The importance of this reasoning for Salvationist reflection becomes particularly evident when illustrated by his account of baptism and the Lord's Supper, as human practices that establish fellowship and as specific ministries that partner with God in witness.[39] In view of the distinctive Salvationist position in relation to these two practices, it is essential that Barth's account is understood, in a final dialogue between Barth, his friends and critics, and The Salvation Army, for these practices articulate *in nuce* Barth's account of theological anthropology.

Baptism and the Lord's Supper

Barth assigns baptism and the Lord's Supper to the Church's action in establishing fellowship.[40] Whilst he sees these actions as essential practices for the Church, he openly acknowledges a significant shift in his thinking, in which he regrets the Church's use of the term sacrament. In relation to the discussion outlined in chapter three, Salvationists should weigh Barth's account carefully for two reasons. Firstly, they should re-assess the value of baptism and the Lord's Supper in the life of the Christian community, and secondly, they should clearly establish, in

35. Ibid.

36. Ibid., 847.

37. Ibid., 849.

38. Ibid., 851.

39. Whilst Barth's account of the Lord's supper was never completed, his account of Spirit and water baptism was his final addition to *Church Dogmatics* within his lifetime. See *CD* IV.4.

40. *CD* IV.3.2, 901.

dialogue with Barth and his critics, whether they hold an understanding of sacrament, and if so, in what sense.

Baptism and the Lord's Supper as Human Actions

In Barth's estimation, baptism and the Lord's Supper are "human actions that follow emphatic divine commands and ordinances,"[41] and so a high view of their value in nurturing fellowship is to be maintained, for they continue to be integral to the life of the church, acting as signs that "are full of meaning and power . . . in their very simplicity the most eloquent, elements in the witness which the community owes to the world."[42] Barth will not relegate them to an archive box of church traditions, as in The Salvation Army's historical development. He is clear, however, that they are simply dramatic human actions, and in this sense it is better not to call them sacraments. This decision is of course highly controversial in the way that it breaks ranks with the Church's theological development of a sacramental understanding of these actions, notwithstanding the excruciatingly divisive nature of that development within the history of the Church. It does, however, illustrate Barth's theological anthropology, the Christologically patterned unity, differentiation, asymmetry and irreversible nature of divine and human action within an analogical understanding of correspondence.

Much attention is given to the question of Barth's consistency within *Church Dogmatics*. His early volumes acknowledge that the revelation or unveiling of God's word comes to us in veiled form through the secular mediation of God's world.[43] Barth is clear that during its writing, he changed his mind about how to give an account of what he now calls the "so called sacraments," for "it will perhaps have been noted in Volumes II and III that I made less and less use—and finally none at all—of the general term 'sacrament,' which was so confidently bandied about in Volume I."[44] Whereas he could acknowledge Jesus Christ as the "first sacrament" with the possibility that "the existence of the man Jesus is a

41. Barth, *The Christian Life*, 45.

42. *CD* IV.3.2, 901.

43. See *CD* I.1, 121, 169, 174. In this sense the church is both "mediate" and "mediating." See *CD* II.2, 196. See also O'Grady, *The Church in the Theology*, 1:106f.

44. *CD* IV.2, xi.

beginning of which there are continuations,"[45] he now presents the event of Jesus Christ's death as the one and only sacrament in which baptism and the Lord's Supper,

> can and should attest this event but only attest it . . . This is the one *mysterium*, the one sacrament, and the one existential fact before and beside and after which there is no room, for any other of the same rank.[46]

The full implications of Barth's understanding, due to what he describes as the incidental treatment in the first three volumes of the doctrine of reconciliation, became apparent in the 1967 publication of his baptismal fragment, (a full revision of his earlier account of baptism),[47] and his posthumously published lecture fragments on the ethics of reconciliation.[48] They reveal the full implications of what he has in mind:

> Baptism and the Lord's Supper are not events, institutions, mediations, or revelations of salvation. They are not representations and actualizations, emanations, repetitions, or extensions, nor indeed guarantees and seals of the work and word of God; nor are they instruments, vehicles, channels, or means of God's reconciling grace. They are not what they have been called since the second century, namely, mysteries or sacraments.[49]

Instead Barth maintains that they are

> actions of human obedience for which Jesus Christ makes his people free and responsible. They refer themselves to God's own work and word, and they correspond to his grace and commands. In so doing they have the promise of the divine good pleasure and they are well done as holy, meaningful, fruitful, human actions, radiant in the shining of the one true light.[50]

This explicit understanding is consistent with Barth's understanding of divine and human agency throughout the doctrine of reconciliation, but accords with his early understanding that "not only the objective but also the subjective element in revelation, not only its actu-

---

45. *CD* II.1, 54.
46. Ibid. IV.1, 296.
47. Barth, *The Teaching of the Church Regarding Baptism.*
48. Barth, *The Christian Life,* 46.
49. Ibid.
50. Ibid.

ality but also its potentiality, is the being and action of the self revealing God alone."[51] Barth can therefore say, in explaining the baptism in the Holy Spirit, that "interceding for us in Jesus Christ, He is now present to us, not at a distance, but in the closest proximity, confronting us in our own being, thought and reflection," and what takes place is "quite simply that *in nobis*, in our heart, at the centre of our existence, there is set a contradiction of our unfaithfulness, a contradiction which we cannot escape, which we have to endorse . . . by which it is not merely forbidden but prevented and rendered impossible."[52] It discounts any of the forms of creaturely representation of Christ's work that Barth perceives either in the Mass or in Bultmann's existentialism.[53] It is the Holy Spirit who subjectively realizes here and now the objective work of Christ there and then:

> The real presentation (*repraesentatio*) of the history of Jesus Christ is that which He Himself accomplishes in the work of His Holy Spirit when he makes Himself the object and origin of faith. Christian faith takes note of this, and clings to it and responds to it, without itself being the thing which accomplishes it, without any identity between the redemptive act of God and faith as the free act of man.[54]

John Webster perceives Barth's final settlement of this matter as "a late flowering of his critique of religion."[55] To Barth's mind, just as religion can become a means of diminishing the present, immediate and self-revealing activity of God, by expressing our encounter with God through the operation of natural factors, so Barth believes that sacraments potentially stray into the area of God's divine sovereignty and the actualization of God's self-communication. As Barth puts it, "God sets among men a fact which speaks for itself."[56] Barth signals the indiscriminate use of infant baptism as an example of the trespassing of human sacramental activity, by which "whole populations of whole countries have automatically been made and can automatically be made the holy

51. *CD* I.2, 280.

52. Ibid. IV.4, 22.

53. Ibid. 5.

54. Ibid. IV.1, 767.

55. Webster, *Barth's Ethics of Reconciliation*, 130. I am indebted to Webster for his clear portrayal of the dignity of human agency in Barth.

56. *CD* IV.3, 221.

community . . . the spiritual mystery of the community being replaced and crowded out by an arrogantly invented sacramental mystery."[57]

Barth does not wish to diminish human agency, since the fundamental theme of the *Dogmatics* is the covenant relationship between God and humanity, where the ethics of reconciliation are intent above all in portraying "God and man" as "two subjects in genuine encounter."[58] According to Webster, Barth "rejects human instrumentality precisely to safeguard the genuineness of human action as just that—*human action*."[59] Barth intends rather to "present Christian ethics as the free and active answer of man to the divine work and word of grace."[60] This means describing baptism as, "God's own work: baptism with the Holy Ghost, and . . . man's liturgical work: baptism with water."[61] He is clear that his "concern" is "with the man who ought to come of age in relation to God and the world,"[62] in which:

> [The] change which God has made is in truth man's liberation. It comes upon him wholly from without, from God. Nevertheless, it is his liberation . . . The divine change in whose accomplishment a man becomes a Christian is an event of true intercourse between God and man. If it undoubtedly has its origin in God's initiative, no less indisputably man is not ignored or passed over in it. He is taken seriously as an independent creature of God.[63]

In this respect, the individual requests baptism of the community and the community facilitates this, as the individual's obedient response and Christian testimony to the divine work of grace mediated by the Holy Spirit.

Barth's Pneumatology Questioned

Before discussing The Salvation Army's non-sacramental practice in relation to Barth's proposal, his critics must be acknowledged, for even

57. Ibid. IV.1, 696.

58. Barth, *The Christian Life*, 27.

59. Webster, *Barth's Ethics of Reconciliation*, 131.

60. *CD* IV.4, ix.

61. Ibid. Barth affirms that, "intelligent readers may deduce from the fragment how I would finally have presented the doctrine of the Lord's Supper."

62. Ibid., x.

63. Ibid., 22.

some of his friends find his radical conclusions difficult to countenance. Two responses in particular may be mentioned. The first suggests that Barth's proposal is indicative of a deficient pneumatology, in which the Spirit is presented more as a "mode" of Christ rather than as a distinctive divine economy. Reinhard Hütter, who has already been shown to be critical of Barth's use of the Chalcedonian principle in an "action-determined" setting, complains of what he calls the "absent center" in the relation between God and human beings 'that can be filled only again and again in the joint acting of these two subjects."[64] He says:

> Yet because precisely this center must always become a new event grounded in God's sovereignty—and thus also in his faithfulness—it can only be remembered and anticipated but never really apprehended. If indeed all human action per se can at best refer either anticipatorily or in response to this event, and yet if God's action in principle has never nor will it ever tie itself to any human action, then God's actions can be conceived only as becoming evident as God's self-manifestation in the interiority of the believer.[65]

He points in particular to Barth's account of baptism, in which he perceives "God's actions have no 'worldly' form and can be attested in a worldly fashion only in the form of human action."[66] His concern is that in Barth's "diastatic logic," "a specific understanding of pneumatology follows that does not allow any creaturely *poiemata* of the Holy Spirit to which the Holy Spirit might tie itself,"[67] undermining the possibility of the Church existing in an embodied form. He follows Robert Jenson[68] in deciding that "the pneumatological *vinculum*-doctrine" is "the decisive problem in Barth's doctrine of the Trinity."[69] He says, "because Barth understands the triune God as having but *one* 'center of action,' and because his understanding of the Holy Spirit remains wholly determined by the *vinculum*-doctrine, Barth cannot overcome

---

64. Hütter, *Suffering Divine Things*, 109.

65. Ibid. See also Rahner, *Theological Investigations*, 2:72, for his understanding of a Protestant view of the sacrament as the "purely internal and subjective sphere of fiduciary faith and of the interior experience of justification."

66. Hütter, *Suffering Divine Things*, 110.

67. Ibid.

68. See Jenson, "You Wonder," 296–304.

69. Hütter, *Suffering Divine Things*, 111.

the diastatic logic of action obtaining between God and human beings, and is able to articulate the Holy Spirit *only* as a *mode* rather than as *Spiritus Creator* having its own salvific-economic mission and its own work."[70] For Hütter the issue at stake is that Barth's "development of the relational nexus of church, church doctrine, and theology ultimately remains ecclesiologically unstable."[71] Hütter wants the relation between the Holy Spirit and the Church "clarified theologically" in order that in turn the "relation between theology and church doctrine (or dogma)"[72] can be established.[73]

Following Hütter, Joseph Mangina is equally concerned with Barth's pneumatology:

> The Spirit can only appear as a predicate of Christ's reconciling work, a *manifestation* of the latter rather than an *agency* of its own. Correspondingly, the church "shows" or signifies Christ but does not serve as the means through which believers begin to participate in the new life he brings.[74]

Mangina believes that concerns expressed by other theologians about Barth's temporality, are misplaced, so that "instead of a general thesis about such matters as experience (Williams), time (Jenson), the future (Moltmann), or human agency (the early Hauerwas), the criticism is better stated as a pneumatological worry and specifically, a worry about the role played by the church in the economy of salvation."[75] Mangina asks:

> Is the church merely a human echo or analogy of Christ's completed work, as in Barth? Or is it also somehow the herald of new

---

70. Ibid. See also Jürgen Moltmann's comments on the direction he took in his theology beyond Barth's Christological "centre" into what he calls the "surrounding area" in which he wished to give "positive answers to the political possibilities and cultural challenges of the post-war period," (Moltmann, *How I Have Changed*, 14f). See also 13–21. See Moltmann, *The Church in the Power of the Spirit*.

71. Hütter, *Suffering Divine Things*, 112.

72. Ibid., 113.

73. See Webster, *Barth's Moral Theology*, 170 n. 77, for his response to Hütter's criticism of Barth, suggesting that "the separation of divine and human action is undertaken, not in order to disqualify human agency, but precisely in order to establish it in its proper, limited but nevertheless real, human sphere."

74. Mangina, "Bearing the Marks of Jesus," 270.

75. Ibid., 282.

activity in which God is engaged between now and the eschaton, the view that I would favour?[76]

Stanley Hauerwas adds that "Barth is not sufficiently catholic just to the extent that his critique and rejection of Protestant liberalism make it difficult for him to acknowledge that, through the work of the Holy Spirit, we are made part of God's care of the world through the church" and that "Barth never quite brings himself to explain how our human agency is involved in the Spirit's work."[77] Hauerwas, Mangina and Hütter all wish to see Barth more committed to an undialectical account of the Holy Spirit's agency in what Mangina calls "the ordinary, empirical practices of the Christian community across time."[78] Whilst Barth can clearly say that, "the Church is the historical form of the work of the Holy Spirit and therefore the historical form of the faith,"[79] his analogical correspondence is not considered by his critics an adequate enough account of that relationship, even though he develops this in twelve specific church practices.[80]

Nicholas Healy, on the other hand, originally expressed his criticism and proposed modifications of Barth's ecclesiology,[81] yet ten years later has reconsidered those criticisms.[82] Without discussing Barth's pneumatology in depth, he suggests that Barth's fundamental difference with Hauerwas and critics such as Hütter, is the doctrine of the Church.[83] The main body of Healy's essay is a comparison of the ecclesiology of Barth and Hauerwas, in which he finds Barth more convincing.[84] He cites numerous examples of Barth's account of the strong, obedient and corresponding human agency of the Church, in which the Church's "'knowledge,' is heavily freighted . . . for whom it necessarily involves acknowledgement, confession, and therefore obedient action."[85]

76. Ibid.

77. Hauerwas, *With the Grain of the Universe*, 145.

78. Mangina, "Bearing the Marks of Jesus," 270.

79. *CD* II.1, 160.

80. Ibid. IV.3.2, 865–901.

81. Healy, 'The Logic of Karl Barth's Ecclesiology."

82. Healy, "Karl Barth's Ecclesiology Reconsidered."

83. Ibid., 289. See also n. 5, where Healy suggests that modifying Barth's pneumatology might not necessarily alter the differences in ecclesiology.

84. Ibid.

85. Ibid., 290.

He describes Barth's view of the Church "as a genuine and ongoing history of action in and for the world 'in correspondence' to Christ's own 'hidden being.'"[86]

The heart of the disagreement, he suggests, rests in "symptoms of anxiety" in which "from contemporary ecclesiology one gets the impression that the church needs to be especially concerned these days about itself and its self-preservation, rather more perhaps than it need be about the task and cause of God."[87] He perceives, amongst other things, a contemporary concern about "the pervasive failure to obey the church authorities" and suggests that "the concern to distinguish and separate, protect and defend, is widespread" and "surfaces not only in Hauerwas and those he has influenced, but in Radical Orthodoxy, communion ecclesiology, and in some forms of postliberalism, too."[88] Barth is far less anxious about the Church, prepared to engage in constant self-criticism, willing to trust the work of the Word and the Spirit. Healy suggests this confidence "requires us, in faithful and prayerful obedience, to turn cheerfully away from ourselves, away from earnest and anxious attempts at self-preservation, towards the God who alone preserves us."[89]

George Hunsinger, against Hütter, supports what he believes to be Barth's clear and coherent account of the Spirit as a dynamic agency, "the mediator of communion."[90] Describing Barth's understanding of the "subtle, intricate, and complex" relationship between revelation, reconciliation and redemption, it is redemption "which Barth defined as the future of reconciliation," and "was his category for the saving work of the Holy Spirit in its own right," for "whereas reconciliation was redemption's abiding ground and content, redemption was reconciliation's dynamic consequence and goal" in which "the work of Christ served the work of the Spirit."[91] Hunsinger believes that Barth's fifth volume on Redemption would have shown a marked contrast between the doctrine of reconciliation's perspective on Christ's work and the doctrine of re-

---

86. Ibid., 291.

87. Ibid., 297.

88. Ibid.

89. Ibid., 299.

90. For his estimate of seven defining characteristics of Barth's account of the Spirit's mediation of communion see: Hunsinger, *Disruptive Grace*, 184.

91. Hunsinger, *Disruptive Grace*, 149f.

demption's perspective on the Spirit's work.[92] Barth, is himself confident that "a theology of the third article ... everything which needs to be said, considered, and believed about God the Father and God the Son in an understanding of the first and second articles might be shown and il-luminated in its foundations through God the Holy Spirit, the *vinculum pacis inter Patrem et Filium*."[93]

Barth's Differentiation of Spirit and Water Baptism Questioned

A second response comes from those who find themselves broadly in accord with Barth, but think his separation of spirit and water baptism too harsh. Webster suggests:

> It would not be impossible to construct an account of Spirit-baptism and water-baptism as a differentiated unity without threatening either the uniqueness and incommunicability of the work of Jesus Christ or the full reality of the human response. A carefully phrased notion of sacramental mediation could allay Barth's fears about overinflation of ecclesial activity, and at the same time, avoid the overschematic separation of divine and human work which afflicts his exegesis.[94]

Equally, Paul Molnar regrets Barth's eventual abandoning of the term "sacrament." Whilst inconsistent with the rest of the *Dogmatics* in rejecting this term, he finds Barth to be consistent in the reasons he gives for doing so. Molnar accepts Barth's reasoning that, "according to the New Testament, man's cleansing and renewal take place in the history of Jesus Christ which culminates in his death, and they are mediated through the work of the Holy Spirit."[95] He wants to add, however, that "the continuing work of the Spirit takes place in the form of Christ's con-tinued presence in history, i.e., the church, scripture, preaching, and the sacraments."[96] Whilst Christ can admittedly still work apart from these forms, he commends them as "events through which God has objec-

---

92. See Busch, *The Great Passion*, 221, who suggests that Barth did not neglect the doctrine, but sought to correct "a loss of the knowledge of the deity of the Holy Spirit." See Barth, *Evangelical Theology*, 58.

93. Barth, "Concluding Unscientific Postscript," 88.

94. Webster, *Barth's Ethics of Reconciliation*, 172. See also in this respect Migliore, "Reforming the Theology," 506.

95. *CD* IV.4, 128.

96. Molnar, *Karl Barth*, 305.

tively chosen to mediate our renewal in the history of Christ" in which "God is freely bound to this form but not by it." He suggests that "the power of his living Word can also reach us through our being taught and through baptism and the celebration of the Lord's Supper as the events in and through which God includes us in his own knowledge and love."[97]

George Hunsinger[98] and John Yocum,[99] in line with Webster, both argue that Barth unnecessarily breaks with his early, qualified acceptance of the term sacrament as carefully demonstrated in his concept of the three-fold form of God's Word.[100] Here scripture and preaching are secondary, and totally dependent upon Christ himself. Yocum agrees with Webster that a carefully phrased notion of sacramentality can be maintained, and highlights the work of Yves Congar in this respect.

Hunsinger demonstrates how a parallel section on the three-fold form of God's Sacrament could be developed from Barth's three-fold form of God's Word,[101] in which baptism and the Lord's Supper run parallel to preaching and proclamation, as the third form of the Word. Conceived in the normal Augustinian tradition as "visible Words," he envisions an ecumenical possibility: "true doctrinal reconciliation might become possible without the more worrisome liabilities of potential ecumenical agreements, like capitulation, compromise, equivocation or evasion" in a form in which "no existing known position would remain exactly as it now stands."[102] Hunsinger suggests he actually learned of this possibility from reading Barth,[103] that "a conception of *non-synergistic co-operation* is possible," in which "faith and freedom in the mode of pure human reception (*receptus purus*) go hand in hand with divine grace as a miraculous and perpetual operation (*operatione mirabilis et perpetua*) in and through the church's proclamation."[104] In this conception, "witness represents the 'upward vector' that moves from the human plane to the divine; mediation represents the 'downward vector'

---

97. Ibid., 306.

98. Hunsinger, "Baptism and the Soteriology of Forgiveness," 247–69.

99. Yocum, *Ecclesial Mediation in Karl Barth.*

100. See *CD* I.1, 88–124.

101. See Hunsinger, "Baptism and the Soteriology of Forgiveness," 254ff.

102. Ibid., 255.

103. Ibid., 266.

104. Ibid., 259.

that moves from the divine plane to the human."[105] Hunsinger adds that, "mediation no less than witness occurs under only one condition—by grace alone (*sola gratia*)."[106]

Hunsinger explains how Spirit and water baptism may be held together in a true differentiated unity as a *koinonia* relation, of mutual coinherence and asymmetry, in which "the principle of strict irreversibility of the movement from the divine to the creaturely is what upholds the anti-synergistic grammar of baptism in both its forms (Spirit and water)."[107] Whilst he considers Barth's account "confused" and over-schematized, Barth is however correct in maintaining that:

> [T]he efficacy of Spirit baptism is definitive. Spirit baptism stands on its own and does not require water baptism for its efficacy. Water baptism is best understood as the fulfilment of Spirit baptism. Dominically appointed it is the normal consequence of Spirit baptism. Spirit baptism can be and is (in principle) efficacious without water baptism, but water baptism is not efficacious without Spirit baptism.[108]

Hunsinger suggests that "the *koinonia*-theme in Barth may be what unifies the *Church Dogmatics*" for whilst "it is not always as thematically explicit as the theme of witness and correspondence . . . it is never absent."[109]

In contrast, Paul Nimmo finds Barth's account of baptism to be wholly consistent with his account of the doctrine of *concursus Dei*— God's accompanying of human action.[110] In this account Barth suggests that "the activity of the creature takes place in its co-existence with God, in the presence of God, His *praesentia actuosa*" and "is therefore accompanied and surrounded by God's own activity" in which "the history of the covenant of grace accompanies the act of the creature from first to last."[111] Barth's concept of divine accompanying forms the basis of a real differentiated unity and asymmetry between divine and human agency, between Spirit and water baptism in which in the relation of creator to creature, God "co-operates with it, preceding, accompanying and fol-

105. Ibid., 258.
106. Ibid.
107. Ibid., 257.
108. Ibid.
109. Ibid., 266.
110. Nimmo, *Being In Action*, 126. See 118–30.
111. *CD* III.3, 92.

lowing all its being and activity, so that all the activity of the creature is primarily and simultaneously and subsequently His own activity, and therefore a part of the actualisation of His own will revealed and triumphant in Jesus."[112] In this sense "we have to understand the activity of God and that of the creature as a single action ... that His own action takes place in and with and over the activity of the creature."[113] Barth is adamant that this does not diminish human agency. Rather, within the true freedom of the fatherly relation of creator and creature, God "affirms and approves and recognises and respects the autonomous actuality and therefore the autonomous activity of the creature as such," for "just as He Himself is active in His freedom, the creature can also be active in its freedom."[114] In this relation Barth asserts:

> The work of the Holy Spirit ... is to bring and to hold together ... the divine working, being and action on the one side and the human on the other ... not to identify, intermingle nor confound them, not to change the one into the other nor to merge the one into the other, but to co-ordinate them, to make them parallel, to bring them into harmony and therefore to bind them into a true unity.[115]

Nimmo confirms that in Barth's concept of *concursus Dei*, whilst "the humanity of Jesus Christ is the only element in creation to which God is irrevocably bound, by virtue of the eternal decision of God's will," this does not mean that God is not present in human action, for "within the actualistic ontology of Barth, God can bind Godself to the Church, Scripture, preaching, baptism, or the Lord's Supper ... but there can be no objective sense in which God is bound to them in substantialistic terms."[116] Barth explains that:

> There is obviously no baptism or Lord's Supper without His real presence as very God and very Man, both body and soul. But this presence cannot be regarded as restricted to what were later called the "sacraments."[117]

112. Ibid., 105.
113. Ibid., 132.
114. Ibid., 92.
115. *CD* IV.3.2, 761.
116. Nimmo, *Being In Action,* 126 n. 164.
117. *CD* III.2, 467.

Barth is clear that sacraments are "these remarkable relics . . . of the idea that by our own actions—whether in proclamation or in the sacraments—we could, as it were, set the divine allocation in motion."[118]

To Eberhard Jüngel he writes:

> I could wish, of course, that the word sacrament could be commemorated in Evangelical theology for some decades only for irenical and polemical purposes but not used any more constitutively. A languages hostel might well be the right place for such a purification.[119]

He was aware that this view challenged his doctrine of the three-fold form of the Word of God in I. 1, § 4,[120] but was prepared to revise his earlier work.[121]

Which Way Forward for The Salvation Army?

This study suggests that The Salvation Army should, in expressing what it means to be the Church, re-instate the practices of baptism and the Lord's Supper as constitutive of the Church, in the way that they establish *koinonia* at the heart of the Christian community. Reflection on Barth's account of these practices and the ensuing discussion it generates is helpful in establishing exactly what Salvationists believe about these practices, in what appears to be a confused account of the sacramental life. Their present confusion is clearly demonstrated in an account which seeks to explain to Salvationists in what sense they are sacramental. General Shaw Clifton builds on the *Book of Common Prayer* definition that:

> A sacrament is "an outward and visible sign of an inward and spiritual grace." Salvationist sacramentalism carries this to its logical conclusion and says that a person can be such a sign, derivatively from Christ, the one True Sacrament. You can be a sacrament. I can be a sacrament.[122]

118. Barth, *Fragments Grave and Gay*, 88.

119. Barth, *Letters, 1961–68*, 192. See also Letter to Dr. Herman Bizer, March 29, 1963, in ibid., 96.

120. Ibid., 300.

121. See Klappert, *Promissio und Bund* cited in Hütter, *Suffering Divine Things*, 110.

122. Clifton, *Who Are These Salvationists?*, 64. Clifton cites *The Book of Common Prayer*, 294.

By "sign," Clifton means more than the customary Salvationist sense of "a mere reminder of the grace or presence of God," for "it is the Army's belief that such a life actually imparts and channels grace to others since, by the Holy Spirit, the real presence of Christ indwells the believer."[123] Three factors stand out in Clifton's assertion. Firstly, he asserts that a Salvationist is a sacrament, who mediates grace. Secondly, he advances this mediation of God's grace, whilst still affirming the immediacy of grace from Christ in the Spirit. Thirdly, he is firmly resolved that the sacraments of baptism and the Lord's Supper should not be reintroduced into the life of The Salvation Army, for "you do not need ceremonial or ritual sacraments in order to be an authentic church body," and "Salvationists are called of God to do without the symbolism of the sacraments or anything that could be mistaken for a sacrament" for "to act otherwise is to mislead and confuse the people."[124] Nevertheless, it must be confusing for Salvationists to hear that "the number of possible sacraments is infinite, for the potential number of Christlike believers is infinite,"[125] an infinity of people without baptism and the Lord's Supper. Clifton fails to acknowledge that the concept of sacrament that extends from the grace of Christ as sacrament, in his incarnate life, death and resurrection, finds expression through reflection upon the elements of water, bread and wine which act as visible words of that event of grace.

Paul Fiddes, in his chapter "The Incarnate God and the Sacramental Life,"[126] explores the suggestion that a Christian pastor or minister may be a sacrament. He explains that his understanding of sacrament rests not on "substance language which is static" but on "dynamic ideas of movement and relationship" in which "God *happens*, in an interweaving flow of relationship," and the signs of water, bread and wine "enable us to participate in the drama of death and resurrection which is happening in the heart of God."[127] There is no confusion between the material signs and the grace they convey. Rather, "the earthly substance, the material stuff, is a means of being drawn into the movements of the divine life."[128]

---

123. Ibid., 65.

124. Clifton, "People of God," 5.

125. Clifton, *Who Are These Salvationists?*, 65.

126. In Fiddes, *Participating in God*, 278–304.

127. Ibid., 281.

128. Ibid., 282.

Fiddes is able, by carefully working from the particular to the general, to extend from Christ's resurrection body, to communion bread, to the Church as the body of Christ, to the whole body of the world. "The particular moment of encounter with God through the elements of eucharist and baptism can thus awaken us to the God who can be met through the many bodies of the world."[129] In this way, where "sacraments are always to be placed in the context of the sacramental life of the community" and where "pastoral care must be shared by the whole people" he carefully proposes that "we may regard the pastor as a living sacrament, *embodying* the accepting and healing love of God" in which "she embodies the presence of God in the sense that *in her body there is a place of encounter* an interface, with the movements of God's life of love."[130] In similar careful fashion, it might be possible to extend this concept to the life of the Salvationist engaged in active, committed, loving and caring ministry in the community, for as Fiddes remarks "the whole point of a sacrament is that it is a piece of weak, created and fallible stuff in itself, but it is a doorway into the life of the triune God."[131]

Barth and Fiddes help Salvationists to reflect on what some Salvationist accounts mean in the articulation of a sacramental life. Are they in effect suggesting that the Church might participate in the Divine life through the stuff of earth as meeting places, which Fiddes suggests are "doors into the dance of perichoresis in God?"[132] Or, have they simply been tempted, under ecumenical isolation, to stray into sacramental language that holds little real meaning for the Salvationist who does not use the sacraments? In that respect is it more meaningful for the Salvationist to view their sacrificial yet joyful life of witness and testimony more properly, as Barth suggests, as an obedient human response to God's initiative within the Divine accompanying, in which God's self-communication of grace is immediate and mediate in Jesus Christ alone, through the work of the Holy Spirit? Certainly, in neither account can Clifton's insistence be tenable, that the Army's apparent position of a non-sacramental, sacramental life, represents a God-given calling, the abandonment of which would be an act of disobedience.[133] Clifton

129. Ibid., 283.
130. Ibid., 295f.
131. Ibid., 295.
132. Ibid., 281.
133. Clifton remarks, "We are not suddenly going to tell him that we refuse to do so

proposes the concept of a human sacrament that is divorced from the sacramental life of the rest of the Church, and on this basis asserts that The Salvation Army represents God's Church in every locality.

Faced with this confusion, and contemplating the reversal of 130 years of suspension, the Army's leadership might find Barth's account of baptism and the Lord's Supper more amenable and readily understood by Salvationists who do not hold a sacramental understanding of these practices. In this respect there are three specific ways in which Barth could be drawn upon in re-introducing baptism and the Lord's Supper.

Firstly, Barth's view that these practices represent an obedient witness to the "direct self-attestation and self-impartation of the living Jesus Christ, in His active Word of power which goes forth *hic et nunc* to specific men in the work of the Holy Ghost,"[134] would affirm a Salvationist view of God's immediacy, mediate in Jesus Christ alone, through the presence of the Spirit. Admittedly Barth's expression of immediacy could be construed as one that this study has been critical of in early individualistic Salvationist expressions, and one certainly criticised by Rahner and Hütter for its "interiority," as indicated. This is a distinct weakness which Hunsinger suggests, fails to follow through with the logic of a *koinonia* relation in allowing an account of "non-synergistic cooperation" between divine and human agency. Whilst Barth clearly maintains the primacy of the community over the individual, and in this sense corrects early Salvationist individualistic expressions of immediacy, he nevertheless, as Webster suggests, creates an unnecessarily schematic separation of divine and human agency. On the other hand, whilst the Booths were guilty at times of their own unhealthy synergistic expressions, Salvationists would hear an echo of William and Catherine Booth in Barth's insistence that:

> The Church is neither author, dispenser, nor mediator of grace and its revelation ... It cannot act as such. It cannot strut about as such, as though this were its calling. Its work and action in all forms, even in the best possibilities, stands or falls with the self-attestation and self-impartation of Jesus Christ, in which it can only participate as assistant and minister.[135]

---

any longer"(Clifton, "People of God," 5).

134. *CD* IV.4, 31.

135. Ibid., 32.

Secondly, Barth's account of the miraculous intervention and trans-forming power of the Holy Spirit, as demonstrated in the lives of the first Salvationists on their knees before God in nights of prayer, sup-ports their subsequent dissatisfaction with the over-inflation of what Barth refers to as the "so called sacraments" of baptism and the Lord's Supper. This dissatisfaction led to the abandonment of their sacramental Wesleyan Methodist roots. Holiness revivalism was extreme, in some respects in error, but in its acknowledgement of the liberating joy of the creature humbly obedient before God in daily invocation upon the Holy Spirit's presence and power, it grasps Barth's account of the life of the obedient community wholeheartedly. Furthermore Barth includes, from a Salvationist viewpoint, a sympathetic account of the Holy Spirit in which the Spirit continues to bring fresh and ever deepening, miracu-lous outpourings of God's grace:

> In all its actions the work of the Holy Spirit is always and every-where a wholly new thing. At each moment of its occurrence it is itself another change, a conversion, which calls for even more radical conversion. As the change to the Christian life was radical in its inception, so it must and will always be in its continuation.[136]

Barth affirms the Salvationist expectation that God's joyful and liberated people are sent out to obediently witness and serve, in word and deed, without the supposed benefit of a sacramental concept of mediation.

Thirdly, Barth's theological anthropology speaks directly into an ironically overly subjective and synergistic Salvationist account of hu-man agency, from their roots in holiness revivalism. Barth is consistently anxious not to allow either God's monistic agency nor the creature's syn-ergistic agency, in his expression of correspondence in which "the om-nicausality of God must not be construed as His sole causality," for "the divine change in whose accomplishment a man becomes a Christian is an event of true intercourse between God and man."[137] Salvationists can learn much from Barth's objectivity, including his positive embrace of the practices of baptism and the Lord's Supper in the objective apprecia-tion of the fellowship that they establish, from Christ's initiative.

The rationale of Barth's theological anthropology could therefore liberate Salvationists to find new meaning and purpose in baptism and

136. Ibid., 39.
137. Ibid., 23.

the Lord's Supper, as human actions of thanksgiving and testimony, clear sign and witness to God's grace. Since "the Holy Spirit feeds him with the body of Jesus Christ which was given for him, and strengthens him with the blood of Jesus which was shed for him, to nourish and sustain him for eternal life in which God will be all in all, and thus in him too,"[138] the Salvationist can celebrate the Lord's Supper without fearing it polemically as a ritual that obscures the receiving of God's grace, but as a confident celebration and witness to God's grace.

Equally, the re-introduction of baptism can help Salvationists to overcome those problems discussed in relation to equating the enrolment of Soldiers, and its emphasis on "church membership plus," with baptism. This would undoubtedly remain an adult baptism in which, as Barth suggests, the believer in an expression of Christian faith, asks the church to facilitate this human testimony to God's grace. Nevertheless, they should not seek to fracture the Church of God further by insisting on the re-baptism of adults, as is presently the case when they enrol Soldiers who may previously have been baptized as infants, and attempt to equate it with adult baptism. As an ecumenical imperative they should learn to understand and respect the practice of infant baptism in other churches, and in their own service for the dedication of infants, lay greater emphasis upon an objective appreciation of God's prevenient grace, as they more clearly should have learnt to do from Wesley.

Having acknowledged these points of harmony with Barth, his account remains unsatisfactory for many as an ecumenical expression of how the Christian community may move forward in visible unity as the one, holy, catholic and apostolic Church. There are good reasons why Salvationists should ultimately move beyond it. Whilst the re-introduction of baptism and the Lord's Supper will overcome an inconsistent Salvationist exegesis that justifies their removal, Barth is criticized for an exegesis that squeezes the texts into his scheme of Spirit and water baptism.[139] Barth's proposals are radical and strike at the heart of the Church's theological reflection on baptism and the Lord's Supper.[140] Barth acknowledges that he might be labelled "Neo-Zwinglian" even though he believes that his account "does not in fact owe anything to

138. Ibid., 40.

139. See for example, Yocum, *Ecclesial Mediation*, 154–56.

140. See Marshall, *Last Supper and Lord's Supper*, 154–55, for his comments on the sacraments being at the heart of early theological reflection in the Church.

Zwingli's influence,"[141] but is an attempt "to understand Zwingli better than he understood himself or could make himself understood."[142] Nevertheless, John Webster finds in Barth's 1922–23 Zwingli lectures, evidence of Zwingli's lasting influence on Barth in "a deep seated aversion for some ways of coordinating God and creatures, and an acute awareness of the potential losses entailed by a theology of mediation . . . either a collapse of the divine into creaturely action . . . or an undermining of the integrity of creatures."[143]

Salvationists, who now confusingly promote the "sacramental life" without any reference to the sacraments of baptism and the Lord's Supper, would be advised to consider Webster's proposal that "a carefully phrased notion of sacramental mediation'" could take account of Barth's (and the Booths') fears about these practices being overinflated in the life of the Church. Such a consideration would have three positive consequences. Firstly, it would ultimately avoid Barth's harsh separation of divine and human agency. Secondly, it would objectively compensate for the Booths' subjective and individualistic expression of the individual's sacrificial life laid upon God's altar, which they developed, from holiness revivalism, as an alternative to the objective sacraments.[144] Thirdly, it would hold positive promise for the development of a more coherent Salvationist ecclesiology, based on the Church as *koinonia*.

In this respect, Hunsinger's ecumenical attempt to articulate how God's mediation and human witness may be more integrally bound together, as a "*koinonia* relation," bearing in mind Barth's insistence that baptism and the Lord's Supper never take place without God's real presence, should be recommended for Salvationist reflection.[145] Hunsinger upholds the Augustinian tradition of perceiving them as "visible words," and promotes what he believes to be a real ecumenical possibility for agreement. Migliore affirms that "many Protestant and Catholic theologians would now agree, the meaning of the sacraments must be redefined in terms of the activity of God in Jesus Christ, who is the fundamental sacrament,"[146] a view that would support Fiddes' account of these prac-

---

141. *CD* IV.4, 130.

142. Ibid. See 128–30.

143. Webster, *Barth's Earlier Theology*, 37. See 15–39.

144. See Webster, *Barth's Ethics of Reconciliation*, 172.

145. See Hunsinger, "Baptism and the Soteriology of Forgiveness," 247–69.

146. Migliore, "Reforming the Theology," 507.

tices as "windows" or "doors" into our participation in the Trinitarian life of God.[147]

Ultimately, whilst Barth's theological anthropology has been received in this study as a genuine and insightful attempt to avoid unhelpful synergistic accounts of divine and human agency, his conception of the parallelism[148] of divine and human agency is an unnecessarily harsh separation of what may more helpfully be conceived as a *koinonia* relation, along the lines that Hunsinger, Webster, Yocum and Fiddes have suggested. In this respect, Salvationists may ultimately learn much from both a renewal of their understanding of Wesley and from engaging in dialogue with Barth, about a more objective appreciation of God's grace.

Conclusion

The Salvation Army's dialogue with Karl Barth in the complex and as Bender calls it "derived" area of ecclesiology, reveals Barth's coherent if contested ecclesiology, as the outworking of his highly innovative theological anthropology. This places the Chalcedonian Christological reasoning of Jesus Christ's two natures at the heart of Barth's account of the partnership between God and God's creatures, conceiving human agency as correspondent to divine agency in a relation of precedence and subsequence. There are a number of key areas of similarity and difference between Barth's account and the development of Salvationist belief and practice. The differences stem principally from Barth's re-working of the Reformed themes of election and reconciliation, in which he challenges a Wesleyan Arminian polemical view of soteriology that took shape in Wesley's imagination against what he perceived as Calvinistic determinism.

Barth's doctrine of election offers The Salvation Army a fresh working of divine and human agency that avoids both monism and what Barth sees as an unsatisfactory synergistic account of Arminian free-will, which he believes is unhelpfully influenced by Enlightenment philosophical reasoning rather than a theological account of God's sovereignty. Equally Barth offers The Salvation Army an innovative and fresh account of God's sanctification. It understands Salvationist aspirations, to speak of the grace of God that enables the high potential of

147. See also Forsyth, *The Church and the Sacraments*, 130–50.
148. *CD* IV.3.2, 761.

human response in the life of the community, without falling victim to its impossible subjective view of entire sanctification. Barth's focus on the objectivity of prevenient entire sanctification in Christ, to be lived subjectively in the Spirit's enabling as obedient human response, is a welcome new route out of the *cul de sac* of an anthropologically centered account, providing his undeveloped account of spiritual growth is attended to.

Barth's Christological ecclesiology with its Chalcedonian account of the partnership between divine and human agency offers The Salvation Army a way to view and untangle those cords of mission, army and church from its historical development. The church strand is affirmed, both in Barth's account of the precedence of divine agency in electing, reconciling and gathering the Christian community, and in the way it responds faithfully and obediently to Barth's portrayal of the appropriate corresponding human agency in witness and service. The difficulties associated with the concept of the Church as an army are revealed in Barth's account of the Church's temptation to unreflectively embrace a movement of "secularization" and "defect," and, or, a movement towards "sacralization" and "excess" that recasts human work as divine revelation. In this respect The Salvation Army is offered opportunity to reflect upon aspects of a military metaphor not centered on Christ, such as hierarchical autocracy and uniformity, together with other threats to the unity, holiness, catholicity and apostolicity of the Church, such as centralized bureaucratic control, lifestyle rules and regulations and the loss of the unifying signs of baptism and the Lord's Supper.

Finally, Barth's account of the Holy Spirit's agency in the self-attestation of God's grace could offer The Salvation Army a more coherently theological framework in which to articulate its historical non-sacramental understanding of God's self-attestation apart from human mediation; and this whilst adding to Barth's contested and largely overlooked account the example of over a century of sacrificial love and service in the guise of The Salvation Army's international missionary activity in word and deed, and in the life of thousands of local Christian communities. Nevertheless, in view of recent Salvationist attempts to explore an understanding of their life and ministry as sacramental, it is possible to keep Barth's non-synergistic understanding of divine and human agency, yet move beyond him, re-introducing baptism and the Lord's Supper as visible words. Such an approach will offer a surer footing for developing their understanding of the sacramental life, and their development of a more coherent ecclesiology in search of ecumenical unity in diversity.

Conclusion

A t the heart of this study has been an examination of the Salvationist conviction that Salvation Army equals Church. As Needham puts it, "in truth, when we have said 'Army' we have said 'Church'... we have said something about how we understand 'Church.'"[1] The emergence of the concept of the Church as an army, or more specifically The Salvation Army, has been traced from its roots in nineteenth-century trans-Atlantic holiness revivalism, through its incipient and institutionalizing phases, into a contemporary reflection on a Salvationist expression of the nature, form and mission of God's Church. Three intertwined ecclesial strands are identified that broadly relate to three phases in the historical development of The Salvation Army and its ecclesiological convictions. It is suggested that these strands, identified as "mission," "army" and "church," persist into the life of the contemporary Salvation Army, are unhelpfully tangled and continue to create ecclesiological tension.

The Salvation Army began, as an expression of trans-Atlantic holiness revivalism, a style of evangelistic endeavor characterized as "aggressive Christianity." These are the roots of what has been termed the incipient "mission" strand. It was a combination of an evangelistic mission and a "higher life" movement which aimed to renew the fortunes of the Church and revive the spiritual life of the nations. In many respects it was a lay movement of individuals escaping from the constraints of denominationalism, in order to pursue a spiritual agenda of revivalism in seeking the salvation and the sanctification of all, across the denominations and beyond. It was a post-millennial movement of evangelists and social reformers, intent on creating a better society and ushering in the millennium. Invariably these spiritual revivalist efforts resulted in the establishment of new denominations, as in the case of the Booths,

---

1. Needham, "Integrating Holiness and Community," 5.

who along with fellow revivalists commenced a holiness mission in the East End of London. They galvanized the aggressive insights of Finney's new means and measures in greater soul winning and soul sanctifying endeavor, with a mission of "full salvation" for all, especially those most marginalized and impoverished.

It is fully acknowledged that on the journey, and by the grace of God, many inspired and inspiring examples of Christian community have been created; nothing less than this would be expected in the enunciation, from John Wesley, of holiness as "perfect love." Holiness revivalism is noted for an emphasis upon social justice, upon the dignity of human beings, whether slaves requiring emancipation, women requiring affirmation in Christian ministry and leadership or homeless alcoholics requiring acceptance, love and rehabilitation. Nonetheless, in the way that it was adopted by the Booths, holiness revivalism, or the call to "full salvation," had an individualistic focus upon the personal salvation and subsequent purity of the individual, including a disciplined devotion to the aggressive task of saving other souls. Furthermore, it was a highly subjective movement. The individual was encouraged to meet a set of human conditions and ethical standards in order to appropriate the immediacy of God's entirely sanctifying grace. This underlying missionary individualism and subjectivism was to have a significant impact upon the visible form of the community that took shape.

In the popular culture of urban Victorian Britain, in London, at the heart of the British Empire, the holiness revivalist Christian Mission eventually took the most logically aggressive form available—a military army—called The Salvation Army. This has been called the institutionalizing "army" strand. It is critically suggested that this metaphor, an extreme version of Finney's new means and measures, was not chosen with an explicit theological desire to give visible expression to the Church, but primarily as a functional organizational vehicle to "save souls," through the pragmatic methods of holiness revivalism. The metaphor of an army, whilst it was superficially an expression of community, it appealed to a secular enlightenment philosophy of individual freedom. Individuals entered into a voluntary alliance to accomplish a task. This individualism was marshalled as an army, under the charismatic and visionary leadership of William Booth. By his admission, his autocratic leadership gave him the power to make quick decisions, and to get something done. As Needham admits, in the hierarchical structure that ensues, "the organization becomes more important than the body,"[2] in which "we have been strong on compassion for the lone outsider but weak on nurturing the community of faith where members care for and support one another."[3]

This phase represents the establishment of visible military characteristics such as hierarchical officer ranks, uniformity, legalism and an organizational model that would later provide the foundation for a burgeoning bureaucracy. The rule of law was established in the detailing of Orders and Regulations for Officers and Soldiers. The Soldier was initially enlisted as a fully mobilized disciple of Christ among a "priesthood of all believers," but was increasingly characterized as an obedient foot-soldier in submission to the command structure of an autocratic and hierarchical system of military ranks. In this respect she was definitely not expected to ask strategic questions, but obediently to submit to the wisdom of her leaders. Furthermore, her submission was not based simply upon her obedience to Christ, but upon her obedience to the human rules and regulations of a military order, in which practical holiness subjectively included the imposition of particular lifestyle choices and practices that her leaders considered worthy of her military calling, in the service of Christ and The Salvation Army.

Finally, the two strands of mission and army, with their underlying individualistic and subjective tendencies, were illustrated by the Booths' decision to abandon the objective sacramental symbols of water, bread and wine, which could have properly protected an understanding of unity and diversity through an emphasis upon the mutuality and interdependence of *koinonia* community. These were replaced by the more subjective living symbol of the lone individual's life laid upon God's altar as the necessary conditional pre-requisite to experiencing the immediacy of God's entirely sanctifying grace.

The third phase, concerns a process of self-evaluation influenced by the development of the ecumenical movement, in which The Salvation Army ultimately brings the deeply ingrained and particularistic identity of an army, with what it admits to be an emphasis upon "church membership plus,"[4] into its reckoning of what it means to be the Church; the Church as an army. This is what is called the contemporary "church"

2. Ibid., 9.

3. Ibid., 8.

4. Thurian, *Ecumenical Perspectives*, 162.

strand. It is argued that this Salvationist ecclesiology has failed to grapple with and reflect upon the character of those two ecclesial strands, from historical development, of individualistic mission and military army, which compete with a true understanding of God's Church. Needham's study, *Community in Mission*, comes closest to recognizing the need for re-evaluation, and ten years after its writing he acknowledges:

> Our adoption of the hierarchical-institutional metaphor as the organizing principle of our movement and its processes has worked against our ability to integrate holiness and community. Since we look at ourselves as an organization rather than an organic body, our relationships with one another are defined more impersonally in terms of keeping the organization running . . . In hierarchical institutions emphasis is on position and status, with decision making being power-based. In the Body of Christ emphasis is on servanthood and shared power. To the extent that our functional ecclesiology is hierarchical, holiness is severed from Salvationist practice.[5]

Needham reveals the confusion that exists for Salvationists who increasingly wish to reflect theologically upon their ecclesiological practice, but are hampered by the historical baggage from which they find it difficult to cut loose. Needham's account of Salvationist ecclesiology lacks the theological concept of the Church as *koinonia*. Whilst he describes holiness as a corporate and personal reality from the free gift of transforming love that God shares with God's people, the grace of the Lord Jesus Christ and the unity and fellowship of the Holy Spirit, he does not explore the nature of that holy life in community as expressed in the NT word *koinonia*. It is at the heart of Barth's dynamic and "actualistic" conception of the Church, the congregation or community as event, gathered, built up and sent out by Christ, in the power of the Holy Spirit. It is also the concept that continues to focus the ecumenical community upon its journey towards visible unity; the one, holy, catholic and apostolic Church living in mutual recognition, respect and participation, as local or denominational churches that faithfully express the nature, form and mission of God's one Church.

Fundamentally, neither Needham nor Salvationist reflection in general has actively questioned the military metaphor itself. It is a weakness that results partly from an almost dualistic Salvationist focus upon

---

5. Needham, "Integrating Holiness and Community," 8.

what it articulates as the priority of the "spiritual reality," in which the visible form is pragmatically chosen for effective Christian mission, without reflection upon its theological credibility in shaping the community of God's people. Whilst the Army's hierarchy is questioned, there is a lack of Salvationist comprehension as to how the movement could function effectively without this military command system. Whilst in theory the visible form is pragmatic, in practice, over time, it assumes a form of divine revelation. To reform the metaphor would be to strike too deeply at the God-given identity of the people. For example, the revivalist method of wearing a uniform as a visible witness to Christ, quickly assumes within the military metaphor the character of a uniformity that is legalistically buttressed by rules and regulations, and competes against a theological concept of the Church's unity and diversity. Whilst the Church's form and order is properly a sociological reality that is drawn from human life and culture, a residual dualistic tendency from holiness revivalism has not encouraged Salvationist theological reflection upon that visible form.

In contrast, the theological concept of *koinonia*, as a relational quality of God's shared life and love is grounded in practical human form and action. In this respect the Church is called faithfully to express in visible form and order a theological understanding of the *koinonia* that properly exists at the heart of all the key metaphors of God's community, whether the People Of God, the Body of Christ or the Temple of the Holy Spirit. Salvationists cannot be faulted for developing the very powerful metaphor of the "soldier of Christ," as an obedient disciple who lays down her life for her friends and neighbors, in which the Church militant is depicted as a holy people who are called to deny themselves and follow the lordship of Christ into the *missio Dei*, in the power of the Holy Spirit. The militant nature of the Church is, however, something markedly different from the comprehensive development of a military model, almost to the exclusion of all other models, and in competition with a meaningful ecumenical discussion on the pilgrim journey towards the visible unity of the Church.

Karl Barth is a helpful dialogue partner for Salvationists intent on addressing difficulties that stem from their individualistic and subjective roots. He brings objectivity to Salvationist ecclesiological reflection and a renewed understanding of the Church's essential communal nature. Barth's theological anthropology and his regulative Chalcedonian

Christology, offer The Salvation Army a thoroughly theological understanding of the Church, and a foundation for future dialogue amongst
the churches. His distinctive account of the "special visibility" of the
Church, what Barth sees as its essential invisibility and appropriate
corresponding visibility, enables Salvationists to unravel those tangled
strands of mission, army and church that are confused, in which the
Army's visibility has been more sociologically pragmatic than theologically credible.

In particular, Barth's Christologically patterned account of heretical positions to the left and right, offer insight into the Church's potential
docetic escape into invisibility and defect, or the excesses of an overinflated visibility. Barth characterises these two movements as the closely related, twin errors, of secularization and sacralization. They speak
directly into aspects of the Army's visible form. Under the spotlight of
Barth's theological reasoning, it is possible to see that holiness revivalism's retreat into the spiritual invisibility of a "higher life" mission, with
its subjective and individualistic tendencies, enabled the Booths in due
course to establish a sociological military metaphor without adequate
objective theological reflection upon this secularizing influence. The military metaphor was more attuned, within Enlightenment reasoning, to
a philosophical understanding of voluntarism, than to a theological and
biblical concept of covenant. The resulting difficulties for The Salvation
Army's form have correspondingly been those secularized concepts of
hierarchy, uniformity, legalism and bureaucracy, together with the loss
of the objective sacramental symbols of water, bread and wine.

According to Barth's Christological reasoning and insight, the difficulties are more deep rooted than simply recognition of the secularization of Salvation Army life and theology that has taken place. In a closely
related way, this secularized human work can potentially, over time,
become sacralized as divine revelation. At such a point it is stubbornly
resistant to attempts to reform, without incurring the risk of undermining the deeply held identity of people who have assumed this God-given
revelation. It is only when both insights are acknowledged that progress
can be made. Then Barth's vision of a truly "lightweight" ecclesiology
may be embraced, of the pilgrim people of God, *ecclesia semper reformanda*, with Christ at the head of the Church, and the Holy Spirit free
to gather, grow and send the Church, God's human partner, into God's
world. The sending of this dynamic community is both a positive ex-

pression of, and testimony to, the power of the gospel of God's grace and generosity, in the life of the obedient and faithful human partner.

Salvationists, therefore, need to renew their objectivity in understanding the priority of God's initiative, in the face of what has tended to be an unhealthy and unbalanced pre-occupation with human decision and the human conditions of grace. They can at least begin with a rediscovery of Wesley's objectivity in his insistence upon God's prevenient grace. It lies at the heart of what McGonigle calls Wesleyan evangelical Arminianism, and it has not until recently been explicitly acknowledged in The Salvation Army's *Handbook of Doctrine*. Further to this understanding of prevenient grace, Barth offers Salvationists a challenging theological view of human freedom, not as an individual right to be able to choose evil, but as God's liberating grace for the individual's and the Church's partnership with God as an act of obedient and joyful thanksgiving and witness. In the understanding that this theological anthropology offers the Church as corresponding human partner, there are multiple reforms that The Salvation Army will need to consider in its visible form and order, reforms that will not be easily accomplished.

In the first instance, Salvationists who objectively appreciate the initiative that the Trinitarian God takes in opening the divine life to human encounter, inclusion and participation, might focus their ecclesiological reflection upon what it means for the obedient human response to be militant rather than military. A more limited focus upon the metaphor of the self-sacrificing "soldier of Christ" would enable Salvationists to move beyond the Church as an army, to embrace the primary metaphors of the Church as the pilgrim people of God, the body of Christ and the temple of the Holy Spirit. In each of these metaphors *koinonia*, both as gift and goal, is the essential characteristic of the life that God shares with God's people.

This broader and deeper reflection must have as its ultimate goal the practical inverting of the top-down hierarchical structure. This will enhance the possibility for the vision of servants walking together to be fully realized, in which the status of military ranks is effectively replaced by the language of servanthood. Inevitably, this must radically alter the military metaphor as Salvationists know it. The concept of service is not unfamiliar to Salvationists, who already effectively serve the local communities in which their congregations are situated. The Salvation Army in the UK, is recognized to be one of the largest providers of social services next to the Government.[6] In accord with Avery Dulles maxim that the "servant notion of the Kingdom . . . goes astray if it seeks to set itself up in opposition to the kerygmatic,"[7] Salvationist proclamation has been closely allied to, indeed has directed the Servant vision in so far as the preaching of the *kerygma* has been undertaken in faithfulness to the example of Jesus, in "word and deed."

Several desirable consequences may emerge from this focus upon Christ as servant, in the heralding of the gospel. Firstly, it will in the words of Needham, help to place the emphasis upon the "organic body" rather than the "organization," in particular the local congregation rather than the bureaucracy that has burgeoned within the organization. Officers would be encouraged to serve primarily within, and in extension from, a local community, in opposition to the organizational model that entices them to focus upon a "career path" within the organizational bureaucracy, effectively removing them from the concerns of the local community.

Secondly, it will help to focus Salvationists upon the unity and diversity of God's people, rather than their uniformity, in which God may be free to speak equally from the so called bottom upwards. Officers serving within and from a local community must divest themselves of the power that inhibits the flourishing of the "priesthood of all believers." This flourishing may further encourage the Christian community in what Newbigin rightly asserts is "the daily business of the world,"[8] where believers take their ministry seriously in public life. An emphasis upon a diversity of gifts will prevent "a uniform style of Christian discipleship"[9] in which a church or denomination suggests that every believer should be an evangelist, or engaged in social action, or speaking in tongues, or even dressed in Salvation Army uniform.

Thirdly, an emphasis upon the local body of believers will encourage a deeper understanding of the integral relationship between community and mission. Newbigin suggests that "the only possible hermeneutic of the gospel is a congregation which believes it,"[10] and in which "the Church cannot accept as its role simply the winning of individuals to

6. The Salvation Army, *The Salvation Army: Annual Report*.

7. Dulles, *Models of the Church*, 102.

8. Newbigin, *The Gospel in a Pluralist Society*, 230.

9. Ibid., 231.

10. Ibid., 232. See 222–33.

a kind of Christian discipleship which concerns only the private and domestic aspects of life."[11]

Fourthly, this emphasis on the body will encourage the development of the Church's law to be radically centered on Christ as Head, in which human authority does not develop for the community a legalism of rules, regulations and lifestyle choices, in addition to the "living law" of Christ.

Finally, a focus upon service and the Servant Lord cannot help but renew the Christian practices of baptism and the Lord's Supper. These practices, and their rich theological significance, will not undermine the Christian life as a living sacrament, but underline the authentic nature of *koinonia*, which is at the heart and center of life lived sacrificially for others. Salvationist fears about the likely divisiveness of the re-introduction of such practices, may welcome Barth's emphasis upon them as testimony to God's "self-attestation." Nonetheless, Salvationist reflection upon the *koinonia* relation of divine initiative and human response, in which these practices are visible words, will at the same time considerably enhance the recent Salvationist emphasis upon the sacramental life, and encourage Salvationists to both coherently develop their own ecclesiology and engage more fully with the sacramental understanding of others within the Church, as they journey together towards visible unity.

These proposed reforms may offer scant encouragement to those Salvation Army leaders who perceive them as the breaking of a sacred trust. Such fear is based on the assumption that The Salvation Army might become just another church, in which distinctive aspects of its life and mission might be lost. In this study, these fears have been examined and found to be based upon a false premise as to the nature, form and mission of the Church. On the contrary, these reforms can keep the focus of Salvationists truly upon holy and sacramental living, enhance their joining God's mission in God's world, and keep them in the will and purpose of God. How much of the military metaphor remains intact over time is less important than that the visible expression of the community seeks to be faithful to the divine initiative and calling upon their lives, in the age, geographical location and culture in which they find themselves, in which they express the one, holy, catholic and apostolic Church.

11. Ibid., 222.

Bibliography

Abbott, Walter, M., ed. *The Documents of Vatican II*. London: Geoffrey Chapman, 1966.

Aram I, Catholicos of Cilicia. "Report of the Moderator." In *God, In Your Grace . . . : Official Report of the Ninth Assembly of the World Council of Churches*, edited by Luis N. Rivera-Pagán, 112–35. Geneva: WCC, 2007.

Aulén, Gustaf. *Christus Victor: An Historical Study of the Three Main Types of the Idea of the Atonement*. London: SPCK, 1975.

Avery, Gordon. *Companion to the Song Book of The Salvation Army*. London: Salvationist Publishing and Supplies, 1961.

Baillie, D. M. *God Was In Christ: An Essay on Incarnation and Atonement*. London: Faber and Faber, 1961.

Barclay, Robert. *An Apology for the True Christian Divinity, as the Same is Held Forth . . . by the . . . Quakers*. 7th ed. Dublin, 1737.

Barth, Karl. *Against The Stream: Shorter Post War Writings, 1946–1952*. London: SCM, 1954.

———. *The Christian Life: Church Dogmatics*. IV, 4 Lecture Fragments. Translated by G. W. Bromiley. Edinburgh: T. & T. Clark, 1981.

———. "The Church." In *God In Action: Theological Addresses*, translated by E. G. Hominghansen and Karl J. Ernst, 20–38. Edinburgh: T. & T. Clark, 1936.

———. *The Church and the Churches*. Grand Rapids: Eerdmans, 2005.

———. *Church Dogmatics*. 4 vols. Edited by G. W. Bromiley and T. F. Torrance. Translated by G. W. Bromiley et al. London: T. & T. Clark, 2009.

———. *Church Dogmatics*. Vol. IV. 1. Translated by G. W. Bromiley. Edinburgh: T. & T. Clark, 1956.

———. *Church Dogmatics*. Vol. IV. 2. Translated by G. W. Bromiley. Edinburgh: T. & T. Clark, 1958.

———. "Concluding Unscientific Postscript on Schleiermacher." In *Karl Barth: Theologian of Freedom*, edited by Clifford Green, 66–90. London: Collins, 1989.

———. *Dogmatics in Outline*. Translated by G. T. Thomson. London: SCM, 1949.

———. *Evangelical Theology: An Introduction*. Translated by Foley Grover. Grand Rapids: Eerdmans, 1963.

———. *Fragments Grave and Gay*. Translated by Eric Mosbacher. London: Collins, 1971.

———. *God Here and Now*. London: Routledge Classics, 2003.

———. *God In Action: Theological Addresses*. Translated by E. G. Hominghansen and Karl J. Ernst. Edinburgh: T. & T. Clark, 1936.

———. *The Holy Ghost and the Christian Life*. Translated by R. Birch Hoyle. London: Frederick Muller, 1938.

————. *The Humanity of God.* London: Collins, 1961.

————. *Letters, 1961–1968.* Translated by G. W. Bromiley. Edinburgh: T. & T. Clark, 1981.

————. "An Outing to the Bruderholz." In *Fragments Grave and Gay,* 71–94. Translated by Eric Mosbacher. London: Collins, 1971.

————. "The Real Church." In *Against The Stream: Shorter Post War Writings, 1946–1952,* 62–77. London: SCM, 1954.

————. *Table Talk.* Edited by John D. Godsey. Scottish Journal of Theology Occasional Papers 10. Edinburgh: Oliver and Boyd, 1963.

————. *The Teaching of the Church Regarding Baptism.* London: SCM, 1948.

————. *Theology and Church: Shorter Writings, 1920–1928.* Translated by Louise Pettibone Smith. London: SCM, 1962.

Barth, Markus. *Rediscovering the Lord's Supper: Communion with Israel, with Christ, and Among the Guests.* Atlanta: John Knox, 1988.

Bebbington, D. W. *Evangelicalism in Modern Britain: A History from the 1730s to the 1930s.* London: Routledge, 1989.

————. *Holiness in Nineteenth-Century England.* The 1998 Didsbury Lectures. Carlisle, UK: Paternoster, 2000.

Begbie, Harold. *Life of William Booth: The Founder of The Salvation Army.* 2 vols. London: Macmillan, 1920.

Bell, G. K. A. *Randall Davidson: Archbishop of Canterbury.* Vol. 1. London: Oxford University Press, 1935.

Bender, Kimlyn J. *Karl Barth's Christological Ecclesiology.* Aldershot: Ashgate, 2005.

Bennett, David M. *The General: William Booth.* 2 vols. Maitland, FL: Xulon, 2003.

————, ed. *The Letters of William and Catherine Booth.* Extracted from the Booth Papers in the British Library and other sources. Brisbane: Camp Hill, 2003.

Benson, Arthur Christopher. *The Life of Edward White Benson, Sometime Archbishop of Canterbury.* Vol. 1. London: Macmillan, 1899.

Berkouwer, G. C. *The Triumph of Grace in the Theology of Karl Barth.* Grand Rapids: Eerdmans, 1956.

Best, Thomas F., ed. *Faith and Order at the Crossroads: The Plenary Commission Meeting, Kuala Lumpur 2004.* Faith and Order Paper 196. Geneva: WCC, 2005.

Best, Thomas F., and Günther Gassmann, eds. *On the Way to Fuller Koinonia: Official Report of the Fifth World Conference on Faith and Order.* Faith and Order Paper 166. Geneva: WCC, 1994.

Best, Thomas F., and Tamara Grdzelidze, eds. *BEM at 25: Critical Insights Into a Continuing Legacy.* Faith and Order Paper 205. Geneva: WCC, 2007.

Bettenson, Henry, ed. *Documents of the Christian Church.* 2nd ed. London: Oxford University Press, 1963.

————, ed. *The Early Christian Fathers: A Selection from the Writings of the Fathers from St. Clement of Rome to St. Athanasius.* Oxford: Oxford University Press, 1956.

Bettis, Joseph D. "Is Karl Barth a Universalist?" *Scottish Journal of Theology* 20 (1967) 423–36.

Biggar, Nigel, ed. *The Hastening that Waits: Karl Barth's Ethics.* Oxford: Clarendon, 1995.

————. *Reckoning with Barth: Essays in Commemoration of the Centenary of Karl Barth's Birth.* London: Mowbray, 1988.

The Book of Common Prayer. London: Cambridge University Press, 1962.

Booth, Bramwell. *Echoes and Memories.* London: Hodder and Stoughton, 1977.

————. "Sacraments: A Chapter of Reminiscences." *The Staff Review* (January 1923) 51–60.

————. "Sanctification." *The Christian Mission Magazine* (February 1878) 29–33.

————. *These Fifty Years.* London: Cassell, 1929.

Booth, Catherine. *Address on Holiness, Delivered in St. James' Hall Piccadilly.* London: The Salvation Army, 1887.

————. "Aggression." *The Christian Mission Magazine* (August 1874) 205–7.

————. "Conquest." *The War Cry* (November 3, 1881) 2–3.

————. "Dealing with Anxious Souls: An Address to the Workers in the Christian Mission." *The Christian Mission Magazine* (March/April 1875) 57–60, 85–90.

————. *The Diary and the Reminiscences of Catherine Booth.* Edited by David M. Bennett. Brisbane: Camp Hill, 2005.

————. "Female Ministry, or, Woman's Right to Preach the Gospel." In *Papers on Practical Religion,* 95–123. London: The Salvation Army, 1890.

————. *Female Teaching: Or the Rev. A. A. Rees versus Mrs. Palmer, Being A Reply to a Pamphlet by the Above Gentleman on the Sunderland Revival.* London: G. J. Stevenson, 1861.

————. "The Holy Ghost." *All The World* (June 1900) 339–42.

————. "The Kingdom of Christ." *All The World* (August/September 1885) 183–84, 207–9.

————. "Letter from Mrs. Booth." *The Christian Mission Magazine* (August 1878) 181.

————. "Letter to Her Parents." Held on microfilm at The Salvation Army's International Heritage Centre, February 11, 1861.

————. "Mrs. Booth's Address at Exeter Hall." *The War Cry* 29 (September 1881) 2–3.

————. "Our Commission." *All the World* (April 6, 1885) 83–85.

————. *Papers on Aggressive Christianity.* London: Salvationist, 1880.

————. *Papers On Godliness: Being Reports of a Series of Addresses Delivered at James's Hall, London, During 1881.* London: Salvation Army International Headquarters, 1890.

————. *Papers On Practical Religion.* London: The Salvation Army, 1890.

————. *Popular Christianity: A Series of Lectures Delivered in Princes Hall, Piccadilly.* London: Salvation Army International Headquarters, 1887.

————. *The Salvation Army in Relation to Church and State and Other Addresses.* London: S. W. Partridge, 1883.

————. "Unpublished Letters by the Army Mother." *The Staff Review* (January 1928) 8–10.

————. "Wake Them Up!" *The War Cry* (November 24, 1881) 2.

Booth, William. "Dedication." *The East London Evangelist* (October 1868) 1–2.

————. "A General Order Against Starvation." *The Christian Mission Magazine* (December 1878) 317–18.

————. "The General's Address at Exeter Hall, on Monday Evening." *The War Cry* (June 12, 1886) 9–10.

————. "The General's Address at the Wesleyan Conference." *The War Cry* (August , 14, 1880) 1–2.

————. "The General's New Year Address to Officers." *The War Cry* (January 17, 1883) 4–5.

————. "Hell!" *The Christian Mission Magazine* (July 1878) 169–71.

———. "Holiness: An Address at the Conference." *The Christian Mission Magazine* (August 1877) 193–8.

———. "How We Began." In *Twenty One Years Salvation Army, Under the Generalship of William Booth*, edited by George Scott Railton, 7–23. London: Salvation Army, 1879.

———. *In Darkest England and the Way Out*. London: Salvation Army International, 1891.

———. *A Ladder to Holiness: Being Seven Steps Leading to Full Salvation*. London: SA Book Dept., n.d.

———. "Letter from William Booth to the Brethren and Sisters Labouring for Jesus in Connection with the Dunedin Hall Christian Mission, Edinburgh." *The East London Evangelist* (April 1869) 103–5.

———. *Letters to Salvationists on Religion for Every Day*. 2 vols. London: SA Book Dept., 1902.

———. "The Millennium; or, The Ultimate Triumph of Salvation Army Principles." *All The World* (August 1890) 337–43.

———. "The Past of the War." *The Christian Mission Magazine* (August 1878) 236–45.

———. *Purity of Heart: Letters by General Booth to Salvationists and Others*. London: The Salvation Army, 1902.

———. "The Salvation Army." *The Contemporary Review* 42 (July/December 1882) 175–82.

———. "The Salvation Army." *The Salvationist* (February 1, 1879) 29–33.

———. "Salvation For Both Worlds: A Retrospect." *All The World* (January 1889) 1–6.

———. *Salvation Soldiery: A Series of Addresses on the Requirements of Jesus Christ's Service*. London: Salvation Army International, 1890.

———. *Talks with Officers of The Salvation Army: Being Interviews Reprinted from "The Officer Magazine."* London: The Salvation Army Book Department, 1921.

———. "What Do We Mean by Inspiration?" In *The Bible: Its Divine Revelation, Inspiration and Authority*, edited by Alfred G. Cunningham, 12–14. London: Salvationist Publishing and Supplies, 1961.

Booth-Tucker, Frederick De Latour. *The Life of Catherine Booth: The Mother of the Salvation Army*. 2 vols. London: The Salvation Army, 1892.

Bovey, Nigel. *The Mercy Seat Revisited*. London: The Salvation Army, 2010.

Bradshaw, Timothy. *The Olive Branch: An Evangelical Anglican Doctrine of the Church*. Carlisle, UK: Paternoster, 1992.

Bramwell-Booth, Catherine. *Bramwell Booth*. London: Rich & Cowan, 1933.

———. *Catherine Booth: The Story of Her Loves*. London: Hodder and Stoughton, 1970.

———. *Messages to the Messengers*. London: The Salvation Army, 1921.

Brengle, Samuel L. *The Guest of the Soul*. London: Marshall, Morgan & Scott, 1934.

———. *Heart Talks on Holiness*. London: S. P. & S., 1925.

———. *Helps To Holiness*. London: S. P. & S., 1896.

———. *Resurrection Life and Power*. London: S. P. & S., 1925.

———. *When the Holy Ghost Is Come*. London: S. P. & S., 1909.

Bretherton, Luke. "Beyond the Emerging Church." In *Remembering Our Future: Explorations in Deep Church*, 30–58. London: Paternoster, 2007.

Briggs, J. H. Y. *The English Baptists of the Nineteenth Century*. London: Historical Baptist Society, 1994.

The British Council of Churches. *Reflections: How Twenty-Six Churches See Their Life and Mission*. London: British Council of Churches, 1986.

Brown, Arnold. *The Gate and the Light: Recollections of Another Pilgrim.* Toronto: Bookwright, 1984.

————. "Letter to Dr. Potter." Held in Salvation Army International Heritage Centre, World Council Churches Box 1, October 3, 1979.

————. "Letter to Lt. Colonel Lyndon Taylor, Officer Commanding, Zambia." Held personally, September 8, 1978.

Brown, Callum G. *The Death of Christian Britain: Understanding Secularisation, 1800–2000.* London: Routledge, 2001.

Brunner, Emil. *Dogmatics I: The Christian Doctrine of God.* Translated by Olive Wyon. Philadephia: Westminter, 1950.

————. *The Misunderstanding of the Church.* London: Lutterworth, 1952.

Buckley, James J. "Christian Community, Baptism and Lord's Supper." In *Cambridge Companion to Karl Barth*, edited by John Webster, 195–211. Cambridge: University Press, 2000.

Bulley, Colin. *The Priesthood of Some Believers: Developments from the General to the Special Priesthood in the Christian Literature of the First Three Centuries.* Carlisle, UK: Paternoster Press, 2000.

Busch, Eberhard. *The Great Passion: An Introduction to Karl Barth's Theology.* Translated by G. W. Bromiley. Grand Rapids: Eerdmans, 2004.

————. *Karl Barth: His Life from Letters and Autobiographical Texts.* Grand Rapids: Eerdmans, 1994.

Cadman, Elijah. "The New Kingdom." *All The World* (July 1895) 1–4.

Calvin, John. *Institutes of the Christian Religion.* Edited by John T. McNeill.Translated by Ford Lewis Battles. 2 vols. Louisville: Westminster John Knox, 2006.

Carlile, Wilson. "The Church Army." In *Modern Evangelistic Movements*, edited by D. P. Thomson and Hubert Louis Simpson, 36–47. London: Thomas and Cowan, 1924.

Carpenter, Minnie Lindsay. *William Booth: Founder of The Salvation Army.* London: Epworth Press, n.d.

Carwardine, Richard. *Trans-Atlantic Revivalism: Popular Evangelicalism in Britain and America, 1790–1865.* Westport, CT: Greenwood, 1978.

Chadwick, Owen. *The Victorian Church: Part One, 1829–1859.* London: SCM, 1987.

————. *The Victorian Church: Part Two, 1860–1901.* London: SCM, 1987.

The Christian Mission. *Minutes of the First Conference of the Christian Mission.* Held on microfilm at The Salvation Army's International Heritage Centre, London 1870.

Clifton, Shaw. "People of God: Salvationist Ecclesiology." Unpublished paper delivered at the Salvation Army's International Theology and Ethics Symposium, Johannesburg, South Africa, August 9–13, 2006.

————. *Who Are these Salvationists? An Analysis for the 21st Century.* Alexandria, VA: The Salvation Army Crest, 1999.

Cobbe, Frances Power. "The Last Revival." *The Contemporary Review* (July/December 1882) 182–89.

Collins, Kenneth J. *The Theology of John Wesley: Holy Love and the Shape of Grace.* Nashville: Abingdon, 2007.

Coutts, Frederick. *Bread For My Neighbour: An Appreciation of the Social Action and Influence of William Booth.* London: Hodder and Stoughton, 1978.

————. *Essentials of Christian Experience.* London: Salvationist Publishing and Supplies, 1969.

————. *No Discharge In This War.* London: Hodder and Stoughton, 1974.

————. "The Salvation Army and Its Relation to the Churches." *The Officer* (October 1964) 649–54.

————. *The Salvation Army in Relation to the Church*. London: The Salvation Army, 1978.

Coutts, John. "The Army's Contribution to the Churches." *The Officer* 16/9 (1965) 597–605.

————. *The Salvationists*. London: Mowbrays, 1977.

Cox, Harvey. *God's Revolution and Man's Responsibility*. London: SCM, 1969.

Cross, Whitney R. *The Burned-Over District: The Social and Intellectual History of Enthusiastic Religion in Western New York, 1800–1850*. Ithaca: Cornell University Press, 1950.

Cunningham, Alfred G. "The Army's Attitude Toward 'The Sacraments': Considered in the Light of Scripture." *The Staff Review* (May 1929) 163–69.

————. *The Bible: Its Divine Revelation, Inspiration and Authority*. London: Salvationist Publishing and Supplies, 1961.

————. "Letter to General Albert Orsborn." Held in Salvation Army International Heritage Centre, World Council Churches Box 1, March 21, 1948.

————. "Letter to General Albert Orsborn." Held in Salvation Army International Heritage Centre, World Council Churches Box 1, April 24, 1948.

Dalferth, Ingolf U. "Karl Barth's Eschatological Realism." In *Karl Barth: Centenary Essays*, edited by S. W. Sykes, 14–45. Cambridge: Cambridge University Press, 1989.

Davidson, Randall Thomas. "The Methods of the Salvation Army." *The Contemporary Review* (July/December 1882) 189–99.

Davidson, Randall Thomas, and William Benham. *Life of Archibald Campbell Tait: Archbishop of Canterbury*. 2 vols. London: Macmillan, 1891.

Dayton, Donald W. "Asa Mahan and the Development of American Holiness Theology." *Wesleyan Theological Journal* 9/1 (Spring 1974) 60–69.

Dean, Harry. "What is the Church?" *The Officer* 20/10 (1969) 697–99.

Dieter, Melvin Easterday. "The Development of Nineteenth-Century Holiness Theology." *Wesleyan Theological Journal* 20/1 (Spring 1985) 61–77.

————. *The Holiness Revival of the Nineteenth Century*. Metuchen, NJ: Scarecrow, 1980.

————. "The Wesleyan Perspective." In *Five Views on Sanctification*, edited by Stanley N. Gundry, 11–55. Grand Rapids: Zondervan, 1987.

Douglas, J. D. "Nazirite." In *New Bible Dictionary*, 819–20. 2nd ed. Leicester: InterVarsity, 1962.

Dulles, Avery. *Models of the Church: A Critical Assessment of the Church in All Its Aspects*. 2nd ed. Dublin: Gill and Macmillan, 1987.

Dunn, James D. G. *Unity and Diversity in the New Testament: An Inquiry into the Character of Earliest Christianity*. London: SCM, 1977.

Eller, Vernard. *In Place of Sacraments: A Study of Baptism and the Lord's Supper*. Grand Rapids: Eerdmans, 1972.

Ervine, St. John. *God's Soldier: General William Booth*. 2 vols. London: William Heinemann, 1934.

The Evangelical Alliance. *The Nature of Hell: A Report by the Evangelical Alliance Commission on Unity and Truth Among Evangelicals (ACUTE)*. London: Evangelical Alliance, 2000.

Fairbank, Jenty. *Booth's Boots: The Beginnings of Salvation Army Social Work*. London: Salvation Army International Headquarters, 1983.

Falconer, Alan. "Introduction." In *One, Holy, Catholic and Apostolic: Ecumenical Reflections On the Church*, edited by Tamara Grdzelidze, 1–13. Faith and Order Paper 197. Geneva: WCC, 2005.

Fiddes, Paul S. *Participating in God: A Pastoral Doctrine of the Trinity*. Louisville: Westminster John Knox, 2000.

———. *Tracks and Traces: Baptist Identity in Church and Theology*. Carlisle, UK: Paternoster, 2003.

"Final Report of the Special Commission on Orthodox Participation in the WCC." *The Ecumenical Review* 55/1 (2003) 4–38.

Finney, Charles G. *Finney's Systematic Theology*. Edited by Dennis Carroll et al. Minneapolis: Bethany, 2004.

———. *Lectures On Revivals of Religion*. Edited by William G. McLoughlin. Cambridge, MA: Belknap, 1960.

———. *The Memoirs of Charles G. Finney: The Complete Restored Text*. Edited by Garth M. Rosell and Richard A. G. Dupuis. Grand Rapids: Zondervan, 1989.

———. "The Pernicious Attitude of the Church on the Reforms of the Age." *The Oberlin Evangelist* (January 21, 1846) 11–12.

Flew, R. Newton. *The Idea of Perfection in Christian Theology*. London: Oxford University Press, 1934.

Forsyth, P. T. *The Church and the Sacraments*. London: Independent, 1917.

Gauntlett, Caughey. "Letter to: All Delegates Berlin Conference." Held in Salvation Army International Heritage Centre, World Council Churches Box 1, April 2, 1984.

———. *Today In Darkest Britain*. Eastbourne, UK: Monarch, 1990.

George, Timothy. "The Sacramentality of the Church: An Evangelical Baptist Perspective." In *One Holy, Catholic and Apostolic: Ecumenical Reflections on the Church*, edited by Tamara Grdzelidze, 27–39. Faith and Order Paper 197. Geneva: WCC, 2005.

Gassmann, Günther, and John A. Radano, eds. *The Unity of the Church as Koinonia: Ecumenical Perspectives on the 1991 Canberra Statement on Unity*. Faith and Order paper 163. Geneva: WCC, 1993.

Geernaert, Donna. "Church as Koinonia/Church as Sacrament." In *The Unity of the Church as Koinonia: Ecumenical Perspectives on the 1991 Canberra Statement on Unity*, edited by Günther Gassmann and John A. Radano, 62–77. Faith and Order paper 163. Geneva: WCC, 1993.

Giles, Kevin. *What on Earth is the Church? A Biblical and Theological Inquiry*. London: SPCK, 1995.

Grdzelidze, Tamara, ed. *One, Holy, Catholic and Apostolic: Ecumenical Reflections on the Church*. Faith and Order Paper 197. WCC, 2005.

Green, Clifford, ed. *Karl Barth: Theologian of Freedom*. London: Collins, 1989.

Green, Roger J. *Catherine Booth: A Biography of the Co-Founder of The Salvation Army*. Crowborough, UK: Monarch, 1997.

———. *The Life and Ministry of William Booth Founder of The Salvation Army*. Nashville: Abingdon, 2005.

———. "The Salvation Army and the Evangelical Tradition." *Word and Deed* (May 2003) 51–69.

———. *War On Two Fronts: The Redemptive Theology of William Booth*. Atlanta: The Salvation Army Supplies, 1989.

———. "William Booth and Methodism." Unpublished Paper Delivered to The Salvation Army/World Methodist Council Bilateral Theological Dialogue, Sunbury Court, Middlesex, England, June 2–5, 2003.

Gros, Jeffrey, et al., eds. *Growth In Agreement II: Reports and Agreed Statements of Ecumenical Conversations on a World Level, 1982–1998.* Faith and Order Paper 187. Geneva: WCC, 2000.

Gundry, Stanley N., ed. *Five Views on Sanctification.* Grand Rapids: Zondervan, 1987.

Hardesty, Nancy A. *Your Daughters Shall Prophesy: Revivalism and Feminism in the Age of Finney.* New York: Carlson, 1991.

Hardman, Keith J. *Charles Grandison Finney 1792–1875: Revivalist and Reformer.* Darlington, UK: Evangelical, 1990.

Harries, Richard. *Questioning Belief.* London: SPCK, 1995.

Hart, Trevor. *Regarding Karl Barth: Essays Toward a Reading of his Theology.* Carlisle, UK: Paternoster, 1999.

Hartwell, Herbert. *The Theology of Karl Barth.* London: Gerald Duckworth, 1964.

Hattersley, Roy. *Blood and Fire: William and Catherine Booth and Their Salvation Army.* London: Abacus, 1999.

Hauerwas, Stanley. *With the Grain of the Universe: The Church's Witness and Natural Theology.* The Gifford Lectures delivered at the University of St. Andrews in 2001. London: SCM, 2002.

Headlam, Arthur C. *The Doctrine of the Church and Christian Reunion.* The Bampton Lectures for the year 1920. 2nd ed. London: John Murray, 1921.

Healy, Nicholas M. "Karl Barth's Ecclesiology Reconsidered." *Scottish Journal of Theology* 57/3 (2004) 287–99.

———. "The Logic of Karl Barth's Ecclesiology: Analysis, Assessment, and Proposed Modifications." *Modern Theology* 10/3 (July 1994) 253–70.

Heelas, Paul, et al., eds. *Detraditionalization: Critical Reflections on Authority and Identity at a Time of Uncertainty.* Oxford: Blackwell, 1996.

Heitzenrater, Richard P. *Wesley and the People Called Methodists.* Nashville: Abingdon, 1995.

Held, Heinz Joachim. "A Remarkable Document: Reflections on the Final Report of the Special Commission on Orthodox Participation in the WCC." *The Ecumenical Review* 55/1 (2003) 56–66.

Higgins, Edward J. *Stewards of God: A Series of Papers Specially Compiled for the Help and Guidance of the Corps Officers of The Salvation Army.* London: Salvationist Publishing and Supplies, n.d.

Hill, Harold. "The Language of Ordination: The Clericalising of The Salvation Army." The Frederick Coutts Memorial Lecture, Sydney, Australia. N.p. http://www.therubicon.org/2009/12/ordination5-hill.htm.

———. *Leadership in the Salvation Army: A Case Study in Clericalisation.* London: Paternoster, 2006.

Hill, Michael. *The Religious Order.* London: Heineman Educational, 1973.

Hunsberger, George R. "Evangelical Conversion Toward a Missional Ecclesiology." In *Evangelical Ecclesiology*, edited by John G. Stackhouse Jr., 105–32. Grand Rapids: Baker Academic, 2003.

Hunsinger, George. "Baptism and the Soteriology of Forgiveness." *International Journal of Systematic Theology* 2/3 (November 2000) 247–69.

———. *Disruptive Grace: Studies in the Theology of Karl Barth.* Grand Rapids: Eerdmans, 2000.

———. *How To Read Karl Barth: The Shape of His Theology.* Oxford: Oxford University Press, 1991.

————. "A Tale of Two Simultaneities: Justification and Sanctification in Calvin and Barth." In *Conversing With Barth*, edited by John C. McDowell and Mike Higton, 68–89. Aldershot: Ashgate, 2004.

Hütter, Reinhard. *Suffering Divine Things: Theology as Church Practice*. Translated by Doug Stott. Grand Rapids: Eerdmans, 1997.

Inglis, K. S. *Churches and the Working Classes in Victorian England*. London: Routledge and Kegan Paul, 1963.

Jenson, Robert. "You Wonder Where the Spirit Went." *Pro Ecclesia* 2/3 (1993) 296–304.

Jewett, Vern. "An Examination of Ecclesiastical Authority in The Salvation Army." *Word and Deed* (November 1999) 49–65.

Jones, Charles Edwin. "The Inverted Shadow of Phoebe Palmer." *Wesleyan Theological Journal* 31/2 (Fall 1996) 118–31.

Jüngel, Eberhard. *Karl Barth: A Theological Legacy*. Translated by Garret E. Paul. Philadelphia: Westminster, 1986.

Kent, John. *Holding The Fort: Studies in Victorian Revivalism*. London: Epworth, 1978.

Kew, Clifford W., ed. *Catherine Booth—Her Continuing Relevance: A Collection of Essays*. London: The Salvation Army, 1990.

————. *Closer Communion*. London: S. P. & S., 1980.

Kirk-Smith, H. *William Thomson Archbishop of York: His Life and Times, 1819–90*. London: SPCK, 1958.

Klappert, Bertold. *Promissio und Bund: Gesetz und Evangelium bei Luther und Barth*. Forschungen zur systematischen und ökumenischen Theologie 34. Göttingen: Vandenhoeck & Ruprecht, 1976.

Kung, Hans. *The Church*. Tunbridge Wells, UK: Search Press, 1968.

Lang, U. M. "Anhypostatos-Enhypostatos: Church Fathers, Protestant Orthodoxy and Karl Barth." *Journal of Theological Studies* n.s. 49/2 (October 1998) 630–57.

Larsson, John. "Being True to Ourselves." *The Officer* (November/December 2004) 2–3.

————. *1929: A Crisis That Shaped The Salvation Army's Future*. London: Salvation Books, 2009.

————. "Salvationist Theology and Ethics for the New Millennium." *Word and Deed* (November 2001) 9–24.

Locke, John. *A Letter Concerning Toleration*. London, 1689.

Lunn, Henry S. *Chapters From My Life: With Special Reference to Reunion*. London: Cassell, 1918.

Mackenzie, F. A. *The Clash of the Cymbals: The Secret History of the Revolt in The Salvation Army*. London: Brentano's, 1929.

Macquarrie, John. *Principles of Christian Theology*. 2nd ed. London: SCM, 1977.

Mangina, Joseph L. "Bearing the Marks of Jesus: The Church in the Economy of Salvation in Barth and Hauerwas." *Scottish Journal of Theology* 52/3 (1999) 269–305.

————. *Karl Barth: Theologian of Christian Witness*. Aldershot: Ashgate, 2004.

Manning, Henry Edward. "The Salvation Army." *The Contemporary Review* 42 (July/December 1882) 335–42.

Marsh, P. T. *The Victorian Church in Decline: Archbishop Tait and the Church of England 1868–1882*. London: Routledge & Kegan Paul, 1969.

Marshall, I. Howard. *Last Supper and Lord's Supper*. Carlisle, UK: Paternoster, 1980.

Marshall, Norman. "Letter to Commissioner Stanley Cottrill." Held in Salvation Army International Heritage Centre, World Council of Churches Box 1, August 17, 1978.

McClelland, Vincent Alan. *Cardinal Manning: His Public Life and Influence, 1865–1892*. London: Oxford University Press, 1962.

McCormack, Bruce. "Grace and Being: The Role of God's Gracious Election in Karl Barth's Theological Ontology." In *Cambridge Companion to Karl Barth*, edited by John Webster, 92–110. Cambridge: University Press, 2000.

———. *Karl Barth's Critically Realistic Dialectical Theology: Its Genesis and Development 1909–1936*. Oxford: Clarendon, 1997.

McDowell, John C., and Mike Higton, eds. *Conversing With Barth*. Aldershot: Ashgate, 2004.

McGonigle, Herbert Boyd. "Pneumatological Nomenclature in Early Methodism." *Wesleyan Theological Journal* 8/1 (Spring 1973) 61–72.

———. *Sufficient Saving Grace: John Wesley's Evangelical Arminianism*. Carlisle, UK: Paternoster, 2001.

McKinley, Edward. "Quaker Influence on the Early Salvation Army." In *Heritage of Holiness: A Compilation of Papers on the Historical Background of Holiness Teaching*, edited by The Salvation Army, Eastern Territory, USA, 47–56. New York: The Salvation Army, 1977.

McLeod, Hugh. *Class and Religion in the Late Victorian City*. London: Croom Helm, 1974.

Metcalf, William. *The Salvationist and the Sacraments*. London: S. P. & S., 1965.

Migliore, Daniel. "Reforming the Theology and Practice of Baptism: The Challenge of Karl Barth." In *Toward the Future of Reformed Theology: Tasks, Topics, Traditions*, edited by David Willis and Michael Welker, 494–511. Grand Rapids: Eerdmans, 1999.

Molnar, Paul D. *Karl Barth and the Theology of the Lord's Supper: A Systematic Investigation*. New York: Peter Lang, 1996.

Moltmann, Jürgen. *The Church in the Power of the Spirit: A Contribution to Messianic Ecclesiology*. London: SCM, 1977.

———, ed. *How I Have Changed: Reflections on Thirty Years of Theology*. London: SCM, 1997.

Morgan, Richard Cope. "Letter to William Booth." Held at Salvation Army International Heritage Centre, June 11, 1881.

Murdoch, Norman H. "Evangelical Sources of Salvation Army Doctrine." *Evangelical Quarterly* 59/3 (July 1987) 235–44.

———. *Origins of The Salvation Army*. Knoxville: University Press of Tennessee, 1994.

Needham, Phil. *Community in Mission: A Salvationist Ecclesiology*. London: Campfield, 1987.

———. "Integrating Holiness and Community: The Task of an Evolving Salvation Army." *Word and Deed* (November 2000) 5–20.

Neill, S. C. *A History of Christian Missions*. Harmondsworth, UK: Penguin, 1964.

Newbigin, Lesslie. *The Gospel in a Pluralist Society*. London: SPCK, 1989.

———. *The Household of God: Lectures on the Nature of the Church*. London: SCM, 1953.

Nicol, A. M. *General Booth and The Salvation Army*. London: Herbert and Daniel, 1910.

Nimmo, Paul T. *Being In Action: The Theological Shape of Barth's Ethical Vision*. London: T. & T. Clark, 2007.

Nissiotis, Nikos, and Lukas Vischer. "Letter to Commissioner Williams." Held in the Salvation Army International Heritage Centre, World Council of Churches Box 1, March 15, 1978.

Ocheltree, Carolyn. "Wesleyan Methodist Perceptions of William Booth." *Methodist History* 28/4 (July 1990) 262–76.

O'Grady, Colm. *The Church in Catholic Theology: Dialogue with Karl Barth*. London: Chapman, 1970.

———. *The Church in the Theology of Karl Barth*. London: Chapman, 1970.

Orr, James Edwin. *The Light of the Nations: Progress and Achievement in the Nineteenth Century*. London: Paternoster, 1965.

———. *The Second Evangelical Awakening in Britain*. London: Marshall, Morgan & Scott, 1949.

Orsborn, Albert. "Letter to Commissioner Cunningham." Held in Salvation Army International Heritage Centre, World Council Churches Box 1, April 6, 1948.

———. "The World Council of Churches." *The Officer* (March/April 1954) 73–78.

Palmer, Phoebe. *The Promise of the Father: Or A Neglected Specialty of the Last Days*. Boston: Henry V. Degen, 1859.

———. *Way Of Holiness: A Narrative of Religious Experience Resulting From A Determination To Be A Bible Christian*. New York: Lane & Scott, 1849.

Pentecost, John. "William Booth and the Doctrine of Holiness." PhD diss., Sydney University, Australia, 1997.

Pollock, John C. *The Keswick Story: The Authorized History of the Keswick Convention—Updated*. Fort Washington, PA: CLC, 2006.

Potter, Philip. "Letter to General Arnold Brown." Held in Salvation Army International Heritage Centre, World Council Churches Box 1, May 18, 1981.

———. "Letter to General Arnold Brown." Held in Salvation Army International Heritage Centre, World Council Churches Box 1, August 24, 1981.

Rack, Henry D. *Reasonable Enthusiast: John Wesley and the Rise of Methodism*. London: Epworth, 1989.

Rader, Paul. "Holiness, Revival and Mission in the 19th Century." In *Heritage of Holiness: A Compilation of Papers on the Historical Background of Holiness Teaching*, edited by The Salvation Army, Eastern Territory, USA, 71–93. New York: The Salvation Army, 1977.

Rahner, Karl. *The Church and the Sacraments*. Translated by W. J. O'Hara. Quaestiones Disputatae 9. London: Burns & Oates, 1963.

———. *Theological Investigations: Man in the Church*. Vol. 2. London: Darton, Longman & Todd, 1963.

———. *Theological Investigations: More Recent Writings*. Vol 4. London: Darton, Longman & Todd, 1966.

Railton, George Scott. *The Authoritative Life of General William Booth Founder of The Salvation Army*. New York: Reliance Trading, 1912.

———. *Heathen England: And What To Do For It*. 3rd ed. London: S. W. Partridge, 1877.

———. *Heathen England: And What To Do For It*. 5th ed. London: S. W. Partridge, 1880.

———. *Twenty One Years Salvation Army: Under the Generalship of William Booth*. London: Salvation Army, 1879.

Ratzinger, Joseph. *Church, Ecumenism and Politics: New Essays in Ecclesiology*. Slough, UK: St. Paul, 1988.

Redwood, Hugh. *God in the Slums*. London: Hodder and Stoughton, 1930.

Rees, Arthur Augustus. *Reasons for Not Co-Operating in the Alleged "Sunderland Revivals", in an Address to his Congregation*. Sunderland: William Henry Hills, 1859.

"The Reverend W. Booth in Whitechapel." *The Revival* 314 (July 27, 1865) 59–60.

Rhemick, John R. *A New People of God: A Study in Salvationism*. Des Plaines, IL: The Salvation Army, 1984.

Rightmire, David R. *Sacraments and The Salvation Army: Pneumatological Foundations*. Metuchen, NJ: Scarecrow, 1990.

Rivera-Pagán, Luis N., ed. *God, in your Grace . . . : Official Report of the Ninth Assembly of the World Council of Churches*. Geneva: WCC, 2007.

Robertson, Roland. "The Salvation Army: The Persistence of Sectarianism." In *Patterns of Sectarianism: Organisation and Ideology in Social Religious Movements*, edited by Bryan R. Wilson, 49–105. London: Heinemann, 1967.

Robinson, Earl. "A Salvation Army Perspective on Baptism: Theological Understanding and Liturgical Practice." In *Baptism Today: Understanding, Practice, Ecumenical Implications*, 173–80. Faith and Order Paper 207. Collegeville, MN: Liturgical, 2008.

Rogers, Eugene F., Jr. "The Eclipse of the Spirit in Karl Barth." In *Conversing With Barth*, edited by John C. McDowell and Mike Higton, 173–90. Aldershot: Ashgate, 2004.

The Salvation Army. "The Army and the World Council of Churches." *The Officer* (September/October 1961) 289–94, 323–24, 361–65.

———. *The Doctrines and Discipline of The Salvation Army: Prepared for the Training Homes*. London: Salvation Army Headquarters, 1881.

———. "Fifty Years Salvation Service: Some of Its Lessons and Results, An Interview with the General." *All The World* (July 1894) 9–11.

———. *Heritage of Holiness: A Compilation of Papers on the Historical Background of Holiness Teaching*. New York: The Salvation Army, 1977.

———. *In Darkest England Now*. London: Hodder and Stoughton, 1974.

———. "Notes of the Meeting of the Advisory Council to the General of The Salvation Army and a Delegation from the World Council of Churches held on 12 December, 1978, at The Salvation Army International Headquarters, London." These notes are held personally. The notes were sent to International Salvation Army Leaders by Commissioner Stan Cottrill, Chief of the Staff, on April 25, 1979.

———. *Orders and Regulations for Field Officers*. London: The Salvation Army, 1886.

———. *Orders and Regulations for The Salvation Army*. London: The Salvation Army, 1878.

———. "Our Library: Finney's Works." *The Officer* (1895) 12–13.

———. *The Sacraments: The Salvationist's Viewpoint*. London: The Salvation Army, 1960.

———. *Salvation Army Act, 1980*. London: Salvation Army International Headquarters, 1980.

———. *The Salvation Army: Annual Report*. London: The Salvation Army, 2002.

———. *The Salvation Army Handbook of Doctrine*. London: Salvation Army International Headquarters, 2010.

———. *The Salvation Army in the Body of Christ: An Ecclesiological Statement*. London: Salvation Army International Headquarters, 2008.

———. "The Salvation Army Response." Unpublished Salvation Army response to *The Nature and Mission of the Church*. 2010.

———. *The Salvation Army Statement on "Baptism, Eucharist and Ministry."* London: Salvation Army International Headquarters, 1986.

———. *The Salvation Army Year Book, 1995*. London: The Salvation Army, 1994.

———. *The Salvation Army Year Book, 2011*. London: The Salvation Army, 2010.

———. *Salvation Story: Salvationist Handbook of Doctrine.* London: Salvation Army, 1998.

———. *The Salvation War 1884: Under the Generalship of William Booth.* London: Salvation Army Book Depot, 1884.

———. *Salvationists and the Sacraments.* London: Salvationist Publishing and Supplies, 1945.

———. *Servants Together: Salvationist Perspectives on Ministry.* London: The Salvation Army, 2002.

———. *The Song Book of The Salvation Army.* London: The Salvation Army, 1986.

Sandall, Robert. *The History of The Salvation Army: Volume I, 1865–1878.* London: Thomas Nelson, 1947.

———. *The History of The Salvation Army: Volume II, 1878–1886.* London: Thomas Nelson, 1950.

———. *The History of The Salvation Army: Volume III, 1883–1953, Social Reform and Welfare Work.* London: Thomas Nelson, 1955.

Schrotenboer, Paul, ed. *An Evangelical Response to Baptism, Eucharist and Ministry.* Carlisle, UK: Paternoster, 1992.

Scotland, Nigel. *Apostles of the Spirit and Fire: American Revivalists and Victorian Britain.* Milton Keynes: Paternoster, 2009.

Sell, Alan P. F. *The Great Debate: Calvinism, Arminianism and Salvation.* Grand Rapids: Baker, 1983.

———. *Saints: Visible, Orderly, and Catholic, the Congregational Idea of the Church.* Geneva: World Alliance Of Reformed Churches, 1986.

Shults, F. LeRon. "A Dubious Christological Formula: From Leontius of Byzantium to Karl Barth." *Theological Studies* 57/3 (September 1996) 431–46.

Smith, Frank. "The Battle-Cry of the Social Reform Wing." *All The World* (August 1890) 355–58.

———. *The Betrayal of Bramwell Booth: The Truth About The Salvation Army Revolt.* London: Jarrolds, 1929.

Smith, Timothy L. "The Doctrine of the Sanctifying Spirit: Charles G. Finney's Synthesis of Wesleyan and Covenant Theology." *Wesleyan Theological Journal* 13 (Spring 1978) 92–113.

———. *Revivalism and Social Reform in Mid-Nineteenth-Century America.* New York: Abingdon, 1957.

Springs, Jason A. "Gender, Equality and Freedom in Karl Barth." *Modern Theology* 28/3 (July 2012) 446–77.

Stackhouse, John G., Jr., ed. *Evangelical Ecclesiology.* Grand Rapids: Baker Academic, 2003.

Stanley, Brian. *The World Missionary Conference, Edinburgh 1910.* Grand Rapids: Eerdmans, 2009.

Stead, W. T. *General Booth: A Biographical Sketch.* London: Isbister, 1891.

———. *Mrs. Booth of The Salvation Army.* London: James Nisbet, 1900.

Street, Robert. *Called to be God's People: The International Spiritual Life Commission—Its Report, Implications and Challenges.* London: The Salvation Army, 1999.

Sykes, S. W., ed. *Karl Barth: Centenary Essays.* Cambridge: Cambridge University Press, 1989.

Taylor, Gordon. *Companion to the Song Book of The Salvation Army.* London: Salvation Army International, 1989.

Thiselton, Anthony C. *Interpreting God and the Postmodern Self: On Meaning, Manipulation and Promise*. Edinburgh: T. & T. Clark, 1995.

Thompson, David M., et al., eds. *Protestant Nonconformist Texts, Twentieth Century*. Vol 4. Aldershot: Ashgate, 2007.

———. "The Salvation Army Act, 1931." In *Protestant Nonconformist Texts, Twentieth Century*, edited by David M. Thompson et al, 4:242–44. Document V.12. Aldershot: Ashgate, 2007.

———. "A United-Reformed Perspective." In *The Unity of the Church as Koinonia: Ecumenical Perspectives on the 1991 Canberra Statement on Unity*, edited by Günther Gassmann and John A. Radano, 25–30. Faith and Order Paper 163. Geneva: WCC, 1993.

Thomson, Robert E. *The Love Feast: Yesterday and Today: A Spiritual Observance for Salvationists in Worship*. Approved by the Commissioners' Conference, 1993. New York: The Salvation Army, 1993.

Thomson, William. *The Atoning Work of God Viewed in Relation to Some Current Theories: In Eight Sermons, Preached Before the University of Oxford, in the Year MDCCCLIII, at the Lecture Founded by the Late Rev. John Bampton, M.A., Canon of Salisbury*. London: Longmans, 1853.

Thurian, Max, ed. *Churches Respond to BEM: Official Responses to the "Baptism, Eucharist and Ministry" Text*. Vol 4. Geneva: WCC, 1987.

———. *Ecumenical Perspectives on Baptism, Eucharist and Ministry*. Faith and Order Paper 116. Geneva: WCC, 1983.

Tomkins, Oliver, ed. *The Third World Conference on Faith and Order, Lund 1952*. London: SCM, 1953.

Torrance, Thomas F. *Karl Barth, Biblical and Evangelical Theologian*. Edinburgh: T. & T. Clark, 1990.

Unsworth, Madge. *Maiden Tribute: A Study in Voluntary Social Service*. London: Salvationist Publishing and Supplies, 1949.

Vickers, Jason E. *Wesley: A Guide for the Perplexed*. London: T. & T. Clark, 2009.

Volf, Miroslav. *After Our Likeness: The Church as the Image of the Trinity*. Grand Rapids: Eerdmans, 1998.

Walker, Andrew. "Deep Church as Paradosis: On Relating Scripture and Tradition." In *Remembering Our Future: Explorations in Deep Church*, edited by Andrew Walker and Luke Bretherton, 59–80. London: Paternoster, 2007.

Walker, Andrew, and Luke Bretherton, eds. *Remembering Our Future: Explorations in Deep Church*. London: Paternoster, 2007.

Warfield, B. B. "Oberlin Perfectionism." *The Princeton Theological Review* 19/1 (1921) 1–63.

Watson, Bernard. *Soldier Saint: George Scott Railton, William Booth's First Lieutenant*. London: Hodder and Stoughton, 1970.

Watts, Kate. "Kate Watts." In *Fighting in Many Lands: Memories of Veteran Salvationists*, 27–30. London: Salvationist Publishing and Supplies, 1946.

Weber, Hans-Ruedi. *Salty Christians*. New York: Seabury, 1963.

Webster, John. *Barth's Earlier Thought: Four Studies*. London: T. & T. Clark, 2005.

———. *Barth's Ethics of Reconciliation*. Cambridge: Cambridge University Press, 1995.

———. *Barth's Moral Theology: Human Action in Barth's Thought*. Edinburgh: T. & T. Clark, 1998.

———, ed. *The Cambridge Companion to Karl Barth*. Cambridge: Cambridge University Press, 2000.

———. "The Christian in Revolt: Some Reflections on The Christian Life." In *Reckoning with Barth: Essays in Commemoration of the Centenary of Karl Barth's Birth*, edited by Nigel Biggar, 119–44. London: Mowbray, 1988.

Wesley, John. *Explanatory Notes Upon the New Testament*. London: Epworth, 1976.

———. *The Letters of the Rev. John Wesley*. Edited by John Telford. Vol. 6. London: Epworth, 1931.

———. *The Works of John Wesley*. Vols. 1–4, *Sermons*. Edited by Albert C. Outler. Bicentennial edition. Nashville: Abingdon, 1987.

———. *The Works of Rev. John Wesley, A. M.* 14 vols. London: Wesleyan Conference Office, 1872.

White, Charles Edward. "Phoebe Palmer and the Development of Pentecostal Pneumatology." *Wesleyan Theological Journal* 23/1–2 (Spring/Fall 1988) 198–212.

Wiggins, Arch R. *The History of The Salvation Army: Volume IV, 1886–1904*. London: Thomas Nelson, 1964.

Williams, Harry. "The W. C. C.—Seeing Ourselves in Context and Role." *The Officer* (February 1976) 61–65.

Williams, Rowan. *Wrestling with Angels: Conversations in Modern Theology*. Edited by Mike Higton. London: SCM, 2007.

Willis, David, and Michael Welker, eds. *Toward the Future of Reformed Theology: Tasks, Topics, Traditions*. Grand Rapids: Eerdmans, 1999.

Wilson, Bryan R. *Patterns of Sectarianism: Organisation and Ideology in Social Religious Movements*. London: Heinemann, 1967.

———. *Religious Sects: A Sociological Study*. London: Weidenfeld and Nicolson, 1970.

Wiseman, Clarence. "Are We a Church?" *The Officer* (October 1976) 435–39, 441.

Workman, H. B. *The Evolution of the Monastic Ideal*. London: Sharp, 1913.

The World Council of Churches. *Baptism, Eucharist and Ministry*. Faith and Order Paper No. 111. Geneva: World Council of Churches, 1982.

———. "Called to be the One Church: An Invitation to the Churches to Renew Their Commitment to the Search for Unity and to Deepen Their Dialogue." In *God, in your Grace . . . : Official Report of the Ninth Assembly of the World Council of Churches*, edited by Luis N. Rivera-Pagán, 255–61. Geneva: WCC, 2007.

———. "The Canberra Statement: The Unity of the Church as Koinonia: Gift and Calling." In *The Unity of the Church as Koinonia: Ecumenical Perspectives on the 1991 Canberra Statement on Unity*, edited by Günther Gassmann and John A. Radano, 2–3 [2.1]. Faith and Order Paper 163. Geneva: WCC, 1993.

———. "The Church: Local and Universal, A Study Document Commissioned and Received by the Joint Working Group, 1990." In *Growth In Agreement II: Reports and Agreed Statements of Ecumenical Conversations on a World Level, 1982–1998*, edited by Jeffrey Gros et al., 862–75. Faith and Order Paper 187. Geneva: WCC, 2000.

———. "The Evangelical-Roman Catholic Dialogue on Mission, 1977–1984." In *Growth In Agreement II: Reports and Agreed Statements of Ecumenical Conversations on a World Level, 1982–1998*, edited by Jeffrey Gros et al., 399–437. Faith and Order Paper 187. Geneva: WCC, 2000.

———. *The Nature and Mission of the Church: A Stage on the Way to a Common Statement*. Faith and Order Paper 198. Geneva: WCC, 2005.

———. "Perspectives on Koinonia: Report from the Third Quinquennium of the Dialogue Between the Pontifical Council for Promoting Christian Unity and Some Classical Pentecostal Churches and Leaders, 1985–1989." In *Growth In Agreement*

II: *Reports and Agreed Statements of Ecumenical Conversations on a World Level, 1982–1998*, edited by Jeffrey Gros et al., 735–52. Faith and Order Paper 187. Geneva: WCC, 2000.

———. "The Salvation Army." In *Churches Respond to BEM: Official Responses to the "Baptism, Eucharist and Ministry" Text*, edited by Max Thurian, 4:230–57. Faith and Order Paper 137. Geneva: WCC, 1987.

———. "Towards Koinonia in Faith, Life and Witness: A Discussion Paper." In *On The Way To Fuller Koinonia: Official Report of the Fifth World Conference on Faith and Order*, edited by Thomas F. Best and Günther Gassmann, 263–95. Faith and Order Paper 166. Geneva: WCC, 1994.

———. "World Council Churches Constitution." Held in International Heritage Centre, WCC Box 1. 1975.

———. "World Council of Churches, 'Toronto Statement'." Held in Salvation Army International Heritage Centre, World Council Churches Box 1.

Yocum, John. *Ecclesial Mediation in Karl Barth*. Aldershot: Ashgate, 2004.

Yuill, Chick *We Need Saints! A Fresh Look at Christian Holiness*. London: The Salvation Army, 1988.

Zizioulas, John. "The Church as Communion: A Presentation on the World Conference Theme." In *On The Way To Fuller Koinonia: Official Report of the Fifth World Conference on Faith and Order*, edited by Thomas F. Best and Günther Gassmann, 103–11. Faith and Order Paper 166. Geneva: WCC, 1994.

Zwingli, Ulrich. "An Account of the Faith of Huldreich Zwingli, Submitted to the German Emperor Charles V, at the Diet of Augsburg, July 3, 1530." In *On Providence and Other Essays*, edited by Samuel Macauley Jackson and William John Hinke, 33–61. Durham, NC: Labyrinth, 1983.

———. *Commentary on True and False Religion*. Edited by Samuel Macauley Jackson and Clarence Nevin Heller. Durham, NC: Labyrinth, 1981.

Index

Lightning Source UK Ltd.
Milton Keynes UK
UKOW07f0846301114

242404UK00001B/131/P